THE
ELEGANCE
OF THE
CAT

An *illustrated* history

THE
ELEGANCE
OF THE
CAT

An *illustrated* history

Tamsin Pickeral
Photography by Astrid Harrisson

BARRON'S

A Quintessence Book

First edition for North America and the Phillipines published in
2013 by Barron's Educational Series, Inc.

All inquiries should be addressed to:
Barron's Educational Series, Inc.
250 Wireless Boulevard
Hauppauge, NY 11788
www.barronseduc.com

ISBN: 978-0-7641-6615-0
Library of Congress Control No.: 2013939118

This book was designed and produced by
Quintessence Editions Ltd
230 City Road, London, EC1V 2TT

Project Editor	Elspeth Beidas
Editor	Jane Simmonds
Designer	Dean Martin
Production Manager	Anna Pauletti
Editorial Director	Jane Laing
Publisher	Mark Fletcher

Color reproduction by KHL Chromagraphics, Singapore
Printed in China by 1010 Printing International Ltd.

9 8 7 6 5 4 3 2 1

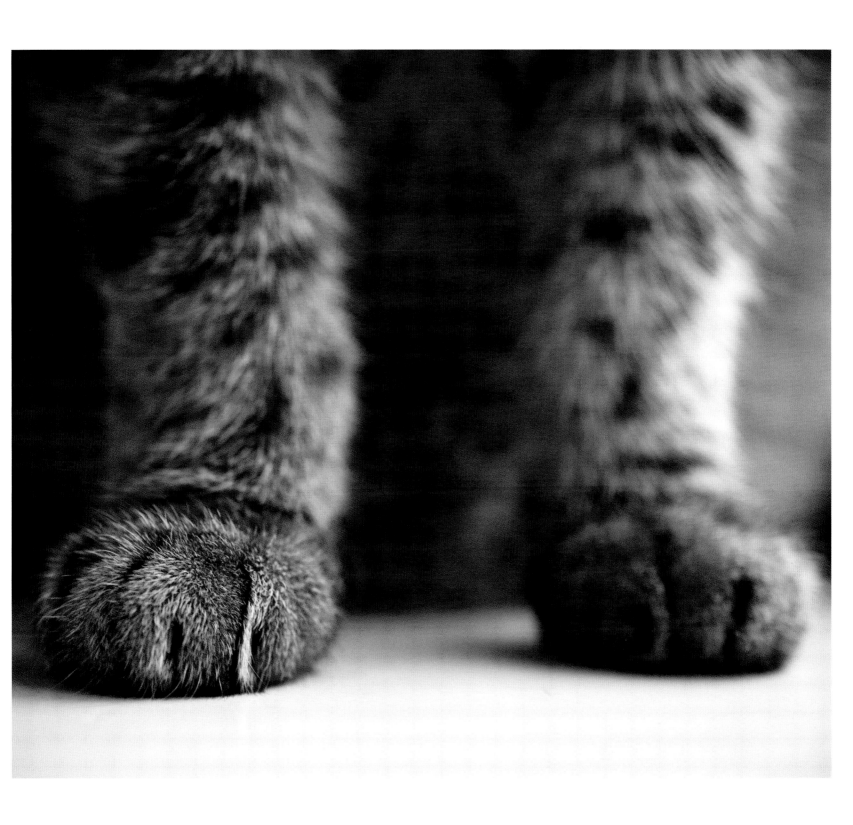

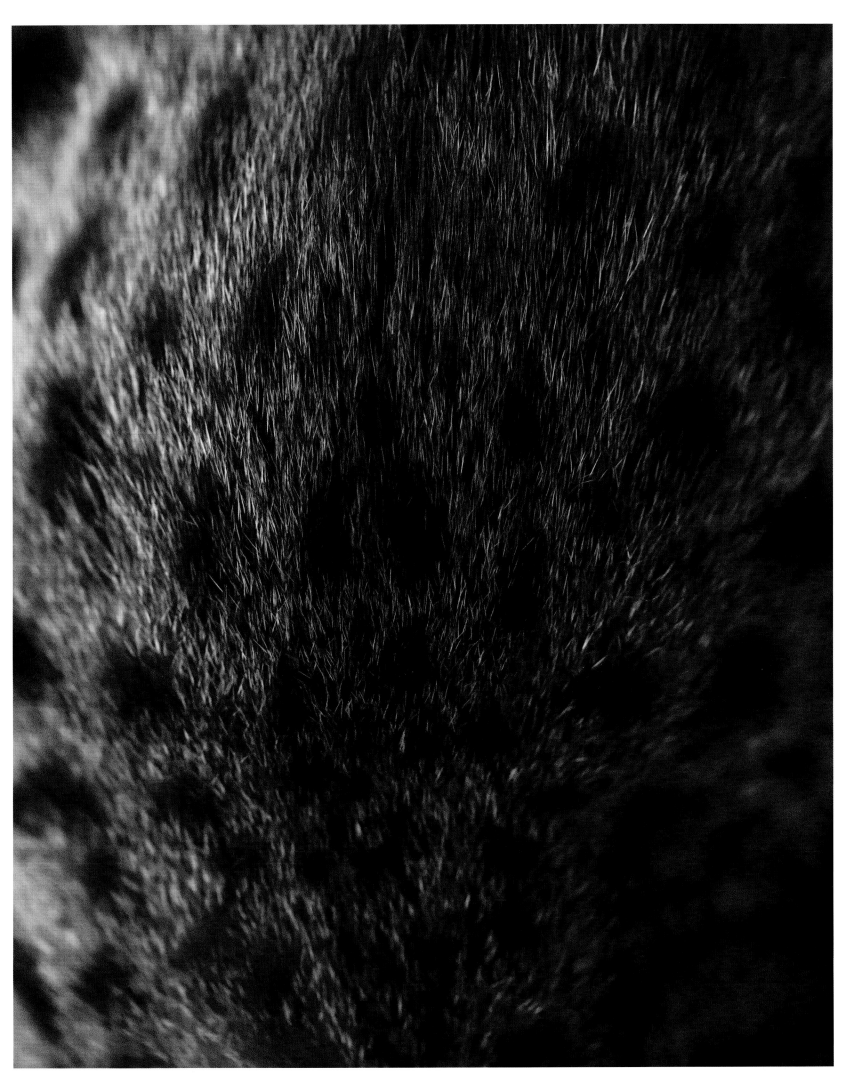

CONTENTS

INTRODUCTION   17

1 | ANCIENT TO MIDDLE AGES   20

2 | MIDDLE AGES TO   82
    NINETEENTH CENTURY

3 | LATE NINETEENTH   118
    CENTURY TO 1959

4 | 1960 TO 1969   160

5 | 1970 TO PRESENT   220

INDEX   282

CREDITS   286

ACKNOWLEDGMENTS   288

INTRODUCTION

Cats are the most enigmatic and alluring of domestic animals; their beguiling beauty, elegance, aloof intelligence, and fierce independence have led in part to the enormously successful and equally tragic episodes throughout their long, exotic history. Cats are extraordinary, mysterious creatures who inspire great depths of feeling; it is relatively unusual to be neutral about cats, instead they are either adored or abhorred. Where dogs and other domesticated animals have proved of infinite use to human development in a myriad of ways, the cat has been far more subtle. Cats have not helped win wars, find new lands, locate missing persons, herd sheep, or fend off burglars—that's dogs' work—mostly they have slept through these trials and tribulations in the choicest spot available. Some might argue that cats have not shaped history at all, although this would be wholly inaccurate. In fact, cats have played a rather more crucial role in history than is at first apparent.

Cats have provoked extreme reactions, ranging from being worshipped as gods and goddesses, to being vilified and hunted down by the thousand. Despite their fluctuating fortunes, they have persisted and gained ground in cultures globally. Through the centuries, and even to a degree today, their important role has been partly based on the "service" that cats provide—their proficiency in rodent control. They cannot be trained to do this, it is of their own volition and undertaken only for their own personal amusement or gain. Historically the role of cats in the control of rodent populations is not to be underestimated. It is no small irony that the mass slaughter of cats across Europe during the Middle Ages neatly coincided with the sweeping devastation of the Black Death, which spread from Asia via fleas carried on rats. Many factors contributed to the spread of the plague, but the scarcity of cats removed another barrier to its progress.

The ability of cats to hunt and kill rodents, combined with their often-exotic appearance, led to the spread of cats across the ancient world, westward from the Middle East and across Europe, and eastward. The establishment of trade routes between Greece and Rome in the west and Mesopotamia, India, and China in the east saw the wide dispersion of cats, traded as valued commodities. Working cats accompanied warring armies, including legions of Romans as their empire expanded, drafted in to protect their food supplies. Additionally, they were welcomed on board early ships by seafaring traders to kill rodents and then kept as lucky mascots, or traded at different ports. Anything remotely edible proves fodder for a rodent, and consequently cats have patrolled museums, government offices, palaces, police stations, hotels, schools, offices, and many other buildings, silently, ruthlessly keeping rodents at bay. The British Royal Mail employed cats in active service from 1868 to 1984, and cats have been widely used in the U.S. Postal Service over the years.

The topic of ownership is one that nearly always accompanies any account of cats, and mostly it seems the cat and its "person" have differing opinions. From the person perspective, the relationship could be construed as a rather unfair marriage that results in footing all bills and providing a full care and entertainment plan, while the cat bestows its affections at whim. The truth is rather different. With the exception of those that are confined indoors, cats are the only domestic pets that have complete free range and independence. Cats can, if they desire, journey wherever they please, and many will cover surprisingly large distances in between returning to their favorite corner of the house. Any cat owner who believes his or her pet does not leave their yard is living under an illusion. The pertinent fact is that cats return to their home and person by choice and, given their self-sufficiency, this is not something they have to do to survive. The cat chooses to live with its favorite person.

Cats can be trained, but generally only if it involves doing something they don't mind doing that perhaps benefits them in some way or appeals to their feline curiosity. More often, the cat trains those around it to facilitate its creature comforts. It is precisely this independent spirit and intelligence that makes cats so entirely captivating—and for non-cat people, frustrating—creatures. Approval from a cat is an unparalleled honor.

This book is a celebration of the cat in its many guises. It looks at the history of a selection of breeds, some well-known, some less so. The chapters have been divided into periods of time to indicate the approximate order of emergence of the different breeds. For most natural breeds, there is little or no specific documentation pertaining to their earliest history. In the case of artificially created breeds, which are the majority, the timeline is based on the start of the breed development, not when it was accepted by a cat association or governing body. At the start of each entry, information is given as to the age of the breed (ancient, historic, or modern), its region of origin, and its rarity (from common to moderate, uncommon, or rare).

The world of cat fancy—that is, the breeding and showing of pedigreed cats—did not develop until the late nineteenth century, and the majority of cat breeds as they are now recognized date to this period or later. The first cat association was the National Cat Club, formed in England in 1887. It began a system of registering purebred cats and in 1910 the Governing Council of the Cat Fancy (GCCF) was founded and took over the breed registers. It also began to regulate cat shows and to protect and promote purebred cats. In the United States the first association was the American Cat Association (ACA), formed in 1899, and in 1906 the Cat Fanciers' Association (CFA) was founded. The CFA is now the world's largest cat association, followed by The International Cat Association (TICA), which was established in the United States in 1979. There are also a great number of smaller associations that hold their own registries and organize their own shows. The Fédération Internationale Féline (FIFe), founded in 1949 in Paris, is a federation of registries affiliated with forty-two different organizations in forty countries. In addition to the multiple associations is the World Cat Congress, which works toward promoting understanding and communication between the major associations, with an emphasis on welfare.

These are interesting times for cats and the world of cat fancy. In the domestic forum the cat has its paws well and truly under the table, and currently ranks as the most populous domestic pet, usurping the dog. Cat welfare and that of other pets is better protected now than it has ever been, although there are still improvements to be made. Many breeds are rare, however, either because they are older and have fallen out of fashion, or because they are still being established; it is hoped that these rare breeds (both old and new) do not disappear. In simple terms the development of new breeds is achieved either through hybridization (crossing two or more existing breeds) or through the perpetuation of spontaneous genetic mutations. All the breeds featured in this book are recognized breeds, meaning that they have been accepted by at least one of the major organizations, either the CFA, TICA, GCCF, or FIFe. The major organizations accept new breeds via a graduated system that differs between them; for example a breed may start its classification as "preliminary" and proceed to "advanced" status. In all cases, achieving "championship" status is the goal for a breed and may take a number of years. There are many experimental breeds currently being developed. These breeds have not yet gained recognition; some of them will do so eventually, while some will not. The requirements for breed recognition by the organizations differ but are based on application letters, proof of a number of breeders, and numbers of the breed itself, a breed standard, and other prerequisites. Different associations can have different breed standards, which might allow variations in physical characteristics such as coat colors, for example. The descriptions that appear in this book are general guidelines and not affiliated to any one organization. For more definitive breed descriptions, it is recommended to consult the standards of each organization. Alternatively, the World Cat Congress website provides a comparison of individual breeds among its member organizations. In addition, there are some differences in nomenclature and classification of breeds between different countries, notably the United States and the United Kingdom. Irrespective of fashion for extremes in conformation or coat, breeders have a clear responsibility to tread carefully when creating new breeds, placing the cat's best interests and health above all else.

Finally, although this book ostensibly showcases recognized, pedigree cats, a cat is a cat is a cat—a creature of infinite grace and character, irrespective of pedigree or show-bench accomplishments. To know a cat is a privilege, but to be loved by a cat is the greatest accolade.

CHAPTER 1
ANCIENT TO MIDDLE AGES

The story of the relationship between cats and humans stretches far back in time, with archaeological evidence indicating that it began around 9,500 to 10,000 years ago. In 2004 a grave was discovered on the island of Cyprus roughly 9,500 years old, containing an adult human skeleton, with that of an eight-month-old kitten close by; both skeletons had been specifically arranged to face westward. Since Cyprus is an island and cats did not evolve there, the kitten must have been brought to the site. It can be conjectured that it was almost certainly already tame, because transporting a wildcat on a small boat would prove difficult, and because it is unlikely that a wildcat would have been buried in such a special manner. It is most probable that the cat came from the Levant—the eastern coast of the Mediterranean from southern Turkey around to northern Egypt—which is part of the larger Fertile Crescent, the productive land from Mesopotamia (modern Iraq and parts of neighboring countries) to the Nile delta of North Africa, or today's Middle East.

Recent scientific studies based on genetic analysis have indicated that the domestic cat developed in the Middle East. This coincides with the establishment of settlements and farming here around 10,000 years ago. As communities made the shift from nomadic life to a settled existence, an entirely new environment arose in terms of the animal and human relationship, allowing animals the opportunity to prosper on the back of human endeavor. One such was the common house mouse (*Mus musculus*), which took up uninvited residence in the newly stable and permanent homesteads of humans. Evidence of these interlopers has been unearthed in Israel, where some of the earliest grain stores have also been discovered. Opting not to compete with other rodents, the house mouse moved into settlements, profiting from shelter and food waste. It can be convincingly theorized that the wildcats (*Felis silvestris lybica*) in this area were also attracted to human settlements, gravitating toward them and in turn profiting from garbage heaps, the accompanying rodents, and other fringe benefits such as some warmth and shelter. Certain cats were temperamentally better equipped to live in close proximity with people and these gradually, over many centuries, developed into domestic cats.

Wildcats posed little threat to people due to their relatively small size, and were seen to be actively ridding communities of rodents. In this way they were able to coexist with human communities in a symbiotic manner until gradually they made the transition from living on the perimeters of societies to living within the domestic forum. It is likely that there was a long period during which cats lived a largely feral existence, within the community but without being "owned" or domesticated. This type of relationship has been seen even within the last century through the discovery of the African Sokoke, which still lives largely on the peripheries of communities in its native Kenya. It is a newly recognized breed, despite its ancient origins, and although it is still rare, it is becoming more popular outside its native home, helped by its inherent affinity for people.

Apart from the burial site in Cyprus, there are few other archaeological finds relating to cats for several thousand years. Other early finds include a feline molar in Jericho, approximately 9,000 years old, and another tooth dated to 4,000 years ago discovered in Harappa in the Indus valley, Pakistan. Two significant discoveries in terms of cat domestication are a slightly primitive ivory statuette of a cat found in Israel, from about 3,700 years ago and currently in the Jerusalem Rockefeller Museum, and a strikingly realistic alabaster statuette found in Egypt and dating to 1990–1800 B.C.E. Both of these carefully crafted statuettes reveal great familiarity with cats, in two separate geographical areas, and imply that cats were firmly integrated in various communities by this time. The alabaster cat is now in the Metropolitan Museum of Art, New York, and has stunning inlaid eyes of copper and rock crystal. Cats' eyes were linked with the movement of the sun and moon, and perceived as all-seeing. This is clearly a piece that was expensive to make and as such must have been of considerable significance.

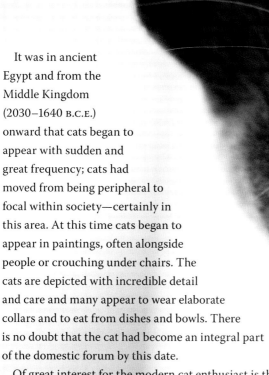

It was in ancient Egypt and from the Middle Kingdom (2030–1640 B.C.E.) onward that cats began to appear with sudden and great frequency; cats had moved from being peripheral to focal within society—certainly in this area. At this time cats began to appear in paintings, often alongside people or crouching under chairs. The cats are depicted with incredible detail and care and many appear to wear elaborate collars and to eat from dishes and bowls. There is no doubt that the cat had become an integral part of the domestic forum by this date.

Of great interest for the modern cat enthusiast is the undeniable similarity between the Egyptian Mau as it is now recognized and the depictions of cats from ancient Egypt. The beautiful Egyptian Mau is one of only two recognized breeds of naturally spotted cat in existence, and these same spotted cats appear in Egyptian works from about 1900 B.C.E. In addition to its very obvious coat pattern, the Mau bears an uncanny physical resemblance to the many images and statuettes from the same period in the shape of its body, head, eyes, and ears, as well as its regal bearing; there seems little doubt that these cats trace back to those of the ancient civilization. The distinctive and majestic Abyssinian cat has also often been likened to the cats of ancient Egypt. Recent genetic studies, however, have indicated that the Abyssinian probably developed along the coastline of the Indian Ocean and in Southeast Asia. Today's Abyssinian is considered a modern breed and is not thought to have descended directly from ancient cats.

From a very early date cats in Egypt were associated with the goddess Isis, who was also an all-encompassing mother and wife figure. Worship of Isis spread throughout the ancient world and many temples were built in her honor; the temples are believed to have been populated by cats, and the spread of the religion is thought to have contributed toward the spread of cats at this date. The goddess Bastet was the daughter of Isis and the sun god Ra and was originally depicted as lion-headed due to the associated qualities of fierceness, bravery, and beauty. By around 950 B.C.E., the cult of Bastet had overtaken all others and she gradually began to be perceived as cat-headed, or often in the complete form of a cat. The ancient Greek historian Herodotus (c. 484–425 B.C.E.) traveled to Egypt in around 450 B.C.E. and described the temple of Bastet in the center of the city of Bubastis. It was apparently a magnificent, square structure built from red granite with carved stone walls, and with a shrine to the goddess at its center. A number of sacred cats were kept in some style at the temple and it was here that one of the main ancient Egyptian festivals took place annually; many cats were ritually sacrificed and according to some accounts, large quantities of wine were drunk.

The cult of Bastet became so embedded in Egyptian society that images of cats appeared everywhere, both painted and as small statuettes. Cat ceremonies were a regular occurrence, particularly along the banks of the Nile, and archaeological digs have uncovered large numbers of cat-shaped amulets and effigies in this area. Cat images were utilized in jewelry making, household objects such as jars were decorated with cats, and many works of art were produced. Cats were also routinely mummified and were often buried alongside their owners. Pet cats were given funeral rites and invariably buried with small bowls of food; their passing was mourned by their family and accounts indicate that families would shave their eyebrows on the death of their cat. Killing a cat was a serious crime and punishable by death. The great irony that runs at the root of this culture of cat-loving people was that cats were also routinely sacrificed as part of the worship of Bastet. Evidently there was a distinction between the ritual sacrifice of these animals by an elected person, and the indiscriminate killing of cats, punishable by death. Given the widespread extent of the cult of Bastet, enormous numbers of cats were killed and mummified. These cats are believed to have been specifically bred in very great numbers for this very reason. Evidence reveals that they were typically killed at a young age, often under one year old, before being embalmed. Excavations at Bubastis and other sites uncovered cat mummies in the hundreds of thousands.

The ancient Egyptians banned the export of their cats due to their venerated nature, but cats were probably smuggled illegally from Egypt, and of course many made their own way across borders. Certainly there is evidence of cats in Greece from around this time and it is thought that grain ships sailing from Alexandria to Roman ports had cats on board to prevent rodent infestation. Cats became widespread across Europe, although they would never be treated in quite the same way again as they had been along the dusty banks of the Nile. Cat images appeared in ancient Roman mosaics and on Greek pottery, perhaps most famously on a Greek vase dating to about

600 B.C.E., which shows two women teasing a cat with a bird. This piece is currently housed in the British Museum in London and clearly depicts a pet cat. The cat also appears to be spotted, perhaps indicating the spread of the Egyptian Mau.

It was through the expansion of the Roman Empire that cats were distributed throughout Europe. Cats were an important component of Roman expeditions, accompanying their food supplies and ridding the armies of rodents. These shorthaired cats are considered the ancestors of the British Shorthair. Cat remains have been discovered at the German site of Tofting in Schleswig-Holstein, dating to around 2,000 years ago. Forty-nine cat skeletons were discovered in a Roman villa settlement at Tac, in Hungary, and other Roman cat remains have been found in various sites in England, including a Roman villa at Lullingstone, Kent. Interestingly, there is some evidence that cats had arrived in Britain before the Romans. It is quite possible that they arrived with the seafaring Phoenicians, whose culture spread across the Mediterranean between 1550 and 300 B.C.E. Turkish Vans are another ancient breed thought to have spread across Europe and into England, but at a later date, during the Crusades (c. 1095–1272). Knights captured the exotic cats, which originated near Lake Van in Turkey, as war bounty.

Just as cats were spreading westward and across Europe, so too were they spreading eastward with the opening of trading routes between Greece and Rome and the Far East. These networks of well-traveled routes reached China via Mesopotamia (Iraq, Syria, Turkey, and Iran) and India by both land and sea routes. Cats arrived in these eastern destinations and over a period of time began to develop very specific characteristics such as coat colors and type through a process known as genetic drift, where traits that are neither beneficial nor maladaptive become fixed in a population. Other characteristics such as long hair are believed to have developed as a result of environmental impact. There are several ancient breeds of longhaired cat, but it is not known with any certainty which gave rise to the longhaired cat seen today, or if in fact this trait caused by a recessive gene occurred in one or several locations. The best-known of the longhaired or semi-longhaired cats today is the Persian, one of the most widespread breeds of current times. It is believed that these distinctive cats developed in the remote, frigid, and mountainous areas of Persia, now Iran. Although the breed is believed to be very old, there are no accounts of it prior to the Middle Ages. The rare and ancient Siberian cat, which is among the largest of the domestic cat breeds, developed its substantial coat in the heart of Russia. Although there is no supporting documentary evidence, this is considered to be one of the naturally occurring ancient longhaired breeds, as are the Norwegian Forest Cat and the Japanese Bobtail (which also occurs as a shorthaired breed). The Japanese Bobtail, with its tail the length of a rabbit's tail, was introduced to Japan from China and Korea and starts to appear in artworks from the sixth century onward. The other ancient short-tailed or tailless cat, which is no relation at all to the Japanese Bobtail, is the Manx (and longhaired variety Cymric). These rare cats developed on the small Isle of Man off the coast of Britain, and are thought to trace back to cats that first arrived either during the time of the Phoenicians (1550–300 B.C.E.) or via the Vikings at the end of the eighth century.

Three ancient breeds developed in Thailand and neighboring Burma. The first two appear in the *Cat Book Poems* (*Tamra Maew*), written by a Buddhist monk possibly as early as 1350. These are the Siamese, known historically as the "royal cat of Siam" and closely associated with the royal houses of Thailand, and the rare Korat, with its distinctive heart-shaped face and silver-blue coat. The third breed is the Birman, which, according to legend, is the sacred cat of Burma. Recent DNA testing (in 1999) by Marilyn Menotti-Raymond, Leslie Lyons *et al.*, has indicated that these breeds date back at least 700 years and shows clear genetic differences between them and European breeds. Cats in the East also had spiritual significance and associations, particularly concerning death and the afterlife, and magical powers. A popular belief in both East and West at various times during history was that of the cat transporting the souls of the dead to their final resting place. In Thailand there was a historical tradition that when a ruler died their spirit entered one of the Royal Cats of Siam (Siamese). The Siamese cat is also said to carry the "temple mark," a dark patch low on the back of the neck. This mark, it is said, was made when a god once picked up a sacred Siamese cat and left the imprint of his hand forever on the cat's descendants.

In ancient China, the home of the rare Chinese Li Hua cat, a common belief was cats had the power to detect and banish evil; it is thought that this might have arisen due to the cat's ability to see in the dark and therefore be all-seeing. Often clay images of cats were placed above the front entrance of houses in ancient China to ward off evil spirits. People employed the same logic to look after their silk crops: cats were profoundly useful to the Chinese in protecting their silkworms from rodents, and when farmers were unable to procure enough cats to protect the crops they would place effigies of cats around the silkworms instead. According to the ancient Chinese *Book of Rites*, Chinese farmers also worshipped the cat goddess Li Shou, who was said to ward off evil spirits and protect crops. In both China and Japan, cats not only banished evil but were positively associated with good fortune and prosperity. The Japanese Bobtail gave rise to the Maneki-Neko, a bobtailed female cat figure who beckons welcomingly. This figure is still seen all over Japan, often as a ceramic statue in an entrance, and has been widely reproduced over time and internationally; it remains one of the most recognizable Japanese symbols of good fortune.

EGYPTIAN MAU

ANCIENT – EGYPT – RARE

APPEARANCE

Elegant and regal. Medium, long, and muscular body with several defining features: random and beautiful spots, distinctive brow line and slightly slanted eye set to give a "worried" look, a loose skin flap extending from flank to hind leg that allows for long stride and jumping ability, "gooseberry-green" eye color and a "tiptoe" stance because hind legs are slightly longer than front legs. Slightly rounded, wedge-shaped head, almond-shaped eyes, *medium to large ears broad at base and may be tufted. Medium long tail.*

SIZE

Medium

COAT

Medium-length coat with lustrous sheen, can be silver, bronze, or smoke for showing; also black and dilutes of primary for nonshowing. Smoke coat is fine and silky, silver and bronze is dense and resilient.

PERSONALITY

Lively, intelligent, intensely loyal, playful, can be wary of strangers

THE EGYPTIAN MAU IS A TRULY CAPTIVATING BREED, one of the oldest domestic cat breeds, and one of only two naturally occurring spotted cats in the world. An immediately arresting feature is their coats, with randomly patterned spots and banded legs and tails. Their eyes are a luminous "gooseberry green." Their characteristic facial markings include an "M" shape across the brow, sometimes referred to as a scarab-beetle mark, and two distinctive "mascara" lines; it is said that ancient Egyptian women fashioned their eye makeup based on the lines of their revered cats. The cats in fact bear a close resemblance to their ancestor, the African wildcat (*Felis silvestris lybica*).

Just as these cats have a unique appearance, they also have a distinctive temperament and will steal their way into heart and home with dexterity. They are graceful, athletic, fairly energetic, extremely playful, and highly engaging. Typically they enjoy any form of play that aligns with their natural hunting instincts; this includes, somewhat unnaturally for a cat, retrieving! Although they can be reserved with strangers and even aloof with those that they know, Egyptian Maus are attentive and crave company and adoration. They are extremely loyal to their family and highly interactive. These charming cats have a tendency to wag their tails at speed when happy, while treading their forepaws, and make soft chortling noises.

The Egyptian Mau is one of the very few breeds whose early history is partially documented. Spotted and distinctive, they can be seen in numerous works of art from ancient Egypt dating from about 1900 B.C.E. The context of these artworks varies, with some depicting domestic scenes. In these the cat is frequently seen alongside a woman and may represent fertility. Others show cats of Egyptian Mau-like appearance representing the Goddess Bastet, Goddess Mafdet, and occasionally the God Ra; a papyrus painting (c. 1100 B.C.E.) depicts the God Ra in the form of a spotted cat killing the evil serpent Apep. A number of images, one a wall painting from the tomb of Nebamun, Thebes (c. 1400 B.C.E.), show the same type of cats in bird-filled marshes accompanying Egyptian hunters—often seemingly retrieving fowl. Their name is derived from the ancient Egyptian word *mau*, meaning "cat."

Ancient Egypt formed the height of the Egyptian Mau's early history. Spotted cats of similar appearance are in just a few images and artifacts from the Classical world, including a Greek vase dated to c. sixth century B.C.E., now in the British Museum, London. On this, two women are shown teasing an athletic-looking spotted cat with a pigeon. Other images of similar cats are found in Roman mosaics.

In the early years of the twentieth century Egyptian Maus were seen in the cat fancy of continental Europe, including France, Italy, and Switzerland, presumably having been imported from Egypt, and efforts were made to consolidate breeding. The years of World War I decimated the breed, and numbers declined until the cats were in danger of disappearing altogether by the end of World War II.

The survival of the breed is commonly attributed to an exiled Russian princess, Nathalie Troubetskoy, who was living in Rome, Italy. She is said to have seen the breed on a trip to Egypt and, through her diplomatic connections, imported two cats from Egypt into Italy. A more romantic account suggests that in the early 1950s, a young boy gave her a silver-spotted kitten that he had been hiding in a box.

The kitten had been given to the boy by a diplomat working at a Middle Eastern embassy. Troubetskoy was so enamored with the cat that she researched its origins, established its breed, and tried to procure more. Her first two cats were a silver-spotted female called Lulu and a black male called Gregorio. She then imported more of them, reputedly via the Syrian Embassy and direct from Egypt, including a smoke-colored male called Geppa. The first litter of kittens was born in 1953, followed by a second in 1954.

Troubetskoy emigrated to the United States in 1956 taking three of her Egyptian Mau cats, and established the Fatima cattery. Her foundation line of traditional Egyptian Mau traces to two of these three cats, the silver female Fatima Baba and her bronze son, Fatima Jojo (Giorgio). Because of this tiny gene pool there was inbreeding and almost certainly some outcrossing to establish the breed, particularly as it was almost impossible to import the cats directly from Egypt. Breeding programs were carefully managed to maintain the qualities of the breed, and to address some initial temperament problems. The breed gradually gained a core following of enthusiasts and by the 1970s there were at least eight significant catteries across North America and Canada breeding Egyptian Maus.

In 1980, to combat the small gene pool, Jean Mill of the Millwood cattery imported two cats of Egyptian type from a zoo in New Delhi, India. These cats, Toby and Tashi, gave rise to the Indian line of Maus, which were accepted by the Cat Fanciers' Association (CFA) in the late 1980s. Some breeders believed that this led to a loss of the traditional Egyptian Mau head, but others maintain that the Indian line has benefited the breed, adding to the clarity of the spots in their coats and the richness of color. In the 1980s the breeder Cathie Rowan imported thirteen Maus directly from Egypt and in the early 1990s the breeder J. Len Davidson imported a further four from Egypt.

The Egyptian Mau in England owes its success to Melissa Bateson. She acquired her first two Egyptian Maus while living in the United States in the 1990s, swiftly followed by three more. Bateson had great success in the show ring in the United States with her cats and bred four litters. She returned to England in 1998 bringing her five cats with her; these were considered the first of the breed in the country. She continues to run her New Kingdom cattery, and there are now a number of other breeders in the United Kingdom.

TURKISH VAN
ANCIENT — TURKEY — RARE

APPEARANCE

Solid, muscular, and semi-longhaired. Substantial cats, broad and muscular through chest, and moderately long in body. Legs are moderately long and muscular, particular hind quarters, which have great power. Head is broad wedge shape with medium-length nose with slight dip below eye level. Ears are moderately large, with rounded tips and set high and well apart. Eyes are relatively large and rounded, set at a slight slant and either blue, amber, or odd colored.

Tail is long with a good brush.

SIZE

Medium to medium-large

COAT

Single coated semi-longhaired with soft, silky cashmere texture. Feathering on insides of ears, legs, feet, belly, neck ruff, and brush tail. Color distinctions vary with associations to include: white; solid and white; tabby and white; particolor and white.

PERSONALITY

Highly intelligent, very active, playful, interactive, mischievous, loving, and loyal

TURKISH VANS ARE A RARE AND DELIGHTFUL TREAT, easily identifiable through their distinctive pattern. The ideal Turkish Van has a pure white body with colored markings only on the head and tail, which also shows darker rings. In addition some will have a "thumb" mark between their shoulder blades and the odd spot. The thumb mark is said to represent the hand of Allah from when he blessed the cats as they left the Ark. The color pattern on this breed is now used as a descriptive—the "van" pattern. The most traditional of the colors is the white-bodied Van with red markings. Alongside their coloration, the Turkish Van has a unique, highly water-repellent coat. Water tends to roll off the surface, which is useful since these cats often enjoy swimming! When they first arrived in Europe in the 1950s and America in the 1970s they were colloquially known as "swimming cats," and it is not unusual for them to take a dip in a pool or bath when the weather is very hot.

The Turkish Van is a natural breed and thought to be ancient—possibly one of the earliest cat breeds. They are believed to be from the Lake Van region of Turkey. Excavations of a Neolithic site near Hacilar, Turkey, by the British Archaeological Institute in Ankara uncovered clay figurines of women with cats from about 5000 B.C.E.; these might represent the ancestors of the Turkish Van. Images of cats with ring marking on their tails appear on Hittite jewelry dating to 1600–1200 B.C.E. Further archaeological finds include a battle standard bearing the image of a distinctive ring-tailed cat that dates to around 75 C.E.

Turkish Vans are thought to have spread across Europe and into England during the time of the Crusades (c. 1095–1272) when knights captured the exotic cats as war bounty. Despite this, it was in Turkey that the cats remained most plentiful, and it seems that gradually they disappeared from the rest of Europe until the twentieth century.

In 1954 two British women, journalist Laura Lushington and photographer Sonia Halliday, were employed by the Turkish Tourist Board to document Turkey for marketing purposes. The two were given a pair of unrelated Turkish Van kittens, and the kittens accompanied them on the rest of their travels, living in their car. They were both the classic white-and-red marked Vans, and were taken back to England at the end of the trip. Sometime later the female had a litter of three kittens, which bred perfectly true to type. Over the next four years the cats continued to breed and produce almost identically marked kittens. In 1959 Lushington and Halliday returned to Turkey and to the city of Van, where they acquired another pair of cats and began the process of getting the breed recognized in England. Breeder Lydia Russell was also influential in this respect and in 1969 the Governing Council of the Cat Fancy (GCCF) awarded the Turkish Van full pedigree status.

Turkish Vans were first imported to the United States during the 1970s but they remained extremely rare until 1982 when Florida couple Barbara and Jack Reark began to promote them. Following much hard work, the breed was recognized by the major cat associations, but even today they are extremely rare. It is only comparatively recently that Vans have attained official recognition in their homeland, despite being greatly prized as pets for centuries. The Turkish College of Agriculture now preserves the breed in conjunction with Ankara Zoo.

SOKOKE

ANCIENT — AFRICA — RARE

APPEARANCE
Elegant and strikingly marked. Lean but muscular and leggy appearance. Head is a modified wedge shape and small in relation to body. Ears are medium large and upright, and eyes are moderately large, slightly almond-shaped, and amber to light green in color. Back is level and body lithe. Tail is medium long and tapers to a point with a hard, muscular feel.

SIZE
Medium

COAT
Single layer, very short and close lying, feels hard to the touch. Any shade of brown in a classic tabby pattern; ticking is found in the ground color and the pattern itself.

PERSONALITY
Highly intelligent, playful, very affectionate, and loyal to its family

THERE IS NO MISTAKING this uniquely marked and captivating breed that balances its regal elegance with a tremendous, playful nature. The Sokoke is lean and lithe in appearance, firm to the touch, with long, slender legs and a moderately long, narrow tail. It has a characteristic tiptoe gait seen in the back legs that becomes more pronounced when it is excited, and its boldly patterned coat is highly distinctive. Sokokes make excellent pets; they relish human company and are not suited to environments where they are left on their own for long periods. They form loyal bonds to their family and are extremely affectionate, but not overly demanding. They are also prone to bouts of extreme playfulness.

This is an unusual and still rare breed. One of the few natural breeds, the Sokoke developed in the greater Arabuko-Sokoke Forest Preserve area in the coastal zone of Kenya, Africa. The cats lived a largely feral existence on the perimeters of the Giriama communities; the Giriama referred to the Sokoke as *Khadzonzo* meaning "come pretty one." It is unclear if the cats were specifically domesticated by the Giriama or if they simply lived a fairly self-sufficient lifestyle. What is clear is that, as a breed, it is inherently amenable and forms close bonds with humans.

Despite the lack of physical evidence surrounding their origins, recent scientific research into the cat genomics by S. J. O'Brien, C. A. Driscoll, J. Clutton-Brock, and others

has shown that the Sokoke shares a genetic affinity with the cats of Lamu Island, off the coast of Kenya, and the street cats of coastal Kenya. All three have been grouped into a separate branch of the Asian Cat Breed Group, and share some genetic similarity to the Arabian wildcat.

The documented history of the breed begins in 1978 when a British woman, Jeni Slater, discovered some wild kittens living on her coconut plantation in Kenya. She was taken by their beautiful appearance and caught two, which she tamed and later bred together. She showed her Sokoke cats to her Danish friend Gloria Moeldrup, who imported two of them to Denmark in 1984. Three more followed in 1991, and in 1992 one was imported to Italy. These cats together were the foundation for the "Old Line" of Sokokes, and were recognized by the Fédération Internationale Féline (FIFe) in January 1994 as a championship breed. These Old Line cats had particularly taut, muscular bodies, almost rigid when standing or crouching, and had thin, whiplike, stiff tails. These traits have been somewhat softened in the New Line. Old Line cats also carried the pointed gene, resulting in the occasional pointed tabby.

Just under a decade after the Sokoke became known in Europe, Jeni Slater's neighbor in Kenya, Jeannie Knocker, also British, began to research the Sokoke breed. She found eight Sokoke cats and began to breed them; they bred true to type, indicating that they were purebred Sokokes. Her son contacted breeders in Europe with the news that his family had a number of the breed; breeders were desperate for new purebred cats to increase the gene pool. Several were imported to Denmark, Sweden, and Norway and were registered with FIFe in 2003. These cats from the Knockers and their progeny became known as the "New Line." Seven were imported to the United States and were accepted by The International Cat Association (TICA) in 2004 as a registration only breed, upgraded in 2008 to preliminary new breed, eligible for showing. Although rare, the breed is increasing in popularity in Europe and the United States.

ANCIENT TO MIDDLE AGES

MANX AND CYMRIC

ANCIENT – ISLE OF MAN – RARE

APPEARANCE

Substantial, rounded appearance. Muscular, strongly built cat with a short back that slopes in a smooth arch from shoulders up to rump. Strongly boned front legs are shorter than the hind legs and set well apart. Flanks are deep. Head is fairly large and round with prominent cheeks, especially in the mature male, with a well-defined strong muzzle and firm chin. The eyes are large and round, color in keeping with the coat color. Can be tailless, or have a short, stumpy tail, or a tail only just shorter than other breeds.

SIZE

Medium

COAT

Double coat with short, dense hair, outer guard hairs appear hard and glossy, undercoat is soft. Longhaired variety called Cymric has a medium-length double coat, often with longer neck ruff and bib. Wide range of colors.

PERSONALITY

Playful, intelligent, sociable, gentle, even-tempered

THE MANX AND ITS LONGHAIRED COUNTERPART, the Cymric, hail from the Isle of Man, a small island in the Irish Sea between Great Britain and Ireland. These extraordinary cats distinguish themselves in a great many ways, not least due to the configuration of their tail—or lack of it. The Manx and Cymric have lovely personalities. They are playful, inquisitive, and intelligent, and will interact and play in an almost doglike manner. It is not unusual for them to retrieve toys or even bury them, and many are fascinated by water. They make devoted pets and are much happier in the company of their family than on their own. They interact well with children due to their phlegmatic temperament, and tolerate other animals. Because of the power in their hind quarters, these are also among the most adept and talented jumpers of the cat world.

The Manx's taillessness is legendary, but not all Manx are without tails. There are four classifications used to describe the Manx and its tail: rumpy, rumpy-riser, stumpy, and longy. The rumpy describes the tailless Manx; it often has a small dimple at the base of the spine where the tail would normally be. Rumpies are the most highly prized for the show ring. The rumpy-riser has a very short tail between one to three vertebrae long. The stumpy has a slightly longer, stumpy tail, which is often kinked or curved. The longy has a tail equivalent to or slightly shorter than those seen in other cat breeds. Manx and Cymric also have a very distinctive conformation. Like the British Shorthair, the Manx has a rounded face with full cheeks. It is a shortbodied but heavy cat, and has a smoothly curving topline from its shoulders upward to the rump. The overall impression of the Manx is of a well-balanced round cat. It is also distinguished by an unusual, stiff-legged gait because of its slightly longer hind legs. The gait when running can also be rabbitlike, sometimes referred to as the Manx- or bunny-hop.

There are a number of myths and stories surrounding the breed's origin. A popular one is that they were the last to board the Ark and, in his hurry to set sail, Noah slammed the door on their tails. Another equally colorful legend recounts that the Manx had their tails cut off by Irish invaders, who wore them as plumes in their helmets. Some claim that Phoenician traders introduced cats to the Isle of Man from the Mediterranean or even Japan at some point during their seafaring height (c. 1500–300 B.C.E.). Others believe that the Vikings took cats to the island when they arrived at the end of the eighth century. Yet another story tells of cats on board one of the ships of the Spanish Armada swimming ashore when their boat was shipwrecked in 1588. Unfortunately there is no evidence to substantiate any of these claims.

What is known is that the taillessness of the Manx is derived through a genetic mutation within the island's cat population and, because the island is small and isolated, the mutation was replicated through the cat community, probably over a long period of time. The Manx and Cymric differ from all other tailless cat breeds in the nature of their mutation: the Manx's taillessness is brought about through a dominant gene while other short-tailed or tailless breeds are governed by a recessive gene. It is the presence of this dominant gene that makes Manx cats difficult to breed, and their numbers remain relatively low. Kittens that inherit the

Manx gene from both parents, known as homozygous Manx kittens, die early in their development, before birth; this accounts for roughly 25 percent of kittens conceived. Even heterozygous kittens—those that inherit the Manx gene from one parent—can be prone to abnormalities, particularly in the formation of the spine and rear end. It is believed that Manx cats share a common ancestry with the British Shorthair because they share a similar look to their heads and weight of frame.

An early account of Manx cats dates to 1844 and the historian Joseph Train, who described seeing the cats on the island and likened them to rabbits, suggesting that their parentage was a mix of both species. One of the earliest written references to the Manx is in C. Lewis Hind's book *Turner's Golden Visions* (1910) about the artist J. M. W. Turner. When Turner was in his mid-thirties in 1810, he claimed that he owned seven cats that came from the Isle of Man. In 1902 the author Frances Simpson wrote an article about the Manx and indicated that it was already being seen in the show ring, making it one of the early breeds to appear. Today only Manx with no tails (rumpies) or rumpy-risers can be shown, but Simpson described those with stumpy tails also making an appearance.

It is not clear when the Manx first made its way to North America. In about 1820 the Hurley family from Toms River, New Jersey, are said to have brought tailless cats from the Isle of Man back to the United States after a sailing trip. The first recognized and recorded Manx arrived in about 1908, with the Cat Fanciers' Association (CFA) recognizing the breed in the 1920s. In the 1930s the Carlson sisters from the Chicago area were noted Manx breeders, owning one of the first Manx grand champions. They also imported a male in 1935, Ginger of Manx of Glen Orry, who was influential in their breeding lines.

Longhaired cats are believed to trace back to early in the history of the Manx on the Isle of Man, but the cats were not actively shown until the 1960s. At first there was debate over their origin, with some suggesting that they were created through crossing Manx with Persian—this outcrossing did occur during the 1930s, but the Cymric was around long before this. For many years they were known simply as longhaired Manx, but two influential breeders, Blair Wright and Leslie Falteisek, instigated Cymric as their name. Cymric is the Welsh word for Wales.

NORWEGIAN FOREST CAT

ANCIENT – NORWAY – MODERATE

APPEARANCE

Substantial with beautiful long-haired coat. Large, muscular, athletic cat with solid bone structure. Characterized by distinctive long coat. Head is the shape of an equilateral triangle; nose is straight from brow ridge to tip of nose. Large ears, broad at base, heavily furnished, often with lynx tips. Eyes are large, luminous, and almond shaped, set at a slight angle. They are any shade of green or gold, green gold, or copper. White cats or cats with white may have blue or odd-colored eyes. Hind legs longer than front, rump slightly higher than shoulders. Medium long tail, broad at base and very bushy.

SIZE

Large to medium

COAT

Magnificent longhaired double coat with dense undercoat and glossy top coat. Large neck ruff, chest ruff, britches on hind legs, ear tufts, and well-haired paws. Any color except chocolate, lilac, Himalayan pattern, or any of these with white.

PERSONALITY

Curious, fun-loving, adaptable, highly affectionate

NORWEGIAN FOREST CATS, affectionately known as Wegies or NFCs, make a wonderful addition to any home. These are charming, phlegmatic cats whose nature allows them to adapt calmly to most situations—dogs, children—activities, and environments, and to do so with unfailing good humor. They are extremely athletic and like to climb to the highest point available to survey all around them; no ledge is safe from the NFC. Their climbing skills are combined with natural curiosity and an innate intelligence. They mature slowly, not reaching full size until they are around five years old, when males range between 12 and 16 lb (5.5–7 kg), and females 9 and 12 lb (4–5 kg). They are affectionate, gregarious cats that will often greet people at the front door, much in the manner of a dog. Although they are great purrers, NFCs tend not to vocalize a great deal and are quiet, serene cats. Their coats are splendid and, despite their long hair, they need little in the way of grooming. An NFC will shed in the spring and fall as it changes its winter coat to summer and back to winter. Grooming at these times is a good idea to remove the dead hair, but once the new coat has come through they require little maintenance.

NFCs, also known as Skogkatt, meaning "forest cat," are a naturally occurring ancient breed in Norway, and developed their unique characteristics over a period of time. The date of their origin is not known, but they are closely linked to the Vikings and appear frequently in Norse mythology. Domestic shorthaired cats were included in the Roman expedition parties to Northern Europe to keep their supplies free from rodent destruction. It is believed that longhaired cats developed from these as a result of environmental impact and the extremely cold, harsh climate of northern Scandinavia. Certainly the Skogkatt of the Norwegian forests developed a thick, weather-resistant coat enabling its survival in the most frigid conditions; these cats have particularly well-furred paws to protect them from snow and ice, which is a distinct advantage in Norwegian winters. They also developed sharply honed survival skills; as a result, today these cats are generally robustly healthy.

There are many references to large cats, which can be assumed to be Skogkatts, in ancient Norse mythology. Although it is not clear when these stories developed, they were first written down by Snorri Sturluson (1179–1241) in his *Prose Edda*. The goddess of love and fertility, Freya, had two such cats that pulled her chariot and are mentioned often. There is also reference to a vast grey cat, which Thor, the god of thunder, was unable to lift from the ground. Cats were popular in Viking culture and were often given to young brides on their wedding day—perhaps because of the association with Freya and love. Realistically, cats were probably most popular because they kept supplies and homes free from rodents; this was why the Vikings took Skogkatts with them on their many warring expeditions.

An early literary description of the Skogkatt was probably made by the Danish clergyman Peter Clausson Friis (1545–1614), who lived most of his life in Norway. Friis translated Sturluson's *Prose Edda* into Danish, but also separately described three types of lynx in his writings: a wolf lynx, a fox lynx, and a cat lynx. It is believed by many that this reference to a "cat lynx" was in fact the Skogkatt.

Centuries later what must surely have been Skogkatts appeared in a book of fairy tales written by Peter Christen Asbjørnsen and Jørgen Moe. Here they were called *huldrekat*, meaning "fairy cat," but were described as living in the forest with long, bushy tails—just like the modern Skogkatt.

It was not until the twentieth century that efforts were made to officially recognize the breed. The first Norwegian Cat Club was formed in 1934 and the first NFC was exhibited at a cat show in Oslo in 1938. The years of World War II halted further efforts to establish the breed and by the end of the war the numbers of NFCs in their homeland were extremely low. It was not until the 1970s that an effort was once again made to recognize Norway's superlative cat. In 1972 the Skogkatt was given the official name "Norsk Skogkatt" and was given a preliminary standard; however, there were virtually none of the purebred cats in existence.

In 1973 Edel Runas and Helen and Carl Frederik Nordane of the Norwegian Cat Association located two pure Skogkatts, Pippa Skogpuss (who belonged to Runas) and Pans Truls. These cats produced a litter of two kittens, Pjewiks Forest Troll and Pjewiks Forest Nisse, which were the beginning of a new breeding initiative. The program was supported by dedicated breeders and by 1975 the Norwegian Forest Cat Club was formed. Before the breed could be officially recognized by the Fédération Internationale Féline (FIFe), three generations had to be authenticated. By 1977 there were about 150 Skogkatts registered in Norway and FIFe sent a German judge to the cat show in Oslo to report on the "new" breed. Later that year Carl Frederik Nordane travelled to Paris to hear the verdict of FIFe, taking photographs of Skogkatts with him, including a picture of Pans Truls. The FIFe judges recognized Pans Truls as the standard by which all Skogkatts would be judged and awarded him championship status. It was a moment of tremendous pride for Norway.

The cats quickly caught the attention of the cat fancy world and in 1979 the first pair were imported to the United States, with a third in 1980. They quickly gained a following and were accepted by the major U.S. cat fancy associations in the 1980s. They arrived in the United Kingdom in 1986 (recognized by the Governing Council of the Cat Fancy in 1990, given championship status in 1997); since then, they have been imported in relatively large numbers to the United Kingdom, continental Europe, Australia, and Japan.

SIBERIAN
ANCIENT – RUSSIA – RARE

APPEARANCE
Large, substantial and powerful. Moderately long in body with barrel-like chest and well-rounded appearance. Strong musculature, moderately long in leg with heavy boning, back legs slightly longer than front, round paws with toe tufts. Head is modified wedge shape with broad, rounded muzzle and slightly curved forehead. Medium to large ears, preferably with Lynx tufts. Eyes large, almost round, wide set, and intelligent. Medium-length tail, broad at

base, covered in long, thick hairs that drape down from the sides.
SIZE
Large to Medium
COAT
Very thick, triple coated with soft dense undercoat, moderately long to long top coat and water resistant oily guard hairs on top. Any color or pattern although some associations will not accept pointed colors.
PERSONALITY
Lively, very playful, highly intelligent, loving, loyal

THERE IS NO MISSING A SIBERIAN CAT—this is one of the largest domestic cat breeds and has a substantial frame with a rounded appearance, and a particularly glorious coat. Males weigh between 17 and 26 lbs (7.5–12 kg) and females slightly less. Given their size, weight, and robust frame, it is surprising that these cats are so extraordinarily agile. They are in fact known for their jumping ability. They are extremely athletic and fairly energetic, enjoying a boisterous game. Water is particularly fascinating for Siberians and they can often be found exploring recently vacated bathtubs or dripping faucets; sometimes they will deliberately drop their toys in their water bowl to play. The Siberian is also a markedly intelligent cat and exhibits a high degree of problem-solving skills. This is both good and bad news for the owner, since these cats will invariably work out a way to access restricted food or areas, including opening latches and doors! They enjoy communicating and have a soft, chirping vocalization as well as a very melodic, deep purr. Siberians are also often described as being doglike, and they do have a tendency to greet one at the front door, much like a dog, to follow their owners around, and even to play fetch. These are very sociable cats that like to interact with those around them, and are noted for their patience with children. Claims have been made for some

time that the coats of Siberians are less likely to cause allergies than those of many other breeds. Studies continue into this.

The history of the Siberian is very poorly documented, although it is believed to be an ancient breed. It developed its unique characteristics in its homeland of Siberia, including the extremely thick coat and well-tufted paws that helped it to survive the cold. Before the twentieth century there was no interest in pedigree cat breeding in Russia and these Siberian cats lived throughout the country, breeding indiscriminately. They were highly valued on farms and in towns for their rodent-killing qualities and thrived in large numbers, many living a semiferal existence. St. Petersburg has a long tradition of being home to many cats; Elizabeth, daughter of Czar Peter the Great, brought cats originally in 1774 to rid the Winter Palace of rats. It is said that the cats were specially brought in from Kazan, and were chosen based on their rodent-killing skills—it is quite possible that these cats were ancestors to the modern Siberian. Cats have been popular in Russia for centuries, and many Russian folktales have characteristically large cats at their foundation—cats that acted as protectors to children and magical beings. Historically, cats have been considered a sign of good luck and prosperity; on moving to a new home, if a cat was allowed in first, the house would be blessed.

In the late nineteenth century a few Siberian cats were brought out of their homeland and into Europe. They were seen in the first official cat show held in 1871 at Crystal Palace in London and were described by the "father of the cat fancy" Harrison Weir in his book *Our Cats and All About Them* (1889). In the book he writes at length about the "Russian Long Haired Cat" and describes seeing them in the first show, which he had in fact organized. Other early cat fanciers and authors include John Jennings, who described the Siberian in his book *Domestic and Fancy Cats* (1901), and Helen Winslow in her book *Concerning*

ANCIENT TO MIDDLE AGES

Cats (1900). During the first decades of the twentieth century, under the Russian Communist regime, keeping domestic pets was banned—in great part as a result of food shortages. So, as Europe and the United States were embracing the world of cat fancy and pedigree breeds, the concept was not allowed to take hold in Russia.

It was not until the 1980s that the cat breeding was taken up with enthusiasm in Russia; at that time they began to realize the magnificence of their native cats. Siberians, many of which had lived a semiferal life, were suddenly ushered into the domestic forum with gusto. People began to keep records and establish pedigrees and the Kotofei Cat Club was established. The first cat show in St. Petersburg was held in 1987, organized by the Kotofei Cat Club, and the city started to become a center for Siberian breeding. The first standard for the breed was written in 1987 based on two cats, Roman, a brown tabby-and-white, and Mars, a blue lynx point. The Soviet Felinology Federation accepted this standard and Roman and Mars, along with Mars's son Nestor, are three of the foundation cats of the breed as it is recognized today. In 1989 at the All-Union Cat Show in Moscow twelve Siberians were exhibited, including Mars, and from this time on entries of Siberians at Russian cat shows have increased rapidly.

In 1988 an American breeder of Himalayans, Elizabeth Terrell from Starpoint Cattery, responded to an article asking people to donate Himalayans to help establish the breed in Russia. Terrell contacted Nelli Sachuk of the Kotofei Cat Club in St. Petersburg and a trade was arranged. Terrell sent four of her Himalayans and in return in 1990 she received three Siberians (Ofelia, Naina, and Kaliostro); these three were offspring of Roman and were the first Siberians to enter the United States. Following Terrell, a number of other breeders began to import Siberians, including Dana Osborn of the Willowbrook Cattery, who imported the first colorpoint Siberians in 1997. In 1991 Terrell founded the TAIGA Siberian Breed Club to promote the breed and to try to maintain its purity. Through the 1990s Siberians began to be exported in relatively large numbers from Russia, and there were instances of mixed breeds being sold as Siberians. They were not bred in the United Kingdom until 2002 but have quickly gained an enthusiastic following. Now the Siberian can be found in Europe, North America, and most countries of the world.

BRITISH SHORTHAIR
ANCIENT — BRITAIN — COMMON

APPEARANCE
Powerful, cobby, solid body type with short to medium length, well-boned legs and a medium length tail that is rounded at the tip. The head is round and massive with a well-developed chin, short nose, and round, alert eyes. Ears are set far apart, broad at base and rounded at tip.

SIZE
Medium to large
COAT
Distinctive, short, and very dense coat, firm to the touch with no woolly undercoat. Many different colors and patterns with eye color dependent on coat color.
PERSONALITY
Calm, dignified, loyal, affectionate

THE LOVELY BRITISH SHORTHAIR is a quiet, undemanding cat that enjoys company but is equally self-sufficient. It is affectionate and loyal to its family, not just to an individual, and enjoys attention without making a fuss. Although it is not excessively active, it is prone to short bursts of playing. These are particularly dignified cats and can be relatively shy with those not known to them. The distinctive coat of the British Shorthair is exceptionally dense and firm to the touch and has no undercoat or woolliness. This makes upkeep and grooming easy. The most popular and commonly seen color is a beautiful blue, but the breed does exhibit an enormous range of colors. These cats, perhaps due to their rugged early history as working farm cats, are incredibly sound in their health and very robust, making superb family pets.

The Romans are believed to have introduced the ancestors of the British Shorthair into England during their conquests beginning in 55 B.C.E. They had long welcomed cats into their culture following the ancient Egyptian precedent, although in a secularized manner. Cats were used for protecting stores and supplies from rodents, and were taken with the Romans on their expeditions for this very reason. In this way the shorthaired cats from Italy were spread across much of Europe and finally introduced into England. Here they thrived, many living a largely feral existence on the fringes of communities before they gradually crept into the household. The relationship between home owner and cat was largely symbiotic and different in nature to that between people and their dogs. Cats kept homes and farmyards free of disease-spreading vermin and demanded little in return for their services. The British Shorthair developed over centuries as a self-sufficient, medium to large cat with a tremendous coat that was resilient in any weather. It was not until the nineteenth century, though, that they really began to be noticed, and this was largely due to the influence of Harrison Weir, a man whose name is synonymous with any account of cats.

Weir and Mr. Wilkinson, who was the manager of Crystal Palace, London, set about organizing a cat show, which was eventually staged in 1871, and was the first of its kind in the world. Weir's aim was to bring to the public attention the different breeds and colors of cats, and to set in motion a system of recognition and registration for them through promoting them in shows. Weir was himself a great enthusiast of the British Shorthair, and the winner of Best in Show at the inaugural event was in fact Weir's own female British Shorthair!

It was in the late nineteenth century that people began to breed the British Shorthair for its color, type, and pedigree and to become interested in pedigreed cats. By this time, the British Shorthair had developed into a clear type; most noticeable was its coat, but also its frame, being stocky and muscular, and its characteristic face and head. The British Shorthair has often been likened to the Cheshire Cat from *Alice's Adventures in Wonderland* by Lewis Carroll (1865), and this is due to its rounded, full-cheeked facial appearance and a tendency to appear as if smiling.

By the beginning of the twentieth century the British Shorthair was extremely popular in cat shows and was being exhibited in a number of different color classes. Their popularity was such that by 1910 the most successful show cat in England was a male silver tabby British Shorthair owned by Mrs. Herring; his sister was the most successful female. These two winning cats helped to popularize this particular color, which became greatly sought after. The breed continued to gain in ascendency through the early years of the twentieth century, but was seriously affected during World War I. Following the war, and due to reduced numbers, Persian blood was introduced to the breed, which also brought in the longhaired gene. Although this crossbreeding helped to re-establish numbers, the Governing Council of the Cat Fancy (GCCF) objected to the different blood, and ruled that offspring from these crosses be ineligible for registration as British Shorthairs. Once the offspring had been bred back to registered British Shorthairs for three generations, they would then be allowed to be registered. Coinciding with these setbacks was the increasing popularity of the Persian cat in the show ring; this further affected the popularity and numbers of the British Shorthair.

World War II affected the breed again, and following the war years Chartreux, Burmese, and Russian Blues were used to bolster the British Shorthair. This led to the cats developing a slightly "foreign" appearance; Persian blood was then used again to bring the British Shorthair closer in line with its original appearance. Since that time the breed has greatly increased in popularity.

British Shorthairs, or at least their ancestors, arrived in North America on ships with the colonists in the seventeenth century, but the earliest pedigreed cats did not arrive until the early 1900s. Initially the most prolific were silver tabbies, and these were probably influential in the development of the American Shorthair. Despite the import of British Shorthairs, they were not recognized as a breed in the United States, and instead were registered as "domestic shorthairs." This changed in the 1950s when the blue British Shorthairs began to become popular and were then established as a breed (British Blue), although other color varieties of the British Shorthair continued to fall under domestic shorthairs. It was not until the 1970s that any concerted efforts were made to recognize the British Shorthair in all its color varieties, and then it was down to the sheer determination and hard work of a core group of enthusiasts. From this time, and particularly in the 1980s, the British Shorthair began to become more popular in the United States. The British Longhair, established through the introduction of Persian blood, has also now become popular on both sides of the Atlantic.

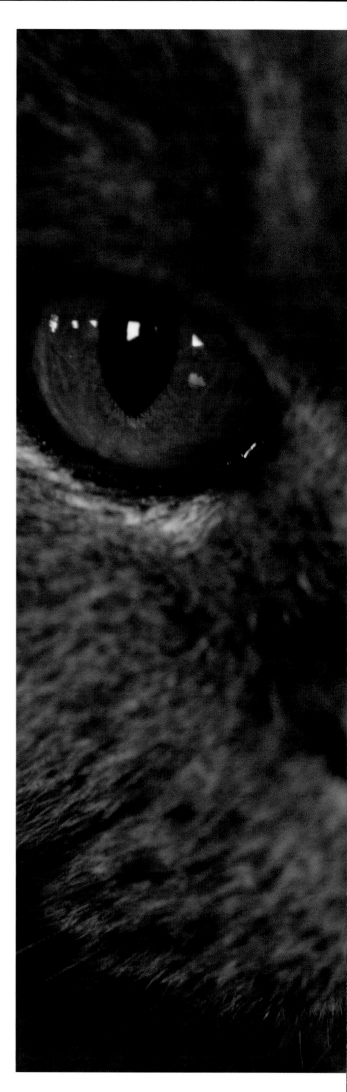

JAPANESE BOBTAIL

ANCIENT – JAPAN – RARE

APPEARANCE
Elegant, lean, and athletic cats, slender but muscular in build with long legs and powerful hindquarters. Back legs are longer than front. Triangular head with high, chiseled cheekbones, eyes set at a slant, and large, upright ears set high. Eye color harmonizes with coat color; each eye can be different in color. Tail is clearly visible and composed of one or more curves, angles, or kinks; it is covered in long hair that gives a pom-pom effect.

SIZE
Medium

COAT
Shorthaired has medium-length soft, silky coat. Longhaired has medium to long soft, silky coat. Neither has a noticeable undercoat. Can be any color.

PERSONALITY
Curious, active, lively, playful, interactive, affectionate

THE JAPANESE BOBTAIL is a hugely charismatic breed with an appearance that is quite unique and unlike other tailless breeds. The Japanese Bobtail (JBT) has no relation to the Manx. The JBT derives its short, pom-pom-like tail through a recessive gene; every JBT's tail is unique in conformation to the particular cat. The Manx, on the other hand, derives the structure of its tail through a dominant gene. When two JBTs are bred they will always produce their distinctive tail configuration. The JBT has a classically Oriental face with its beautiful eyes set on a slant and upright, intelligent ears. These are slender, athletic cats that delight in interactive play including fetch, and sometimes even in water. They also have a characteristic chirping voice often described as "singing." A JBT will become heavily involved in its owner's life, an integral part of every activity.

The JBT is a truly ancient breed and one whose origins are subject to a number of colourful (and wholly untrue) legends. One recounts that a cat lay sleeping by the fireside long ago when a spark leapt from the embers and set its tail alight. The terrified cat jumped up and ran through the Imperial City in Japan, setting fire to all the buildings as it went. By the next day the entire city had been burned to the ground and the furious emperor announced that all cats must have their tails cut off to prevent such a thing happening again—this gave rise to the Japanese Bobtail. Cats are thought to have been introduced to Japan by the sixth century C.E. from China and Korea, and appear frequently in ancient Japanese works of art. Many depict cats with a bobtail and there are also a number of images that clearly show longhaired Bobtail cats, indicating that the longhaired variety has been around just as long as the shorthaired. From early on cats were considered lucky and a sign of prosperity in both China and Japan, possibly because of their rodent-killing ways.

The Japanese Bobtail is most aligned with the famous symbol of welcome and good fortune, the female short-tailed Maneki-Neko, a beckoning cat figure. Over time it has become a hugely reproduced and recognized figure internationally and is first thought to have been introduced during the Edo Period (1603–1868). Works of art from the seventeenth century frequently depict Bobtail cats that are tricolored, being mostly white with patches of red and black. This popular coloration is called mi-ke. Despite these rather grand associations, the JBT was historically a working cat, found throughout Japan. It is consequently extremely hardy and disease resistant.

It was not until the late 1960s under the impetus of Elizabeth Freret that the JBT began to be established in the United States. Freret, who was also an Abyssinian breeder, imported three JBTs in 1968. She was helped through the process by the breeder Judy Crawford, an American living in Japan at the time. These three cats had been chosen from thirty-six kittens in Japan as the best of their kind, and were the foundation for the breed in the United States. At the same time Crawford helped Lynn Beck, a judge with the Cat Fanciers' Association (CFA), to import several more JBTs, and together Beck and Freret wrote the first JBT standard. They were also a driving force in gaining recognition for the breed in American cat fancy circles. Most of the major cat associations recognize the JBT today and, more recently, the longhaired JBT has also been acknowledged; the British Governing Council of the Cat Fancy (GCCF) does not recognize the breed. It remains low in numbers.

CHINESE LI HUA

ANCIENT — CHINA — RARE

APPEARANCE

Cobby and muscular. Strong, rectangular-shaped body with wide chest; the body length is greater than the height. Head is longer than it is wide and rounded between the ears; nose is long and straight with a slight dip at the bridge of nose. Large, almond-shaped eyes, green is preferable, but can be brown or yellow. Legs are strong and straight. Front legs are the same length or slightly shorter than the hind legs. Tail is slightly shorter than length of body.

SIZE

Medium

COAT

Short, thick, and lies close to the body. Always brown mackerel-tabby; each hair is ticked with a black root, lighter middle section, and brown tip, or with a light root, darker middle section, and a black tip. Underbelly is brownish-yellow

PERSONALITY

Amenable, intelligent, mild mannered, loving, loyal, gentle

THE LOVELY AND EXTREMELY RARE CHINESE LI HUA is known for its very phlegmatic character. Not much seems to faze these calm cats, who are also extremely affectionate. They are inherently intelligent and trainable —it is reputed that Zhao Shangzai (1908–1942), a proletarian revolutionary, had a Chinese Li Hua cat, which he trained to fetch the newspaper for him! Given their easy-going nature they get along well with other cats, animals, and children as long as they are treated with respect, and they make charming household companions. Currently, however, they are still extremely rare outside their homeland of China.

The Chinese Li Hua was only recognized in the United States by the Cat Fanciers' Association (CFA) in February 2010. In their homeland, these cats are considered to be one of the oldest natural breeds. Natural breeds are those that have evolved through the centuries without human interference or specialized crossbreeding. One theory of origin suggests that this breed developed from the wild Chinese mountain cat (*Felis silvestris bieti*), and there are considerable similarities between the two. However, there is no scientific data available at the moment to prove or disprove this theory.

There is little documented evidence pertaining to the origins of this strikingly marked breed, although there are references to cats of this type in Chinese folklore that date back many centuries. A great number of these references are particularly colorful, including one that relates how cats were in charge of the world and had the power of speech. Realizing how much work this was, they delegated their leadership to humans, along with speech, so that they could spend their time lazing around! Cats were assigned with special powers, often the ability to foresee the future, and even today a superstition continues that cats can predict earthquakes.

Historically cats were largely viewed as lucky and spiritual beings in China and they were welcomed into homes as pets. Of course their rodent-killing ability was no doubt a contributing factor to their popularity, and the Chinese Li Hua is especially adept in this department. It was also the ancient Chinese who discovered that the time of day could be predicted through watching the pupils in a cat's eye; as the day draws towards noon the pupil narrows until it becomes the width of a hair, and then starts to expand again towards evening.

The Chinese Li Hua is known by a number of different names including Dragon Li, Li Mao, and Li Hua Mao; *mao* means "cat" in Mandarin. The Chinese script for Li Hua Mao was often confused historically and translated as Fox Flower Cat; subsequently the breed has sometimes been called by this name, with the "flower" part of the name a reference to the strongly marked mackerel-tabby coat pattern. More recently the name Dragon Li has become popular in China and abroad since the association of the dragon is a profoundly nationalistic one and, understandably, China is proud of its "new" breed. Reputedly wedding ceremonies are held for mating pairs of the breed!

Despite its ancient origins, the Chinese Li Hua has only been recognized as a distinct breed relatively recently in its homeland as well as the United States, and this has been through the increasing interest in cat fancy in

China. This enthusiasm has been driven by the founding of the Cat Aficionado Association in China in 2001; this is China's largest registry of pedigreed cats and has recognition throughout Asia and internationally. The Chinese Li Hua was first exhibited in 2003 at the Beijing Cat Show where it was entered into the experimental breed class. Two judges from the American CFA were invited to the Beijing show as guest judges. Since that time American judges have been invited to Beijing shows at various intervals to participate in judging the Chinese Li Hua.

In February 2010, Allbreed CFA judge Bob Zenda presented the Chinese Li Hua to the CFA Board of Directors for recognition—this was the first time in its long history that the breed had been seen beyond its homeland. The presentation of the cats to the CFA Board of Directors was made possible through the help of Zhang Li Yu, president of the China Great Wall Cat Fanciers' Club in Beijing, who arranged for club member Yu Yin to transport two Chinese Li Hua cats to the United States for Bob Zenda's breed presentation.

Following their acceptance, two cats were flown from China to Los Angeles International Airport, arriving on October 18, 2010. They debuted at the CFA's Fort Worth Cat Club and Lone Star Cat Club shows in Dallas, Texas, on October 30–31, 2010 in the miscellaneous class. This was a momentous occasion for this little-heard-of breed and was only made possible through the help of Zhang Li Yu, Phebe Lo of the CFA International Division, and sisters Joann and Esther White, who received the cats on arrival in the United States.

From the Dallas show, one of the cats, Lihua China Nao Nao, left for his new home in South Dakota, while the White sisters returned to California with the other one. His name is Lihua China Zhong Guo of C2C, though he is affectionately known as "China." Since his arrival in the United States, China has been doing the rounds of cat shows and attracting a great deal of attention, including newspaper and television publicity. He has also, very recently, been joined by a female, Lihua China Xiao Lan of C2C, and the White sisters now have the only pair in the United States. Currently, there are six Chinese Li Hua living in the United States and each one is co-owned with people in China.

ANCIENT TO MIDDLE AGES

SIAMESE
ANCIENT — THAILAND — COMMON

APPEARANCE

Elegant and svelte. Characterized by long, graceful lines. Slender-framed with long, slim legs and firm muscles through body. Wedge-shaped, long, tapering head; nose is straight, skull flat. Large ears, wide at base, pointed at tip, continue line of the wedge-shaped face. Almond-shaped eyes, blue in color, slant toward nose. Long, tapering tail.

SIZE

Medium

COAT

Short, close lying, and glossy. Different colors accepted by different organizations; CFA recognizes Himalayan pattern in seal, blue, chocolate, and lilac point; GCCF recognizes these and others such as tabby point and red point.

PERSONALITY

Enormous. Highly intelligent, playful, very interactive, demanding, vociferous, very affectionate

THE SIAMESE IS ONE OF THE MOST POPULAR cat breeds in the world and certainly one of the most instantly identifiable. These cats have tremendous personalities, positively brimming with charisma, and are guaranteed to enliven any home. They are therefore only suitable for homes that wish to be actively involved with their cat, on their cat's terms, for extended periods of time! The Siamese is not only a highly intelligent individual but also likes to communicate with those around it—loudly and often at length. These are truly delightful cats and wonderful pets. They are devoted to their owners and do not do well for lengthy periods on their own. The Siamese will engage in all kinds of play, including fetch, and will demand undivided attention. They are frequently amusing and seem to have a sense of humor. When the playing is over, however, they like nothing better than the warmest, most comfortable spot in the house to take a nap, and invariably this will be on a lap.

There is a striking regal quality to the Siamese cat, so it is perhaps unsurprising that their early history is linked to the royal households of Siam, now called Thailand, from where the breed takes its name. It is not known where these elegant cats originated, though some speculate that they first came from Egypt. In Siam, they were associated with the wealthiest or ruling classes, and with the sacred

temples; they have often been referred to as the "royal cats of Siam." The cats were the subject of many superstitions and legends, not least that they housed the souls of the deceased members of royalty as they journeyed to their next world. When a member of the royal household had died, a special Siamese was chosen to house the spirit and was then sent to one of the temples where it lived out its days among the monks. Here the cats were fed only the finest food and were greatly revered on account of their supernatural powers. They are also believed to have acted as guardians to the temples, alerting the monks with their noisy mewling when strangers approached.

One legend about the Siamese cat tells how a sacred cat had been charged with guarding a special vase in a temple. The cat curled its long tail around the vase and stared at it so hard that its eyes became crossed—cross-eyes were seen relatively frequently in early Siamese cats, although successful steps have been taken to breed it out now. Another trait often seen in the cats was a kinked tail—again this is now considered undesirable. One story that explains the kinks in the tail tells how a Siamese was appointed to look after the royal princesses' rings. The cats kept the rings safely on their tails, leading to the kinks. The earliest written reference to the Siamese appeared in the *Cat Book Poems*, now in the Bangkok Library. This ancient book also contains the earliest-known illustration of a Siamese cat, dating from the Ayudhya period (1350–1767).

It was not until the nineteenth century that the breed began to gain any kind of exposure beyond its homeland. Two Siamese cats are listed as being among the exhibits at the very first official cat show, held in London in 1871. The show attracted great attention from the national press, and the two Siamese cats, being unfamiliar to the British public, were described both positively and negatively. *The Daily Telegraph* wrote that the cats were "unprepossessing and their colours completed the resemblance of the little brutes to a pair of pug puppies." Another journalist, however, raved that they were "singular and elegant in their smooth skins." Beyond these remarks, little is known about these two Siamese.

Some of the earliest properly documented Siamese to arrive in the United Kingdown were given in 1884 to Sir Edward Blencowe Gould, the Consul-General in Bangkok, by the Thai royal family. Gould gave the two cats, Pho and Mia, to his sister Lilian Veley. Veley exhibited Pho, Mia, and three of their kittens at the cat show at Crystal Palace, London, in 1885. The first British standard was written in 1892, and in 1901 Veley and another Siamese breeder, Miss Forestier Walker and her sister Mrs. Vyvyan, founded the Siamese Cat Club—one of the first cat registries in the United Kingdom and an early member of the Governing Council of the Cat Fancy (GCCF).

One of the first Siamese to arrive in the United States was a small female called Siam, who was gifted to the wife of American President Rutherford B. Hayes by the U.S. Consul in Bangkok, David Stickles, in 1879. Siam rapidly made herself at home in the White House and became a firm favorite with the first family and all the staff. She was also the first of a number of Siamese cats to live alongside American presidents; Jimmy Carter and Gerald Ford also had Siamese Cats in the White House. The first registered Siamese in the United States, however, belonged to Mrs. Robert Locke, who founded the Beresford Cat Club in 1899.

From this time on, and particularly during the 1940s and 1950s, the breed escalated rapidly in popularity. The Siamese has also been at the foundation of a number of modern cat breeds including the Himalayan, Burmese, Tonkinese, Snowshoe, Ocicat, Balinese, Javanese, Oriental, and Colorpoint Shorthair and Longhair. During the 1960s there was a gradual change in breeding policies that has become extremely controversial among breeders. At that time there was a considered trend towards breeding the Siamese towards the extremely slender and angular form that is recognized today, and away from the slightly heavier build of cat with a more rounded head shape. This has split the Siamese world in two, with the slender frame often described as the Extreme Siamese, or in show circles as Modern or Wedge-shaped. The more robust cat is referred to as the Traditional, Old Style, or Applehead; some lobbied for the Old Style to be given its own breed status and in this book it appears under the entry for the Thai Cat.

KORAT

ANCIENT — THAILAND — RARE

APPEARANCE
Alert and silver blue. Semicobby body with broad chest; heavier than expected when lifted. Compact and muscular. Distinctive heart-shaped face with breadth between eyes curving down to well-developed chin and jaw. Eyes appear slanted when closed, but fully round and large when open and are a luminous peridot green. Tail is medium length, broader at base and tapers to tip.

SIZE
Medium to small

COAT
Single coat, short and glossy. Always silver blue all over, hairs tipped with silver to produce a "halo" effect.

PERSONALITY
Very affectionate, intelligent, playful, and energetic

THE KORAT IS A BEAUTIFUL ANCIENT BREED that hails originally from Siam, now Thailand, and has changed very little in appearance throughout its long history. Historically, and still today, the Korat is considered lucky in its homeland, perhaps in part due to the unique formation of its "heart-shaped" head. It in fact has a number of "hearts" associated with its appearance; one is seen in the shape of the face front on, another when looking down on the top of the head. The shape of the nose forms a third heart, while the fourth Korat heart is seen in the direction of hair growth that occurs across its broad chest. Another unique feature of this lovely breed is the color. The Korat is always silver blue with no tabby markings or shadings. Each hair shaft is lighter at the root and a darker shade of blue toward the tip, while the tip itself is silver, which gives the coat a silvery sheen. This, combined with stunning luminous green eyes, makes these cats immensely striking.

Korats are the most delightful companions, being extremely affectionate, playful—they will play fetch—and interactive. They are very loyal to their loved ones and, although not tolerant of loud noise, are good with children. They also cope relatively well with other pets and cats, though show a preference for their own breed.

The documented history of the Korat traces back many hundreds of years to an ancient book of paintings and verses called the *Cat Book Poems*, which dates from the Ayudhya period of Siamese history (1350–1767), and is now in the Bangkok National Library. There are also fifteen or so ancient manuscripts pertaining to animals in the library, of which nine contain images of cats, giving some indication of the esteem in which cats were held in their native home. In the nineteenth century King Rama V (1853–1910) commissioned a monk to copy the original *Cat Book Poems*. This new copy was called the *Smud Khoi of Cats* and can be found in the Bangkok's National Museum. A further copy was made in the twentieth century, depicting seventeen different types of cat that are considered lucky, with accompanying verses. The Korat appears as one of the lucky breeds and is described thus: "The cat Maled has a body color like Dok Lao. The hairs are smooth, with roots like clouds and tips like silver. The eyes shine like dewdrops on the lotus leaf ..." *Dok* translates as "flower," while *lao* translates as "lemongrass," "pampas grass," or "reed blossom," all of which are silvery in color and similar to the Korat's coat.

King Rama V is said to have given the Korat its name when he inquired where the pretty cats came from and was told they had come from the Khorat region—a colloquial term for the northeastern province of Nakhon Ratchasima. This area is home to great rocky, granite outcrops and it is said that the Korat's silver-blue coloring provided it with perfect camouflage in this habitat, and perhaps saved its life during conflicts. More often than not, in Thailand, the cats are referred to as Si Sawat. *Si* means "color" and *sawat* can mean "good fortune" or a mingled color of gray and light green.

A number of superstitions are attached to the Korat or Si Sawat in its homeland. Its silver-tipped fur is said to represent wealth and good fortune, its green eyes are linked to the greenness of young plants, indicating a good harvest, while the silver-blue coat is said to symbolize rain clouds—also important for a profitable harvest. Interestingly, too, in Thailand a Korat with a kink in its tail

is considered lucky, although in the West any sign of a kink is highly undesirable. The breed is greatly prized in Thailand, and even there is relatively rare. Korats have historically been extremely difficult to come by for foreigners, and they pass among Thai families, often as cherished gifts and as presents to newlywed couples to promote a fortuitous union.

There are reports that a Korat was exhibited in England in 1896; the cat was described as "a blue cat from Siam" and was exhibited as a Siamese. It was apparently disqualified from its class by the famous judge Louis Wain on account of its blue coloring (being in the Siamese class, it should have been biscuit fawn). However it is generally held that the first Korats imported to the United Kingdom arrived in 1972, and these are listed as the female Brandywood Saeng Duan and the two males Samelko Sahm and Saang Jahn's Tee Rahk. The same year Saeng Duan had the first litter of kittens in the United Kingdom and just two years later there were more than twenty Korats in the country.

It was due to the efforts of Jean Johnson in 1959 that the first Korats arrived in the United States. Johnson had lived in Bangkok for some years and had tried to procure some Korats while there, with no success. Due to her perseverance she was eventually given two Korats, Nara and Darra, that had come from the respected Mahajaya cattery of Khunying Abhibal Rajamaitri. Johnson owned the Cedar Glen cattery and began a breeding program there to establish the Korat. The breed began to attract attention and by 1962 another breeder, Gail Lankenau Woodward, had imported a further female from the Mahajaya cattery, Mahajaya Dok Rak of Gala and a male, Nai Sri Sawat Miow of Gala from Cholburi. An additional female, Me-Luk of Tru-Lu, was imported by Gertrude Gecking Sellars, and these cats together formed the foundation for the Korat breed in the United States. Another important pioneer in the breed, Daphne Negus, also imported nine Korats—nine being a lucky number in Thailand. By 1965 there were enough breeders and supporters to establish the Korat Cat Fanciers Association, which then set about writing a standard, and by the end of that year the Korat had been accepted by most cat associations in Canada and the United States.

BIRMAN

ANCIENT – BURMA – COMMON

APPEARANCE
Stocky with magnificent coat. Long and stocky through the body, substantial build with good musculature and solid bone, particularly in the legs. Head is broad and slightly rounded, Roman nose profile with full cheeks and strong chin. Ears are broad at base and almost as wide at base as they are tall. Eyes are almost round, set well apart, and always blue. Legs are medium length and muscular; paws are large and round. Tail is medium length and in balance with body.

SIZE
Medium to medium large

COAT
Beautiful medium long to long silky coat with ruff around the neck. Accepted colors vary between registries; the traditional colors are seal point, chocolate point, blue point, and lilac point; some registries accept any pointed color. Should have four white paws (gloves) and white markings to back of hind legs to point of hock, called "laces."

PERSONALITY
Gentle, quiet, amenable, loving

THERE ARE MANY TALES RELATING TO THE ORIGINS of the lovely Birman breed, none of which are truly proven. However, the Birman is generally accepted to be descended from the sacred temple cats of ancient Burma—at least by the more romantic enthusiast. These solid cats are distinguished in a number of ways, not least by their unusual markings, which are also part of the fabric of their legendary origins. All Birman cats have pure white markings on their paws, termed "gloves." These cover the toes and, on the front legs, should extend to the second or third joint of the paws. On the hind legs the glove markings can extend higher up the leg than on the front. They must also extend up the back of the hind legs to the hocks, ideally ending in an inverted V shape. These markings are termed "laces." The markings on the front legs should match, as should those on the hind legs. It is every breeder's dream to produce Birmans with perfectly coordinating markings, although this is not often the case. More tantalizing still is the fact that the cats are born white and do not develop the color of their points for a period of time, so the anxious breeder must wait to see how even the glove and lace markings will be. Birmans also have a particularly wonderful coat. Not only is it luxurious and silky to touch and in appearance, but from a practical

point of view, the coat tends not to mat and so requires slightly less maintenance than other long- or semi-longhaired breeds.

These are extremely gentle and placid cats that like nothing better than to be loved and with their families. They are undemanding, although they enjoy interacting with their owners, and eagerly join in a healthy play session. Birmans tend to get along well with children and other pets including dogs; they also do well with a single owner. They are not particularly vociferous, but will become more so if they are spoken to regularly. They like to communicate with their owner and will do this either through purring or through vocalization, provided they receive a response.

There are a number of different variations on the legend of their origin, some much longer and more complex than others. The most frequently related version tells how the holy priest Mun-Ha lived and worshipped in the Temple of Lao-Tsun in a remote, mountainous area of Burma on the mountain of Lugh. The temple was dedicated to Tsun-Kyankse, a goddess with sapphire-blue eyes who watched over the transmigration of souls and who allowed the souls of priests, or Kittahs, to live again in a sacred animal during the animal's natural existence. The temple was also home to one hundred sacred cats and Mun-Ha's special cat Sinh. Sinh was the priest's oracle and had yellow eyes from gazing upon the golden body of the goddess Tsun-Kyankse for so long. Sinh had brown legs, paws, tail, nose, and ears, like the color of earth, and representing the impurity of everything that touches the ground.

One night the temple was ransacked by raiders and Mun-Ha was mortally wounded. Sinh placed his feet on his dying master and, facing the goddess, underwent a miraculous transformation as the life of his master ebbed away. Sinh's fur glowed golden, reflecting the goddess's body, and his eyes turned sapphire blue, the same as hers. Where his four paws touched the white hair of his beloved

master they turned white, symbolizing purity. Sinh refused to move from his dead master and seven days later he died, transporting the soul of Mun-Ha to the place of eternal rest. As this happened all the sacred cats in the temple surrounded the other priests and they all took on this new coloration of white paws, blue eyes, and golden bodies. The legend states that these sacred cats carried the souls of all of the priests on their final journey. Legend apart, these cats were very likely kept in temples, as was common in ancient times, to control rodent populations.

The next passage of Birman history took place centuries later, but is equally elusive. One tale recounts that Major Gordon Russell, an officer in the British army, and his friend August Pavie, helped to defend the Temple of Lao-Tsun against attack in 1885 during the third Anglo-Burmese war (1885–87). In thanks for saving their temple the priests made the unprecedented gift of two of their sacred cats to the men, who then transported them back to France. This account is problematic because of the timeline and the identies of the men. August Pavie, a French civil servant, explorer, and diplomat undertook a mission from 1894–5 along the borders of China and Burma along the left bank of the Mekong river and as far as the Red River. Major Gordon Russell is thought by some to be a fictional character, although it is possible he is Major Leonard George Russell (1858–1946), who was in the Rifle Brigade. Since the earliest Birmans to arrive in Europe (Paris) are thought to have done so in 1919, the dates do not seem to match up. Another story, equally suspect, relates how a wealthy American, one of the Vanderbilt family, on an expedition to Burma, obtained two Birmans from a temple employee and smuggled them to France where they were received by Mme. Thadde Haddisch.

The first factual evidence surrounding these cats pertains to a pair who were sent from Burma to France in around 1919. The male Madalpour died in transit, but the pregnant female Sita survived and produced kittens. One of these, a female called Poupée, was then outcrossed, possibly to a Siamese, to try to preserve the breed. Poupée is recognized as the *grande dame* of the breed. She was exhibited at the International Paris Cat Show in 1926, along with two other Birmans, causing quite a sensation. Over three hundred cats took part in the show, including Siamese and Persians, but it was the rare Birmans that the

public found most fascinating. Gradually, through careful breeding, the Birman became established in France and was exported throughout Europe. They suffered a great setback during World War II when their numbers were again much reduced. A second breeding program was instigated in some secrecy, although it is thought that Siamese and Colorpoint Persians might have been used; the first blue point Birmans began to emerge at around this time. Some famous early French catteries producing Birmans were the Madalpour Cattery and the da Kaabaa Cattery, while other key Birman breeders included Simone Poirier, Yvonne Drosier, and Anne Marie Moulin.

Birmans arrived in England in 1965 after Mrs. Elsie Fisher and Margaret Richards fell in love with the breed when they saw them at the Paris Cat Show the same year. They at once imported a seal male from Simone Poirier, called Nouky de Mon Rêve, who went to live with Margaret. She first exhibited him at the Herts & Middlesex Show, followed by the National Show at Olympia. Two females were imported in 1966; they went to Elsie. Margaret and Elsie joined forces and founded the breed in England under the joint prefix Paranjoti, breeding their first Birman litter of eight in 1966. The same year the breed was granted championship status by the General Council of the Cat Fancy (GCCF). The Birman Cat Club was founded in 1968, driven largely by Elsie Fisher, and gradually enthusiasm for the breed began to pick up in Britain. After the Paranjoti partnership came to an end, Elsie Fisher continued to breed Birmans under the Praha prefix, and Margaret Richards bred under the Mei Hua prefix.

Word of the beautiful Birman spread to the United States, and the first cat arrived in 1959, imported by Dr. and Mrs. Seipel. Two more followed in 1961, going to Mrs. Griswold. Mrs. Griswold established the Griswold Cattery, and her cat Korrigan of Clover Creek went on to sire the first Birman grand champion, awarded by the Cat Fanciers' Association (CFA). American Birman breeding was based on cats that were primarily imported from both France and England, including Elsie Fisher's Praha Cattery. Today the popularity of the Birman is firmly established in both Europe and the United States—understandably, given its exquisite looks and equally charming personality.

ANCIENT TO MIDDLE AGES

PERSIAN

ANCIENT – PERSIA/IRAN – COMMON

APPEARANCE

Glamorous and solid. Cobby body type, heavily boned, relatively short in the leg with a substantial body and tail short in proportion to body length. Round face with short, snub nose, large, expressive, round eyes, and a sweet expression. Ears are set far apart, small, and tilted forward.

SIZE

Large to medium

COAT

Magnificent long, thick coat with large ruff around neck. Deep frill between front legs, full brush on tail. Many colors and patterns within the following divisions: solid; silver and gold; shaded and smoke; tabby; parti-color; bicolor; pointed (Himalayan).

PERSONALITY

Sweet, gentle, calm, quiet, attentive, playful, and intelligent

ONE OF THE MOST POPULAR CAT BREEDS in the world, the Persian is unmistakable. It is distinguished by its beautiful long coat, brilliantly colored, expressive eyes, and thoroughly regal manner. These are the Kings and Queens of the cat world. The Persian's long, thick coat requires frequent care and grooming; this is a high-maintenance cat, only suitable for those with time to spend on its care. A very devoted cat by nature, the Persian forms strong, loyal attachments to its family, and has a particularly sweet and gentle disposition. It excels at lounging, generally in the most comfortable spot in the house, but it can also be extremely playful and engage in short bursts of activity—usually followed by a long period of rest.

For many years Persian cats have been bred for their wide variety of different and splendid colors. In England in the early 1900s, the Governing Council of the Cat Fancy (GCCF) decided that Persians should be referred to as Longhairs and that each color variety be considered a separate breed; this policy continues today. In the United States, however, the Persian is viewed as a single breed with a number of color divisions: solid; silver and gold; shaded and smoke; tabby; parti-color; bicolor; and pointed (Himalayan). Within each color division there is an enormous range of color variety that extends from their coats to the color of their eyes. These specific colors are the product of intense and considered breeding, and it is due to

the efforts of breeders that they have been maintained to such degree. Some cat organizations list the Himalayan as a color division within the Persian, while others consider the Himalayan to be a separate breed; for the purposes of this book the Himalayan has been given its own breed entry in Chapter 3.

As is typical for an ancient cat breed, there are no records of the exact origins of these lovely, longhaired cats. The first evidence of their existence dates back to the mid-1500s, but it is possible that Persians developed long before this. Interestingly, the earliest depictions of cats, which trace back to ancient Egypt, all reveal clearly shorthaired animals. *Felis silvestris lybica*, the species from which domestic cats are believed to descend, is also shorthaired. In the late eighteenth century the German naturalist Peter Simon Pallas (1741–1811) suggested that the Persian and Angora had descended from *Felis manul*, which was first described by Pallas in 1776 and is also named Pallas's Cat. Found in Central Asia, Pallas's Cat is longhaired and stout with a flattened face—both similar to the Persian. Pallas's theory was not based on any kind of scientific evidence, however—a fact that Charles Darwin recognized in 1868 when he commented on Pallas's suggestion. At the turn of the twentieth century the theory was rejected based on morphological differences between the skull of the Pallas's Cat and those of the Persian and Angora cats; at this time *Felis manul* was renamed *Octolobus manul*.

The most plausible and commonly accepted explanation for the longhaired coat is due to a genetic mutation that probably occurred in a cold environment as an evolutionary aid for the cats within that habitat. There is, however, further debate over where exactly this mutation might have occurred. Some claim it was in the cold, mountainous areas of Persia (now Iran). Others claim it was in Russia, accounting for the Siberian and Russian Angora breeds, and that once the mutation was fixed through interbreeding, the cats may have spread to surrounding countries, including westward to Persia. It may also have spread to Turkey, where the Angora was established, and eastward to Japan where the Japanese Bobtail was developing. It is possible that the mutation occurred in all these locations and that the longhaired cats spread through the extensive web of land and sea trade routes to enter Europe as well as the Middle and Far East.

One of the earliest documented accounts of these longhaired cats was by the Italian traveler Pietro della Valle (1586–1652), who wrote about Persians and Angoras in his travel journal. He described the Persian cat as having a very long, glossy coat, being gray, and coming from the province of Khorasan in Persia, although he also noted that longhaired cats were brought from India by Portuguese travelers. His writings document the earliest-known import of these longhaired cats into Italy.

French travelers are also credited with bringing Persians and Turkish Angoras back to France with them after their expeditions; some of these cats then found their way to England, where they were often referred to as French Cats. Others were brought from China and termed Chinese Cats; the origin of these is unclear, although it is possible that longhaired cats were gifted by the Kings of Persia to the Chinese Emperors. Certainly cats had been popular in China from at least the fourteenth century, when they appear in many works of art. Specific reference to longhaired Chinese cats was made in the eighteenth century by the Abbé Jean-Baptiste Grosier in his *General Description of China* (1788), when he described longhaired white cats with a very silky coat at the Chinese court. In the 1800s travelling diplomats and explorers saw the exotic-looking cats and brought them back to England and continental Europe. The cats were commonly named after their country of origin, hence the Persian and Turkish Angora, with instances of the longhaired Russian cats being far less frequent. As these longhaired cats arrived in Europe they became instantly popular, at first based on their unusual and lovely looks, swiftly followed by an appreciation for their gentle nature. The modern Persian cat as it is known today was developed through crossbreeding these initial early imports that included cats from Persia, Turkey, and probably also Russia. As interest in these cats grew, people began to breed for specific coat patterns and colors.

Various cat clubs were established to meet the new enthusiasm for cat breeding, and in 1871 the world's first cat show was held at Crystal Palace in London, organized by Harrison Weir. Weir also wrote the book *Our Cats and All About Them* (1889), which contained drawings of the different breeds, and a Standard of Points of Excellence not very far removed from that in use today. His description of the Persian shows that it has changed little since the nineteenth century. He differentiates the Persian quite clearly from the Angora, the latter having longer, silkier hair, and being mostly white and lighter in frame than the Persian. Writings and paintings from this period reveal that the Persian was bred in many colors, with solid colors being preferred, but silvers and smokes, reds, bicolors, parti-colors, and tabbies also popular. Queen Victoria owned two blue Persian cats, which increased the popularity of the breed and the color in England.

In the United States interest in cat shows and breeding was also on the increase. According to Helen Winslow, an early cat fancy historian, the first longhaired cat to be imported was a black Persian called Madam, who came from Spain. The second was a white Persian called Wendell, who was imported by Mrs. Clinton Locke of Chicago directly from Persia in around 1875. Mrs. Clinton Locke was the first woman in America to run a cattery, the Lockehaven Cattery, and was founder of the Beresford Cat Club of Chicago. Her Persians dominated the show ring in the first years of the twentieth century. Another breeder, Frances Simpson, who wrote *The Book of the Cat* (1903), also laid claim to having the first Persians in the country and stated that she had purchased a pair of white Persians with blue eyes in 1869 from a foreign ship that put in to port for repairs after a storm. The first major cat show in the United States was held at Madison Square Garden in New York in May 1895, attracting great public interest and 176 cat exhibits, including a number of white Persians belonging to Mrs. Clinton Locke and others.

In 1909 D. B. Champion wrote *Everybody's Cat Book* in which he described the show-type Persian cat, his description still largely reflecting the current standards. At this time American breeders were still following the English precedent of treating each color as if it were a separate breed, and great importance was placed on the color and pattern of each. Angoras were frequently bred with Persians, to such an extent that the Angora all but disappeared and was only reestablished as a separate breed in the 1960s. The extent of crossbreeding early in the modern development of the Persian cat has recently come to light in scientific terms. A study *The Ascent of Cat Breeds, Genetic Evaluations of Breeds and Worldwide Random Bred Populations* (2008) by Lipinski et al revealed that the Persian is more closely related to random-bred cats from Western Europe and America than to random-bred cats from the Near East. It found that the Persian breed is derived from multiple different lineages, underlining the historic accounts of inbreeding between Turkish and Russian longhaired cats as well as British cats.

One of the many appealing and characteristic aspects of the Persian is its sweet, open facial expression. In the late twentieth century a fashion arose—first in the United States, then in the United Kingdom—for breeding Persians with more extreme head conformation. This included a flattened skull with heavy brows, a narrow, high-set nose, and maloccluded jaws to produce a frowning mouth. These cats are described as having a "piggy" expression, and in severe cases can suffer from upper-respiratory problems because of the conformation of their noses, weeping eyes, and even problems during birth because of the shape of their heads. The Peke-face red Persian, named after the Pekinese dog, was developed in the United States and also has an extreme facial arrangement, differing considerably from the other color divisions of the breed. Its skull structure is very round with a depressed nose and an indentation between widely spaced eyes, with the ears set more highly on the head. The Peke-face arose in the 1950s as a mutation before being established as a type; very few are now registered, and preference has swung back to the open expression of the original Persian.

A Persian of special character should be noted: a cat called Precious, who survived the attacks on New York City on September 11, 2001. Precious was home alone in her apartment directly opposite the Twin Towers when they were attacked. Their collapse caused all the windows in Precious's block to shatter, and the building was damaged so severely that the residents were not allowed back in. Eighteen days later a rescue team found Precious on the roof of her building where she had survived on her own— some feat for a cat that had never previously been outside.

CHAPTER 2
MIDDLE AGES TO NINETEENTH CENTURY

In contrast to the early history of cats as objects of worship and spiritual significance, the Middle Ages saw a marked downturn in feline fortunes, and the start of very polarized attitudes toward cats. In Europe, the rise of Christianity marked the beginning of the serious persecution of cats, partly because of their association with the polytheistic religions of the ancient world. It is unarguable that there is an esoteric quality about cats that is hard to define; it is their very nature that is so alluring for some, and abhorrent to others. Cats were associated with magical powers, and this ultimately led to their demonization. The nature of this antipathy toward cats was not a single sweeping movement, but appears to have ebbed and flowed throughout the centuries with several periods of intensity. Cats, and in particular black cats, became associated with the devil—at times during history black dogs have also suffered a similar though less pervasive prejudice. The Italian poet Dante Alighieri (1265–1321) likened cats to demons in the only time he mentioned them in his poetry.

The impact of rodent infestation throughout the ages has been one of grave consequence, manifested not only in the spreading of disease, but also in destruction of crops, food, household goods, manuscripts, papyrus products, and more. In the fourteenth century the Black Death, carried from Asia by fleas living on rats, decimated Europe, reaching its height between 1347 and 1351 and killing 40 to 60 percent of the European population. At this time, cats were being grotesquely persecuted with thousands being killed. Suddenly, those cats that were still around, with their efficient dispatching of rats, became rather more popular.

There appears to have been a markedly double standard with regard to cats. Some cats of exotic breeds, for example, and those traded from overseas and therefore associated with wealthy homes, were regarded differently to those living a semiferal existence among the lower ranks of society. Despite a general antipathy towards cats, in the tenth century the Welsh laws formulated by Hywel Dda, the king of much of Wales, acknowledge that cats had a worth. The laws were broken down into three different

Codes—of Venedotia (north Wales), Dimetia (south Wales), and Gwent (southeastern Wales)—with each exhibiting slightly different legislation. The Venedotian Code for example proclaimed that once a cat was grown enough to kill mice it was worth four pennies. The Dimetian and Gwentian Codes drew a distinction between cats that worked under the royal banner and those of the commoner—this distinction underlines the notion of different attitudes to cats from different classes.

In another example of differing attitudes in the Middle Ages, cats were also linked to convents. They were kept by convents primarily for rodent control, but interestingly (and not so beneficial to the cats), their fur was considered suitable for trimming nuns' habits. In France the beautiful blue-colored Chartreux was highly valued by furriers, and they were specifically bred from the Middle Ages onward for this purpose. Legends also associate this particular breed with the French monasteries. The Knights Templar reputedly returned from the Crusades having collected cats from the North African coastline and retired to French monasteries to recover. It is from these cats that the Chartreux is said to have developed within the quiet seclusion afforded by the religious orders.

During the fourteenth century, most sources indicate that views toward cats were hostile. While they might have been tolerated on farms, homesteads, religious institutions, and ships for rodent control, they were by and large not greatly loved. The Italian scholar and poet Petrarch (1304–1374) is an exception. He is said to have spent much of his time in his later years with his pet cat, whom he adored. Following Petrarch's death, his cat was (unfortunately for the cat) dispatched, embalmed, and entombed at the scholar's house in Arquá, with a marble cat marking the spot and bearing the inscription "I was the greatest passion, second only to Laura"—Laura had been the subject of many of his poems.

At the same time in the East, and China in particular, cats were still revered. During the Ming Dynasty (1368–1644), cats were especially prominent in the royal palaces

and a favorite with many of the Ming emperors. Here, amid the cool marble interiors of Chinese palaces, pampered cats resided in luxury. They were often painted by the court painters and numerous delightful images of cats date to this era. Accounts show that the royal cats were assigned special eunuchs to look after them and were afforded a very comfortable life. These cats were not expected to earn their living chasing mice, and were certainly regarded differently from those cats beyond the palace walls who did. Cats remained popular in China after 1644 and were frequently kept as playthings for the royal princesses who spent most of their life within the palace confines.

During this period in Europe there was a steady increase in the association of cats with evil and the supernatural. This mirrored the persecution of witches by Christian zealots. Cats were seen as "familiars," supernatural assistants to witches that were capable of shape shifting and harboring spirits. Historically, and even today, cats have been associated with women and often single or elderly women; those same figures were frequently accused of witchcraft. This was compounded by a number of superstitions in Western Europe surrounding childbirth. A pregnant woman who experienced pain was said to be harboring kittens from the devil in her womb, which were scratching; this led to the commonly used expression meaning that someone is upset or panicking—"having kittens." Witchcraft was outlawed in Scotland in 1563, and the last public "witch" death occurred there in 1722. Ritual cat sacrifice formed part of the cultural fabric, with *taigheirm*, an ancient rite involving such sacrifice, taking place in the Highlands until the middle of the seventeenth century. The word *taigheirm* means "cry of a cat."

As cats were systematically slaughtered alongside their accused owners through the sixteenth and seventeenth centuries, they were also subjected to various forms of torture for human entertainment. Given their association with witchcraft, cats—particularly black cats—were sacrificed for various rituals, including the promise of a good harvest. Body parts of cats became important in alchemy and were used to ward off various afflictions. In Edward Topsell's book *The History of Four-footed Beasts* (1607), he describes cats as poisonous and dangerous to the soul. Topsell's book was published during the reign of King James VI and I (1566–1625), who had raised a statute against witchcraft and under whose reign the persecution of witches reached a zenith. In 1644 the Englishman Matthew Hopkins was appointed an official witchfinder, and he traveled the east of the country for two years wreaking a path of terrible savagery on great numbers of innocent women and their cats. The last execution of a witch in the United Kingdom was in the late seventeenth century. In France, Cardinal Richelieu (1585–1642) exemplified the conflicting attitudes to cats. He was

reputedly a cat lover, owning more than fourteen of his own pampered cats, including a Turkish Angora—the breed had by this time found its way to France via Italian merchants and traders. Yet he put numerous cats to death alongside their owners, charged with witchcraft. The persecution of witches continued in Europe until the middle of the eighteenth century when the last "witch" was said to have been executed in Bavaria.

Cats were taken to America with the pilgrims and colonists—there are records of cats on board the *Mayflower* in 1620. These early working cats were on board for their ratting skills and were the ancestors to what would become the American Shorthair and the Maine Coon. Given their working origins, both these breeds are particularly robust and healthy, despite now being very different from those original cats taken over. The time of the pilgrims coincided with the full religious fervor in Europe, and the same preoccupations were slowly transferred to the new continent. The famous Salem Witch Trials in Massachusetts from 1692 to 1693, did not ignite until the persecution in Europe was beginning to wane.

In another link between cats and women, the word "cat" had by the seventeenth century come to be used as a colloquial term for a prostitute. A story that dates to 1876 and the then-notorious gambling town of Deadwood, South Dakota, relates how an enterprising man called Alexander Davidson acquired large numbers of cats and sold them to the town's brothel to combat the rodent infestation. He made substantial profits from the endeavor and the brothel became known as the "cathouse," although this term had in fact been in use long before his venture.

Despite their extensive persecution, cats won themselves many great admirers over the centuries, not least Leonardo da Vinci (1452–1519), who frequently made studies of cats and reputedly said, "even the smallest feline is a masterpiece." Another was Cardinal Wolsey (1473–1530), advisor to Henry VIII; his cat accompanied him to meetings when he was officiating as chancellor of England. The nobleman Sir Henry Wyatt (1460–1536) was imprisoned in London and given barely enough food to subsist but, according to stories, a cat he befriended caught pigeons and brought them back for him. Sir Henry was reputedly able to persuade his jailers to cook the pigeons for him and so he stayed alive. When the third Earl of

Southampton (1573–1624) was incarcerated in the Tower of London, he managed to convince the authorities to allow his cat Trixie to share his prison.

Cats were gradually becoming the companions of writers and artists; perhaps their self-sufficient nature proved a good match with those of creative leanings. François-Augustin de Paradis de Moncrif (1687–1770), French author and historiographer to Louis XV of France wrote *Histoire des Chats* in 1727, looking at the history of cats and their importance to society. It was one of the first works written that wholly applauded cats and Moncrif was widely mocked when it was published. In England the historian Horace Walpole (1717–1797) owned the cat Selima, who became famous posthumously (she drowned in a porcelain goldfish bowl) when the poet Thomas Gray wrote an ode to the cat in 1748, inspired by Walpole's grief. Esteemed author Samuel Johnson (1709–1784) was a devoted cat-lover and fed oysters to his cat Hodge; there is still a statue of Hodge and an oyster outside Johnson's house at 17 Gough Square, London. Other notable cat devotees of the period include the romantic poet Lord Byron (1788–1824), who owned five cats along with various horses, dogs, three monkeys, and assorted birds. John Keats (1795–1821) and his friend and fellow poet Percy Bysshe Shelley (1792–1822) adored cats, as did the Scottish writer Sir Walter Scott (1771–1832), whose cat had the eminently grand name, Hinse of Hinsefeldt. Painters of the late eighteenth and nineteenth century frequently included cats in their works; many had studios that also housed a cat or two.

By the late eighteenth century, the fortunes of cats had more or less definitively changed and they became increasingly popular. This overwhelming change in attitude toward cats was brought about by the brown (or gray) rat. These large rats, thought to have originated in northern China, spread throughout Europe at this time, largely replacing the smaller black rat, and are still the most common rat today. They began to cause widespread devastation, but were kept under control by cats, making cats suddenly appear very useful pets to have. Some years later, their worth was further cemented when the work of the French microbiologist Louis Pasteur (1822–1895) was published. Pasteur's work on microbes highlighted the association between disease and lack of hygiene; since cats are fastidiously clean they became more popular as pets.

Through the late eighteenth and nineteenth centuries cats gained more attention. Charles Dickens (1812–1870) often included cats in his novels and became a reluctant cat owner later in life. When his daughter Mamie's cat had a litter of kittens, he allowed her to keep one. This kitten became known as The Master's Cat, and the literary giant and small feline struck up a devoted relationship. William Makepeace Thackeray (1811–1863) was an ardent cat enthusiast and had a favorite cat called Louise, who spent much of her time with the author and was fed on the choicest delicacies, often from Thackeray's own plate. Thackeray's family were similarly devoted to cats and fed many stray cats daily outside their house. Edward Lear (1812–1888), artist, author, and poet sketched his adored tomcat Foss in a series of hilarious poses published as "The Heraldic Blazon of Foss the Cat." When Foss died Lear held a full burial service for him and erected a tombstone in his honor; Lear himself would die just two months later. Florence Nightingale's (1820–1910) love of cats in combination with her nursing activities reinforces the association of cats with cleanliness. Nightingale is estimated to have owned around sixty cats in her lifetime, with one of her favorites being a large Persian called Mr. Bismarck. French poet Charles Baudelaire (1821–1867) once famously said that he preferred the company of cats to humans. Fellow Frenchman Alexander Dumas (1802–1870) was so devoted to cats that he established a welfare group called the Feline Defense League; Baudelaire and other luminaries joined the League to lend their support.

Great enthusiasm for cats during this period was not restricted to Europe. In the United States there are accounts of cat shows being held at county fairs during the 1860s, where the classes seem mostly to have been for the Maine Coon, and based on size, with the largest being the most prestigious. American author Mark Twain (1835–1910) was a great cat lover and always kept several. He is said to have had nineteen cats at one time. He often referred to cats in his writing; he also gave them long, complicated names such as Zoroaster and Blatherskite so that children could practice their spelling and grasp of difficult words.

By this time, a few people were starting to breed cats and to be interested in more exotic cats. The first Russian Blues and Abyssinians had arrived in the United Kingdom. The popularity of the cat was firmly on the rise.

TURKISH ANGORA

HISTORIC – TURKEY – RARE

APPEARANCE
Slender and elegant. Long bodied and lithe, shoulders the same width as hips, frame is slender and fine boned. Rump slightly higher than shoulders. Legs are long with small, round paws. The head is a medium-long wedge, ears are large, wide at base, pointed, and set close together. Eyes are large and almond shaped and can be any shade of green, green gold, gold, copper, blue, or odd-eyed. Tail is long and tapering with a full brush.

SIZE
Medium

COAT
Single coated and varies in length. Tail, britches, and ruff should be long. Texture extremely silky and fine. Any color or pattern except those showing hybridization.

PERSONALITY
Highly intelligent, very lively, playful, interactive

THE TURKISH ANGORA is one of the most elegant cat breeds; its every move is graceful and often very rapid. This cat is extremely active and likes to be involved in all aspects of its owner's life. Part of its curiosity and natural bounce stems from its high level of intelligence; it will actively solve problems, learn, and understand, and has a strong instinct for self-preservation. This has contributed to its survival through the centuries.

This breed hails from Angora in Turkey, now known as Ankara, and exhibits a beautiful, long, silky coat, which is also seen in rabbits and goats from the same area. Its coat is very distinctive and has a slight sheen that is apparent when the cat is moving. It is also surprisingly low maintenance given its coat length, and does not require disproportionate amounts of grooming. The Turkish Angora is widely held to be one of the earliest longhaired cats. Historically, as cats evolved, they were all shorthaired, but at some point in history, probably due to evolutionary pressure led by geographic location, the recessive mutation for long hair spontaneously occurred. It is no coincidence that the natural longhaired breeds, which include the Siberian and Norwegian Forest Cat, developed in particularly cold areas; the winter climate around Ankara can be very icy.

Longhaired cats have been referred to in Turkey for centuries. It is said that the Prophet Muhammad (c. 570–632 C.E.) was very fond of cats and that his own cat Muezza was a Turkish Angora. A delightful tale relates how one day Muezza was asleep on the sleeve of Muhammad's gown and, rather than disturb the cat, he cut his sleeve off. When the cat woke up he was so grateful that he bowed his head to the Prophet, who stroked his forehead three times and imbued the cat with seven lives and the ability to land on its feet. Muhammad's touch is also said to have given rise to the odd-colored eyes often seen in the white Angoras, and such cats remain the most prized in Turkey.

Longhaired cats of various types, including Angoras, had been imported to Britain and France from Turkey, Persia, and Russia by the seventeenth century. The Italian traveler Pietro della Valle (1586–1652) reputedly took Angoras to Italy, although he is also credited with introducing the first Persian cats to Italy, so there may be confusion over the breeds involved. The French scientist Nicolas-Claude Fabri de Peiresc (1580–1637) is said to have taken Angoras back to France with him in the 1620s, and some sources credit him with introducing the breed to Europe. Peiresc presented one of these Angoras to Cardinal de Richelieu, who was known as a great cat enthusiast and owned about fourteen cats of various breeds at the time of his death. Longhaired cats including Angoras became very popular during this period in Europe and had found their way to America by the late 1700s. By the late 1800s Angoras were commanding high prices, with an offer made on one at a cat show in London in 1890 for the sizeable sum of $5,000.

However, the Persian subsequently overtook the Angora in popularity and Angoras were crossbred to Persians to improve the silkiness of the Persian coat. This crossbreeding was so widespread that the unique Angora breed almost completely disappeared. Its existence as a separate breed was not helped by the generic classification by some associations of all longhaired breeds as simply "Longhaired." There was great confusion over what constituted a Persian and an Angora, which seems hard to fathom now, given the extensive differences between the

two breeds as they appear today. Adding to the problem was a tendency by some breeders to outcross to Russian Longhairs as well, which further diluted the gene pool.

By the 1900s the Angora in its original form had disappeared from the show halls of Europe and North America, and survived only tenuously in its native land. Luckily the Turkish government took steps to save it and a breeding program was initiated at the Ankara Zoo—this program is still in place. The program began by collecting all the available white Angoras with either blue or odd-colored eyes, these color combinations being the most prized. Once the zoo had located a number of these cats, they were able to begin a highly supervised breeding program. The cats were closely guarded by the zoo and very careful records kept of the ancestry.

In 1962, U.S. Army Colonel Walter Grant, who was stationed in Turkey, was successful in obtaining a pair of Angoras from Ankara Zoo; he and his wife brought them home to the United States. These were the odd-eyed, white male Yildiz and the amber-eyed, white female Yildizcek, the first two purebred Turkish Angoras in the United States. These two cats became the foundation for a U.S. breeding program. In 1964, the pair Sam Olgum and Aliya's Snowball were brought over, and they were swiftly followed by further imports. By the 1970s the breed had become well established in North America. However, it was initially recognized only in white; it was not until 1978 that the Cat Fanciers' Association (CFA) began to allow colored Turkish Angoras to compete at cat shows. Today, despite the relatively low numbers of Turkish Angoras, they are accepted by all the main associations in a range of colors.

White Angoras with blue eyes are often partially deaf as a result of a defect linked to the dominant gene that produces a white coat and blue eye color. Although this defect is found in white cats of all breeds, it has received the greatest notice in the Angora breed because of the strong preference for white Angoras. White Angoras with odd-colored eyes are occasionally deaf in one or both ears. This partial deafness does not affect the cats in any other way and they can lead perfectly normal lives if they are kept indoors. Nevertheless, the occurrence of deafness is considered by many breeders as highly undesirable. These breeders have worked hard to promote the colored Turkish Angoras and recommend that white-to-white breedings be avoided.

RUSSIAN BLUE
HISTORIC – RUSSIA – MODERATE

APPEARANCE

Elegant, aristocratic, and silver blue. Fine boned and muscular with a graceful body and carriage and long, fine legs with small, slightly rounded paws. Head is a smooth, medium wedge with a blunt muzzle and medium-length nose. Ears are rather large and set far apart, eyes are set wide apart, rounded, and brilliant green. Tail is long and tapering.

SIZE

Medium

COAT

Very dense, short double coat that stands away from body; a soft, velvety feel. Any shade of blue, lighter preferred; guard hairs have silver tips giving a metallic sheen.

PERSONALITY

Reserved with strangers, loyal and affectionate to loved ones, quiet, intelligent, undemanding, gentle

THE RUSSIAN BLUE IS A DELIGHTFUL and captivating breed with striking looks. It has a particularly short and dense coat that stands away from the body and has a luxurious, velvety quality. Traditionally it is always a blue color with a sleek, silvery sheen caused by silver tipping on the coat hairs. Most striking of all is the vivid, green coloring of its eyes, lending them a jewel-like appearance. It also has a distinctive "smiling" expression, which greatly adds to its appeal and in fact reflects its general disposition. The Russian Blue is an aristocratic cat full of elegance and poise. It is known for being reserved with strangers and will take its time to assess a new situation or person. However, once it has made the decision that all is well, it is an extremely affectionate and loving cat. It bonds very strongly with its owner and loves to accompany them, but equally, can be undemanding. An extremely clean cat in its habits, it is fairly routine driven when it comes to meal times—which it will communicate clearly. This breed is rumored to have been a favorite among the Russian czars.

The Russian Blue is thought to be a naturally occurring breed, and the thickness of its coat attests to its development in a very cold climate. It is believed to have originated in northern Russia, in particular in the White Sea port of Archangel (Arkhangelsk). Some accounts suggest that the cats had lived in the wild for many centuries and were hunted for their enviable pelts—an existence that contributed toward their survival instinct and their inherent intelligence. Given the thriving port at Archangel, it is unsurprising that the cats were taken on board ships by sailors, either to keep rodents at bay, or perhaps to be traded at other ports. Either way, it was via boat that the breed made its way from Russia and into Europe, with the first instances of the cats arriving in Britain dating to the 1860s. Certainly they had arrived by 1871 and the inaugural cat show at Crystal Palace, London, organized by Harrison Weir, since they are recorded as being exhibited there.

In the 1890s the renowned cat breeder Mrs. Constance Carew-Cox, who also bred Abyssinians, British Shorthairs, and Manx, imported several Russian Blues from Russia. Her breeding program included the Russian Blue cats Lingpopo, Olga, Fashoda, Bayard, Muchacho, Ivanovitch, and Peter the Great, and these contributed significantly to the breed in England. Mrs. Carew-Cox described her first Russian Blue called Kolya in 1890. He was sourced from the Kola Peninsula between the White Sea and the Barents Sea, and apparently made the sea crossing to London well. In the 1903 *Book of Cats*, by F. Simpson there is a long description of the Russian Blue, and a number of comments by Mrs. Carew-Cox regarding the difference between the cats that were imported from Russia and those bred in England including, "Some of the imported cats have a more round muzzle and round head with small ears placed apart. Cats imported from Archangel are generally of a deep, firm blue throughout; the eyes and ears rather larger than those of English cats, the head and legs longer."

At this time the Russian Blue was shown in the same category as the British Shorthair (Blue), despite an obvious difference in body type, with the British Shorthair (Blue) being cobby and round headed. The British type was favored and so the Russian Blue, despite its beauty, rarely featured in the prize givings. The Governing Council of the Cat Fancy (GCCF) eventually accepted the clear difference and granted the Russian Blue its own class in 1912.

The impact of both world wars saw breed numbers so greatly reduced that the Russian Blue was in danger of disappearing altogether in England. A famous breeder at this time was Miss Marie Rocheford with her Dunloe Russian Blues. She crossbred several of the breed to a blue point Siamese called Lela Do; Lela Do and his son, the champion Dunloe Domokvitch, can be found in many of the modern pedigrees for the breed. Eventually Russian Blues in England became more foreign in their body type than the original cats of the late nineteenth century.

At the same time, breeders in Scandinavia were also trying to resurrect the Russian Blue through crossbreeding to Siamese and blue cats from Finland. The Scandinavian types were larger than the British, with shorter, denser coats. The British and the Scandinavian types were ultimately bred together to produce the Russian Blue as it is now recognized, with important breeding cats being the English Dunloe, Jennymay, Sylphides, and Windywhistle, and the Swedish cats Molleby, Olsenburg, Finlandia, and Kabbarps.

Russian Blues are thought to have first arrived in North America in the early 1900s, although they did not gain any following for a number of decades and breeding was slow to take off. It was not until 1949 that Russian Blues were accepted by the Cat Fanciers' Association (CFA), with the first two cats registered being Dunloe Jan and Dunloe Blue Silk. During the 1950s most American breeding of the Russian Blue was based on English or Swedish bloodlines, resulting in quite a variance. In the 1960s, the two lines were suitably crossed to produce a more uniform type. In 1964 they were awarded championship status by the CFA, with the first grand champion being the male GC Maja Acre Igor II. Numbers of the breed rose rapidly as they became increasingly popular both in the show ring and as companions until the 1980s when they began to decline in popularity. This is thought to be because of an increasing temperament issue in the show ring—for these naturally reserved and quiet cats, the bustle and noise of showing took its toll. To counteract this, breeders made a concerted effort to breed for temperament and to expose their show cats to greater stimuli from a young age. This has resulted in a complete turnaround in the Russian Blue's show-ring attitude and they have returned to being a judge's favorite.

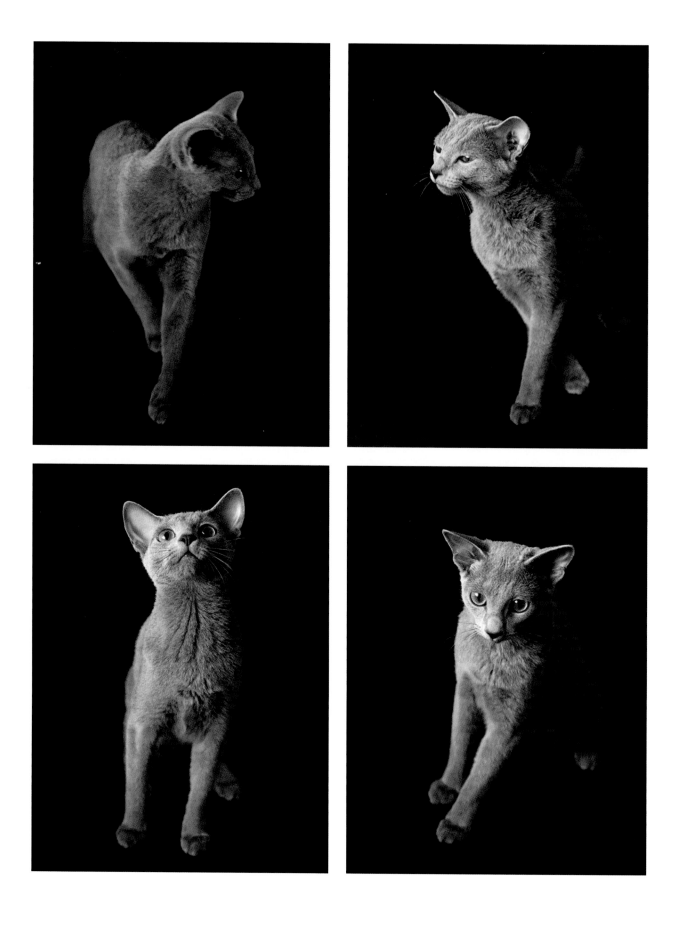

AMERICAN SHORTHAIR
HISTORIC – UNITED STATES – COMMON

APPEARANCE
Muscular, well built, and powerful. Strong body with broad, straight back, medium-length, muscular legs with rounded paws. Head is broad and rounded, with well-developed cheeks and strong jaws. Medium-length nose of even width through entire length and firm chin with moderate stop. Medium-sized ears slightly rounded at tip, eyes are large with color dependent on coat color. Tail is medium long, thick at base and tapers to blunt end.

SIZE
Medium

COAT
Short, thick, dense, and hard to the touch. Wide range of colors including solids, parti-colors, tortoiseshell, and tabby patterns.

PERSONALITY
Easygoing, friendly, sociable, quiet, calm, playful

THIS ALL-AMERICAN BREED is frequently described as a happy medium, and this can aptly be applied to both its personality and its appearance. There is nothing excessive about the American Shorthair. It is a medium-sized cat that is well balanced, robust, and exceptionally healthy. It has a very appealing and undemanding character, and is as comfortable sitting on one's lap as it is making its own entertainment. The American Shorthair is a quiet cat vocally and known for being very adaptable and tolerant. This makes it an ideal cat for families with children, dogs, and other animals.

The breed can be traced back to the first cats brought over by to the United States by European colonists in the seventeenth century. These cats were on board ships to keep the rodent population at bay, and on arrival went to work on farms and in towns, continuing the war on vermin. There is an account of a "shorthaired cat of many colors" on board the *Mayflower* in 1620, which later gave birth to a litter of tabby kittens, indicating that there was also at least one male cat on board the pilgrim's vessel. These ships' cats would no doubt have been largely British Shorthair types, which, after their arrival in the United States, developed their own characteristics. The early stock of cats from which the American Shorthair emerged were working cats, and it is this working foundation over many years that has lent them such good health.

For many years the sturdy American Shorthair was largely neglected by the cat fancy, and it was not until the early 1900s that a group of breeders set out to preserve this all-American cat breed. One of the key problems breeders of the American Shorthair faced was confusion among people over their carefully produced breed and any random shorthaired cat that happened to look like an American Shorthair. The difference was that the American Shorthair would generally breed true to type and had been continually selectively bred to encourage this, whereas random crossbred cats would not.

At first the cats were called simply Shorthair, and appeared in the catalog for the first American cat show at Madison Square Garden in 1895. Forty-six Shorthairs were entered and of these one was listed with a sale price of $1,000—a phenomenal amount of money. At the second show at Madison Square Garden in 1896, thirty-five Shorthairs were entered, with one listed with a sale price of $2,500. The first (American) Shorthair accepted for registration with the Cat Fanciers' Association (CFA) was a male orange tabby called Bell of Bradford, born in 1900 in England. He was imported to the United States in the early 1900s and during nine years of showing was defeated only once. He became the first CFA champion (American) Shorthair, although this was slightly controversial as renowned breeder Mrs. Mitchelson thought her male silver tabby Buzzing Silver was the first champion; he was in fact the first champion of his color, and this magnificent silver color remains the most popular and common today.

The breed name was changed to Domestic Shorthair to differentiate between American shorthaired cats and British imports, but people felt it applied to all shorthaired cats in America. It was not until 1965 that the cats finally earned their proper nomenclature, the American Shorthair. Since then the breed has become one of the most populous in North America, largely based on its easygoing disposition and beautiful appearance.

CHARTREUX
HISTORIC — FRANCE — MODERATE

APPEARANCE
Robust and always a striking blue color. A sturdy cat whose body type is described as primitive, being neither cobby nor classic. Broad shoulders, solid muscle mass, a deep chest, and relatively fine-boned legs. Head is rounded and broad, nose straight, and cheeks full. A "smiling" expression, upright ears set high and rounded, eyes ranging from copper to gold,
brilliant orange preferred. Tail is of moderate length, thick at base and tapering to oval tip.

SIZE
Medium to medium large

COAT
Medium length, dense, woolly, water-resistant outer layer, thick, resilient undercoat. Blue-gray.

PERSONALITY
Sweet, vocally quiet, attentive, loyal, humorous

THE CHARTREUX, informally referred to as the national cat of France, is a magnificent, distinctive breed that can be traced back to at least the Middle Ages. Always blue in color, it has stunning orange-to gold-toned eyes. The unique coat is neither short- nor longhaired, but in-between, and has a particularly woolly feel. There is even some debate over the name of the breed and whether it is linked to the well-known Spanish wool of the same name, popular in the eighteenth century. Its coat is composed of a very dense undercoat covered by a top coat of longer, harder hairs that are somewhat weather resistant. There should be a slight break in the coat at the neck, chest, and flanks.

Chartreux cats were bred in France specifically for their fur and are mentioned in the *Universal Trade Dictionary of Natural History and Applied Arts* by Jacques Savary des Brûlons (1657–1716), published posthumously in 1723. This is the first time that the breed was officially referred to as Chat des Chartreux (Chartreux cat). They were used by the furrier trade up until the beginning of the twentieth century with one of the last published accounts of their use in this industry by Dr. Beauregard in *Our Animals* in 1896.

The earliest origins of the Chartreux are based on guesswork. One story relates that when knights returned from the Crusades, many sought the seclusion of monasteries such as Le Grand Chartreux, perched high in the French Alps. These former warriors brought with them goods from their battles, including cats from along the North African coastline. These cats are said to have been the founders of the Chartreux breed. It is more likely that cats were simply kept in monasteries to control rodent populations and, given the isolated locations, the cats would have developed similar characteristics very quickly.

In the 1700s Comte de Buffon's *Histoire Naturelle* lists four cat breeds common in Europe: the domestic, Chartreux, Angora, and Spanish. Buffon's description of the Chartreux is long and accurate, even today, and was illustrated by plates showing the difference between the breeds. Modern breeding history did not begin until the first half of the twentieth century with the Leger sisters, Christine and Suzanne. The two came across a colony of blue-colored cats on the small Brittany island of Belle-Île off the coast of northern France, and were struck by their uniformity, despite some crossbreeding with European cats on the island. The sisters acquired a number of the blue cats and began to breed them at their de Guerveur Cattery; the first female, Marquise, and male, Conquito, produced the kitten Mignonne, who later became an international champion. In 1931 the sisters were the first to exhibit their cats in France. World War II had a devastating effect on breeding programs and, following the war, breeds such as British Shorthairs, Persians, and Russian Blues were used to boost the numbers of Chartreux. In Europe the Chartreux is shown in the same breed category as the British Shorthair since the breed demarcation is based on color and as such there is a greater diversity in the gene pool.

The breed first arrived in the United States in the early 1970s when Helen and John Gamon from La Jolla, California, brought a male Chartreux from the breeder Madame Bastide's cattery. This cat, Taquin de St. Pierre of Gamonal, went on to become the founding male of the breed in North America. Emphasis is placed on the purity of the breed bloodlines by American associations, and therefore the Chartreux cats in North America are perhaps closer to their origins than those in Europe.

MAINE COON

HISTORIC — NORTH AMERICA — COMMON

APPEARANCE
Large, shaggy coated, and magnificent. Solid, muscular body with broad chest and long body. Legs are wide set and heavily boned with large, round, well-tufted paws. Medium-sized head, slightly longer than it is wide with square muzzle and high cheekbones. Ears are large and well tufted; eyes are large, set well apart, and an open oval shape. Should be green, gold, or copper; blue and odd colored accepted in white cats. Tail is long with long, flowing hair.
SIZE
Medium to large
COAT
Luxuriant, long, and shaggy, being shorter over shoulders. Falls smoothly and with a silky texture. Can be all colors and patterns.
PERSONALITY
Devoted and loyal to loved ones, intelligent, hardy, playful, independent

THE MAINE COON is one of North America's native cat breeds and has, along with the American Shorthair, the longest history on the continent. It is an adventurous, active, independent cat and thrives on outdoor space, the odd tree to climb, and active rodent-control duty. Unlike many breeds, the Maine Coon is untroubled by water, perhaps due to its thick, weatherproof coat. Although the breed enjoys the outdoor life, there are Maine Coons that live inside; because of their flexible and phlegmatic nature they are just as happy with a warm lap and a spot by the fire. Maine Coons have tremendous personalities and will form loyal, deeply loving bonds with their family; they are intelligent and playful, and make wonderful family pets.

The Maine Coon comes from Maine, the most northeasterly state in the United States, and one subject to very cold winters. This is a beautiful, rugged, and isolated part of the country, and here the Maine Coon developed to be an extremely hardy and robust cat with a heavy coat to protect it from the inhospitable weather. Instantly recognizable with its great size and distinctive, tufted ears, the Maine Coon is one of America's best-loved cat breeds, second only in popularity to the Persian. It derives its name from its home state, and "coon" refers to the breed's long, thick, bushy tail that is not dissimilar to that of a raccoon. One unlikely (and genetically impossible) tale of the cat's origins recounts that it is the result of a fortuitous breeding between a large cat and a raccoon. It is said that the cat has inherited the raccoon's tail, its tree-climbing ability, and its fascination with water. A different but equally unlikely account suggests that it is the result of a union between a bobcat (*Lynx rufus*) and a domestic cat, and that this is why the Maine Coon is so much larger than other breeds and exhibits its distinct tufted ears and toes.

Other tales refer to the Vikings sailing to Newfoundland, to the north of Maine, in around 1000 C.E. Their Norwegian Skogkatts (Forest Cats), which kept their boats free from rodents, are said to have traveled ashore and given rise to the Maine Coon. Much later is the tale of Captain Coon, an English sea captain in the 1700s, who is said to have sailed up and down the coast of New England with his many cats of predominantly Persian and Angora lines. When the captain docked his ship and went ashore, his cats followed, and fairly soon local cats began to have longhaired kittens that were described as "Coon's cats."

The most romantic story of the Maine Coon's origins links the breed with the French queen Marie Antoinette in the eighteenth century. Captain Clough from Wiscasset, Maine, was a leading figure in an alleged plot to smuggle the beleaguered queen out of France before she was taken to the guillotine. Clough loaded his ship *Sally* with many of the queen's belongings, including six of her royal cats, said to have been Persian and Angora. The escape plot was too late, and the queen was beheaded; Clough had to set sail quickly before he was arrested. The six longhaired cats were taken to his home in Maine, and bred with the local population, resulting in the Maine Coon.

It is true to say that many seafarers landed along the east coast, and that most of their ships carried cats to take care of the rodents. It is also likely that longhaired cats such as Angoras could have made their way ashore, or even been traded, and established themselves as rodent control on farms. They might have bred and, with the rigors of the

MIDDLE AGES TO NINETEENTH CENTURY

climate, developed into the hardy, weather-resistant cats that are today's Maine Coons. The cats were favored by the Maine farmers, who valued their excellent rodent-killing skills, which, combined with their striking looks and lovely nature, made them an object of great pride. The farmers began to show their cats. The first Maine Coons were exhibited in the 1860s in the Skowhegan Fair, a fair held by Maine farmers (and still held today). Maine Coons from all over the state were shown here and competed for the title of Maine State Champion Coon Cat. They were one of the first cat breeds to be recognized in the United States by the cat fancy in the late nineteenth century.

The author F. R. Pierce, who wrote about cats, particularly the Maine Coon, at the end of the nineteenth century, was also a Maine Coon owner and enthusiast; one of his Maine Coons had the wonderful name Captain Jenks of the Horse Marines. Pierce's accounts reveal that Maine Coons were appearing in cat shows up and down the eastern seaboard and sometimes as far west as Chicago from the 1870s. An important show for the breed was held in Boston from 1878 and attracted large numbers of Maine Coons. The most famous of the early cat shows was held in Madison Square Garden, New York, in 1895, and was won by a Maine Coon called Cosey. Cosey was awarded a silver medal and an engraved silver collar.

The Cat Fanciers' Association (CFA) was formed in 1908 and listed twenty-eight Maine Cats, as they were known then, in its Studbook. Despite the breed's early success and popularity in the show ring, as cat fancy took hold they gradually fell out of favor, being replaced by more exotic breeds. By the 1950s they had all but disappeared and were saved only through the efforts of a number of enthusiasts. The Central Maine Cat Club (CMCC) was formed and began to hold shows and exhibitions of the cats. This helped bring them back to the public's notice and it was through the club that the first standard for the breed was written. In 1968 the Maine Coon Breeders and Fanciers Association was established to preserve, promote, and protect the breed. In 1976 the CFA awarded the Maine Coon championship status, and they have continued to grow in popularity.

The Maine Coon arrived in the United Kingdom in the 1980s and was given championship status by the Governing Council for the Cat Fancy (GCCF) in 1994.

KURILIAN BOBTAIL
HISTORIC — RUSSIA — RARE

APPEARANCE
Strong, robust, distinctive pom-pom tail. Compact, semi-cobby body, broad chest, muscular legs with hind legs slightly longer than front. Head is a large, modified wedge with low cheekbones and straight, broad, medium-length nose. Medium-sized, triangular-shaped ears that tilt slightly forward; eyes are slightly slanted oval on top, rounded at bottom, and clear,

brilliant color. Tail composed of one or more kinks or curves 0.5 to three inches (1.5–8 cm) long and covered in long hair.
SIZE
Medium to large
COAT
Can be shorthaired or semi-longhaired, soft and silky in texture, and in a variety of colors.
PERSONALITY
Gentle, highly intelligent, playful, sociable, adaptable

AN EXTREMELY RARE BREED, the Kurilian Bobtail is still not recognized by many of the major cat associations, yet it is an extraordinary and endearing cat with tremendous character and great intelligence. It is widely considered to be a natural breed that developed and continues to live in an isolated environment; this has led to its particular characteristics and great uniformity in the breed. It originates from a chain of fifty-six islands known as the Kurils, which run from the southern point of the Kamchatka peninsula in Russia to the northeast of Hokkaido, Japan, and separate the Sea of Okhotsk from the North Pacific Ocean. The islands are subject to extremely severe weather conditions—subarctic cold and heavy snowfall throughout the long winter, and prolonged precipitation and fog in the summer months. It is not known how long the Kurilian Bobtail has lived in this difficult habitat, although it is quite possible that it has existed here in the wild for a very long time.

Unsurprisingly, in view of its harsh natural habitat, the Kurilian is an extremely hardy and robust cat, which is also known for its good swimming skills and efficient hunting abilities. It is reported that this cat will not only kill rats, rabbits, and other vermin, but will also catch fish in the shallows. It is a highly resourceful and intelligent cat and has a wildcat appearance that is totally at odds with its very affectionate nature. It bonds quickly and

strongly with its owners and has several quite doglike characteristics, including a meet-and-greet service at the front door! Instead of taking over one's lap, it prefers to lie at its owner's feet, and will often engage in a game of fetch. It also seems to exhibit something of a sense of humor and can be endearingly clownish. The Kurilian Bobtail socializes extremely well with people, other cats, dogs, and children.

Accounts of short-tailed cats were first received in the mid-twentieth century from scientists and military personnel on the Kuril islands, and it appears that a number of the cats were taken back to mainland Russia. Here they proved very popular as pets due to their wonderful temperament, easily adapting to domestic life despite their remote and wild origins.

Given that they are bobtailed and that the islands provide a link between Russia and Japan, parallels have been drawn between them and the Japanese Bobtail. While science has not yet uncovered the genetic relationship between these two breeds, it can be assumed that there is a shared ancestry at some point. Many enthusiasts of the Kurilian Bobtail suggest that this breed gave rise to the Japanese Bobtail. Somewhat confusingly, Russia is also home to the Karelian Bobtail, which is not related to the Kurilian Bobtail. The Karelian derives its short tail from a recessive gene and developed on the opposite side of the country, in the western regions of Russia around St. Petersburg.

The World Cat Federation (WCF) ranks the Kurilian as the fourth breed in cat popularity in Russia. In recent years there has been a concerted effort by enthusiasts to get the breed more firmly established and on an international footing. At present there are between forty and seventy catteries breeding Kurilians in Russia, in both the short- and long-haired varieties. In view of their truly charming qualities it seems likely that this breed will soon be adopted into American and European hearts.

ABYSSINIAN

HISTORIC – SOUTHEAST ASIA – COMMON

APPEARANCE
Regal, recalls wildcat heritage. Medium length, muscular, graceful body, long, slender legs, small, compact, oval paws. Slightly rounded, wedge-shaped head with large, alert ears broad and cupped at base. Large, brilliant eyes accentuated by dark line around rim (eyeliner).

SIZE
Medium

COAT
Shorthaired with distinctive ticked or agouti coat; each hair shaft has alternating dark- and light-colored bands. Hair is soft, fine, and dense with a lustrous sheen. Colors vary in US/UK, can include ruddy, sorrel, blue, fawn, lilac, and chocolate.

PERSONALITY
Vivacious, highly intelligent, playful, loyal, curious

THE ABYSSINIAN is one of the most beautiful and elegant breeds, combining a thoroughly regal appearance with a mercurial, charming nature. It has a huge personality and makes an excellent pet for an active household; with its great athleticism, no ledge is too high or corner inaccessible. Curiosity and an acute sense of fun runs at the core of the Abyssinian, which will crawl under bed sheets, hang around one's shoulders, leap across the furniture, and pounce on unseen shadows with unequalled energy; it has two speeds, fast asleep or full speed ahead! It is tremendously loyal, and typically forms strong bonds with its owner. While it is lively, it is also very affectionate and thrives in human company. The Abyssinian does not like to be left alone or to be confined, and will make this known vociferously. It is also extremely intelligent—it is said that the Abyssinian trains its owner, rather than the other way around.

The history of the Abyssinian's origins is as mysterious and exotic as the cat itself. The most romantic theories go back to Egypt's Blue Nile and to the sacred cats of ancient Egypt, from which the Abyssinian is said to have descended. Although there is no scientific evidence to support this, there is a striking similarity between the Abyssinian and ancient depictions on murals, tombs, and sculptures, the earliest of which date to around 3000 B.C.E. This association has led to the assumption that the breed is ancient, but in truth the modern Abyssinian is most likely much younger than assumed.

These alluring cats did not derive their name until the nineteenth century and this adds further confusion to their origins. The earliest Abyssinians to arrive in England are said to have been brought back by soldiers at the end of the Abyssinian (Ethiopian) War. In particular, a cat named Zula was imported by Mrs. Barrett-Lennard, the wife of a British army captain, in 1868; although, to date, Zula has not been linked genetically to the modern Abyssinian. In fact, it is entirely possible that this cat was not an Abyssinian at all! The first Abyssinians to be exhibited at cat shows were described as such because this was the country from which they had been imported. They were mentioned in *Harper's Weekly*, January 27, 1872, in an article referring to the 1871 cat show at Crystal Palace, London, where an Abyssinian had taken third place; the article was accompanied by an illustration of the breed. Unfortunately, no records exist that trace these early imports from Abyssinia to the modern Abyssinian cat.

In 1889 Harrison Weir, the "father of the cat fancy," published the first standard for the breed in his book *Our Cats and All About Them*, and described the Abyssinian's distinctive ticked coat as resembling "the back of a wild (only not so grey) rabbit." In view of their unusual coats, the cats were often referred to as Hare Cats, Ticks, or Bunny Cats at this time. Also called agouti, the ticked coat is actually a type of tabby and is unusual in that each hair shaft has alternating bands of light and dark, ending in a dark tip with the lighter band closest to the skin. A similar coat is seen in cats native to North Africa, Asia, and the Middle East, most particularly in the African or Egyptian wildcat (*Felis silvestris lybica*), also sometimes called the Caffre Cat. This is commonly cited as the ancestor to all domestic cats, although the Abyssinian bears a far closer resemblance to it than many. Recent genetic studies have shown that the Abyssinian most likely developed along the coast of the Indian Ocean and in parts of Southeast Asia. One of the earliest identifiable Abyssinians is a taxidermal specimen at the Leiden Zoological Museum, Holland, acquired in the mid-1830s and labeled "Patrie, domestica India." It is not a great leap to conclude that the cats were first brought into England from India by merchants. It is also probable that the Egyptians imported them to manage the rodents in their expanding granaries early in history.

What is known is that the breed was developed and refined in England from the late nineteenth century based on cats imported from India, Southeast Asia, and North Africa, and probably native English stock. This base stock included a wide variation, and no early breeding records were kept. The first known records of pedigrees date to 1904 and show many unknown sires and dams, but also some crosses with cats that would not today be considered Abyssinians. This could account for some of the color variety in the breed and also for the possible origin of the Somali breed, which is the longhaired Abyssinian. For the last forty or fifty years, all British-born pedigree Abyssinian cats need to have known antecedents; this has helped to eliminate any undesirable recessive genes from the breed.

Two important cats in the development of the breed were a female called Fancy Free, born in 1903, and the male

Aluminium, born in 1905. Both were bred and owned by the influential breeder Mrs. Carew Cox, and they appear in many of the early pedigrees. The pair produced a male kitten, Aluminium II, born in 1907, and he was sold to Miss Cathcart of the United States. She acquired a further Abyssinian from England called Salt, and these two cats are believed to have been the first of their breed imported to the United States. The breed was established very slowly here, with breeding efforts greatly impacted during World War I. In the 1930s, the breeder Virginia Cobb imported a pair of Abyssinians from England, and these two produced a pair of kittens, which were acquired by Mrs. Metcalfe and Mary Hantzmon. Both these women became extremely important in establishing the breed in the United States, but just as the breed was becoming established, World War II began, and by the end of it there were very few breeding pairs in the United States or England. Enthusiasts of the cats continued their dedicated support and by the 1950s numbers had again picked up. By the late 1980s the Abyssinian ranked among the most popular shorthaired cat breed in the United States, and their popularity has continued to the present day.

CHAPTER 3
LATE NINETEENTH CENTURY TO 1959

By the latter years of the nineteenth century, cats had become more than just pets, and this was reflected in the rise of breeding and showing of cats, known as the "cat fancy." People were becoming increasingly interested in purebred cats and in foreign and exotic breeds. The earliest documented cat show dates to 1598 and took place at the St. Giles Fair in Winchester, England, but cat shows in earnest did not take place until nearly 300 years later. The first official cat show took place in 1871 at Crystal Palace in London. It was staged by Harrison Weir, a noted cat breeder and author. Weir wrote the guidelines against which the cats were judged, calling them the Standards of Excellence or Standards of Points. He also conceived the different classes for cats, basing them on their build, color, and the length of their coat. Weir's work *Our Cats and All About Them* was published in 1889 and became the manual for judges and cat enthusiasts. He is referred to as "the father of the cat fancy" today. His primary aim in promoting cat shows was to improve the welfare of cats by bringing them to public attention, rather than the competitive showing itself. As cat shows took off, however, and became more and more competitive, Weir realized that his objectives had become lost and he distanced himself from the show world.

The first show in London featured an astonishing 170 entries, which included Shorthairs, Manx, Persian, Angora, Russian, and Siamese, and offered 54 prizes. There were even novelty classes such as the fattest cat or biggest cat. The show garnered great media coverage and a wide range of opinions, particularly centered on the Siamese entries, which were equally praised and reviled. The show proved an enormous success and rapidly sparked a fashion for pedigreed cats and for showing, particularly among the middle and upper classes, although subsequent shows also held classes for "Cats belonging to working men." Prize money was significant, which inspired show entries and diverse classes, including those for "hybrid wildcats." In 1887 Weir was key in establishing the British National Cat Club, which began a system of recording pedigrees, and he became the club's first president. He later resigned and the position was taken on by the artist Louis Wain, who is famous for his cat images. Some years later, in 1898, renowned cat breeder Lady Marcus Beresford established a rival organization, The Cat Club, which lasted until 1903. In 1910 the Governing Council of the Cat Fancy (GCCF) was established to promote purebred cats and to take over as the sole registry for purebred cats in Britain. At this time there were only four sections for registering cats: Longhairs, Shorthairs, Abyssinian, and Siamese. Noted judge and breeder Frances Simpson, who was a longhair enthusiast, described Shorthair Tabbies as being the most commonly seen of all cats, followed by Shorthair Black and Whites.

The first official American cat show took place in 1895 in Madison Square Garden, New York, organized by Englishman James Hyde. Four years later the American Cat Association was formed. As in the United Kingdom, many regional cat clubs also developed, including the Chicago Cat Club in 1899 and then the Beresford Cat Club in the same year, named after the English breeder Lady Marcus Beresford. Today there are a great many organizations and clubs in the United States, which share the same underlying motivation of preserving and promoting the different cat breeds, and cat welfare. The main organizations also maintain the pedigrees and records of purebred cats, which is a vital function. The Cat Fanciers' Association (CFA) was established in the United States in 1906. In 1949 the Fédération Internationale Féline (FIFe) was formed in Paris and is an international cat federation that now represents forty-two countries around the world.

Alongside the increasing popularity of pet cats during the nineteenth century and on into the twentieth, they were also being drafted into gainful employment. The notion of cats catching mice was not of course a new one, but they began to be actively sought out by businesses. One such was the British Post Office, which employed cats between 1868 and 1984 to combat their mouse problem. The first cats to be employed in September 1868 were stationed in the Money Order Office in London and paid one shilling a week (to be spent on food). The cats proved a great success and earned a pay rise in 1873. Given their efficiency, post offices around the country began to employ cats. One of the most famous Post Office cats was Tibs, who was born in 1950. Tibs was a substantial cat, weighing in at 23 lb (10.5 kg) when fully grown. He was also an excellent dispatcher of mice and kept the Post Office Headquarters completely mouse-free during his fourteen years of active service.

Theaters on both sides of the Atlantic also kept cats to rid their premises of mice. As the tradition of keeping cats in theaters spread, cats became lucky symbols. Author Carl Van Vechten, who wrote *The Tiger in the House* (1922),

described in detail how theater employees would buy special meat for the resident cats in theaters all across New York. Black cats were apparently the most favored in the U.S. theaters and if the theater cat rubbed around the legs of an actor it was said to predict a favorable reception for the play. Naturally, given the nature of cats, it was not uncommon for the resident feline to make an impromptu appearance during a production.

The British Museum in London kept cats for many years to prevent mice causing damage to the museum exhibits. Exactly when the first cat arrived is not clear, but cats are documented by Sir Frederick Madden, who was Keeper of the Manuscripts and part of the museum staff from 1828 to 1866. The most famous of the museum's cats was Mike, who was a resident from about 1908 to his retirement in 1924. Mike arrived at the museum as a kitten and struck up a great rapport with Sir Ernest Wallis Budge, who was Keeper of the Egyptian Antiquities at the time. Mike was a tremendous character and became a dearly loved member of the museum staff. As he aged, he was looked after by the staff, who fed him fishy delicacies, and on his death in 1929 he was greatly missed. He was followed by a succession of cats that were equally loved, including a large ginger tom cat called Belinda.

The most poignant service in which cats found themselves was the military, particularly during the years of World Wars I and II. Cats were used in the military by many countries including Britain and the United States, and in a number of ways, some more successful than others. Most attempts at training cats to perform a service, such as the delivery of messages, proved unviable given the nature of cats and their distinct lack of interest in doing anything when commanded. However, they proved invaluable in other ways, primarily in the trenches of World War I to try to combat the rat problem. They were also used as gas detectors (not such a good job), and provided great comfort to soldiers. It is said that a number of Russian soldiers when captured were found to be carrying kittens as mascots beneath their coats. There are also innumerable photographs of soldiers with cats and kittens and reports of the therapeutic effect these animals (and others) had on soldiers living under great duress. An estimated 500,000 cats were employed by the British army alone during World War I. Battersea Dogs and Cats Home, England's most famous animal shelter (founded in 1860), provided temporary accommodation in 1917 for dogs and cats belonging to soldiers on active service. Cats also played an important role in both the British and U.S. navies and were kept on board ship for their mousing abilities; they were also kept at air bases where they played a similar role. Old photographs show that cats were used (and loved) by military factions across Europe and as far afield as New Zealand.

Several years before this, one particular cat earned itself a lasting name and led the way for cats in the frozen regions of Antarctica. In 1914 the explorer Ernest Shackleton and his crew set sail from the East India Docks in London on board the *Endurance* heading for Antarctica. A surprise addition to the crew was a large tabby cat who belonged to Henry McNish, the ship's carpenter. McNish found his cat, whom he had been reluctant to leave behind, curled up in his toolbox once on board. The cat was devoted to McNish and followed him around, earning the name Mrs. Chippy ("chippy" being a nickname for a carpenter) despite being a male cat. Mrs. Chippy endeared himself to the crew—though was less fond of the sled dogs on board. When the *Endurance* became trapped in ice and began to break up, Shackleton made the decision to head for the nearest land mass (350 miles away) in three small lifeboats. Mrs. Chippy was shot before departure, something McNish never forgave Shackleton for. In the latter years of World War II the British established two bases in the Antarctic to locate suitable sites for scientific research. The first cat to arrive was Tubby, followed some years later by Tiddles and a series of successors, who seem to have adapted to life in the snow and ice with ease.

Rather less extreme conditions were provided for a working cat in New York in the late 1930s. One day an ill-kempt red tabby cat wandered into the Algonquin Hotel off West 44th Street and was greeted warmly by the hotel owner Frank Case. Frank allowed the cat, who was thought to be an ex-theater cat, to stay and a tradition for the Algonquin cat was born. During the 1930s and 1940s the hotel was host to innumerable stars of the stage, and reputedly one day the actor John Barrymore suggested the red cat be called Hamlet. From that time on there has always been a resident cat at the hotel, with all the males called Hamlet, and all the females Matilda. The current Matilda can be found in the hotel lobby offering a meet and greet service. London's Ritz Hotel was home to an infamous cat called Tiger, and several hotels in Paris also have resident cats.

The Savoy Hotel in London has a resident "cat" dating from 1926—a black statue of a cat 3 ft (1 m) high, carved by architect Basil Ionides. The cat, called Kaspar, is the fourteenth guest whenever he is needed at a table of thirteen. The tradition stemmed from an incident in 1898 when a South African businessman named Woolf Joel held a banquet at the Savoy. At the last minute one of his guests dropped out, leaving thirteen around the table, a fact which one of the guests remarked upon as being unlucky. As Joel rose to leave at the end of the evening, the same guest is said to have commented that the first person to leave was also unlucky and would be the first of all those present to die. Some weeks later Joel was shot dead in Johannesburg. For some years after that the Savoy, wishing to avoid any bad publicity, would provide a member of staff to sit in on any dinner that involved only thirteen people. Guests wishing to talk privately did not appreciate this, so from 1926 onward, Kaspar, who resides in the hotel lobby, always sits at the table at any dinner for thirteen. He became a great favorite of Sir Winston Churchill who insisted that he was always present at meetings of his political club, The Other Club.

The effects of the two World Wars were catastrophic for cat breeding for many reasons: there were terrible food shortages, lost families, war casualties, and more pressing matters than cat breeding. By the 1940s some breeds had all but disappeared, including the Siamese, and breeders had to crossbreed to other breeds to boost numbers. This is one of the explanations for the arrival of the Balinese, the longhaired Siamese. It is suggested that crossbreeding introduced the longhair gene to the Siamese, resulting in the creation of the Balinese during the 1950s (although there is also some evidence of longhaired Siamese before this time). By the end of World War II there were estimated to be only twelve Abyssinians in Britain and breeders are thought to have crossbred these cats, which also resulted in the introduction of the longhaired gene. This eventually led to the establishment of the Somali breed—the longhaired Abyssinian—in the United States and United Kingdom.

The periods directly following the wars, and in particular World War II, saw a boom in the development of new cat breeds, partly based on a return to the enthusiasm of cat breeding and showing and also based on an increasing understanding of genetics and specific breeding for type. This led to the development of new breeds such as the Colorpoint Shorthair, the Javanese, and the Oriental. All these breeds are the result of breeders wishing to create Siamese-type cats in a variety of colors, leading to cats with the exquisite features of the Siamese, but in a wide range of colors and patterns; the Javanese is the longhaired equivalent of the Colorpoint Shorthair and is included in the same entry in this chapter. Another involved and deliberate breeding program between Persian and Siamese resulted in the Himalayan, which is a longhaired cat of Persian character, but with Siamese coloring. Not all organizations recognize the Himalayan as a separate breed; some classify it as a color division of the Persian.

Some modern breeds such as the Burmese, Havana Brown, and Thai originated from cats tracing back to the much-revered cats of Thailand and Indonesia, which were closely associated with the royal courts and temples. Despite their ancient origins, these cats were developed and specifically bred for certain characteristics by modern breeders, and were not established as purebreds until the early to middle decades of the twentieth century. A particularly interesting breed of this time period is the Cornish Rex, a delightful cat with a distinctive wavy coat. The breed can be traced to a farmhouse kitchen on July 21, 1950 when a cat had a litter of kittens with one exhibiting a curly coat. This was as a result of a spontaneous genetic mutation and it took much trial and error, and great efforts from enthusiasts, before the breed was established. The Bombay breed, which was also founded in the 1950s was a more deliberate attempt to manipulate cat genetics to produce a domestic cat with the appearance in miniature of a wildcat. This was a start of a major trend for cats with a wild look that was to come to prominence in cat breeding in the next decade.

THAI

MODERN – UNITED STATES – MODERATE

APPEARANCE
Elegant, lithe, but with substance. Slightly to moderately long through the body, which is firm; athletic in appearance with medium boning. Medium-length, graceful legs with medium-sized oval paws. Unique head shape with long, flat forehead and wedge-shaped muzzle. Ears are medium to slightly large, wide at base with oval tips. Eyes are medium to slightly large, full almond shape, and blue in color. Tail is same length as torso and tapers to end.

SIZE
Medium to slightly large

COAT
Short, silky, and close lying with very little undercoat. Any point color, solid points, tabby, tortie, or torbie points, no white markings.

PERSONALITY
Intelligent, chatty, highly affectionate, loyal, sense of humor

THE THAI IS ESSENTIALLY THE ORIGINAL POINTED CAT of Thailand (formerly called Siam), whereas its close relative the Siamese has been bred outside its homeland to exhibit more extreme physical characteristics. Like the Siamese, the Thai makes a wonderful and entertaining companion with a definite sense of humor. Athletic and active, it is very people-oriented and thrives in company, particularly when interacting with its loved ones. It tends to chat away and is marginally quieter than the Siamese.

Although the Thai has only been recognized by The International Cat Association (TICA) relatively recently, the breed is ancient and is descended from the native cats of Thailand. Descriptions of the Thai cat appear in the famous *Cat Book Poems* that date from the Ayudhya period (1350–1767). The cats were originally called Wichienmaat, which roughly translates as "diamond gold." Despite descriptions of these cats, there are no records documenting how they were bred and whether they were bred for color and pattern or body type. During the nineteenth century the British discovered the Wichienmaat cats in what was then Siam. Descriptions of them dating back to this period describe pale-colored cats with dark points and striking blue eyes. The British began to import the cats in the 1870s and called them Siamese after their country of origin; all Siamese today include among their ancestors around eleven cats that were imported to England from Thailand in the 1880s. The few surviving photographs of the first cats brought over from Thailand show cats with a medium-boned frame and somewhat rounded head with a wedge-shaped muzzle.

An influential Siamese breeder was Greta Hindley, who was living in Malaya in the first decades of the twentieth century. When she returned to England in 1919 she brought with her two Wichienmaat cats, one of which was the female Puteh. This cat went on to found the Prestwick Cattery, and her champion daughter Prestwick Perak was described as having the "perfect head shape for a Siamese cat." Photographs of Perak show a cat with a moderate, non-extreme body, and a head like that of the Thai as it is now called. It seems that British breeders did not begin to breed the extreme body type now associated with the Siamese until just before World War II, and in 1966 the Cat Fanciers' Association (CFA) issued a preface to their breed standard for the Siamese that endorsed a more extreme body type. By the 1980s this more extreme type was common for the Siamese cat, certainly in the show world.

However, there were still breeders of what was known as the "Old-Style Siamese." These cats resembled the original cats from Thailand such as Greta Hindley's champion Prestwick Perak. In the 1980s dedicated breeders of these old-style cats in Europe and North America established breed clubs to try and preserve the type, and in 1990 the World Cat Federation (WCF) changed the name to the Thai and granted them breed championship status. U.S. and U.K. breeders began in 1999 to share bloodlines and information to help the breed; at this time the cats were referred to as both the Thai and the Old-Style Siamese. In 2001 breeders began to import pointed cats from Thailand to bolster the gene pool for the breed and to preserve the original genes of Thailand's native cats. Breeders began a dialogue with TICA in 2006, and the following year the breed was granted preliminary new breed status with the nomenclature of Thai; this was extended to advanced new breed in 2009 and to championship status in 2010.

LATE NINETEENTH CENTURY TO 1959

BALINESE

MODERN – UNITED STATES – RARE

APPEARANCE
Dignified, long coated, and elegant. Long, tubular, lithe body with firm muscles and fine bone structure. Legs are long and slender, hind legs slightly longer than front, and paws are small and oval. Long, tapering wedge-shaped head set to slender neck. Muzzle is fine and wedge shaped, large ears pointed at tip and medium-sized almond-shaped eyes that are a vivid blue.

Tail is long, slender, and tapers to a point; covered with long, plume-like coat.
SIZE
Medium
COAT
Single coated, medium length, close lying, and very silky. Pointed colors with even body color and clearly defined point color.
PERSONALITY
Vocal, demanding, affectionate, playful, intelligent

THE BALINESE is the longhaired version of the Siamese, sharing the same qualities from its long and elegant frame to its captivating personality, differing only in the length of its luxuriant, silky coat. These are not only exquisite in appearance, but have a delightful nature and make loyal and devoted companions. Quite when and how longhaired Siamese originated is contested. One theory is that the longhaired gene is present as a natural mutation, and that longhaired Siamese cats have appeared sporadically over centuries. Such cats can be seen in Chinese tapestries but it is difficult to tell if they are actually Siamese or not. The earliest hard evidence for the longhaired variety dates to 1928 when the Cat Fanciers' Federation (CFF) registered one. The second theory is based on the floundering Siamese population in Europe following World War II. At this time breeders may have crossbred to other breeds to increase the Siamese numbers and this might be how the longhaired gene entered the Siamese bloodlines.

Either way, instances of longhaired kittens alongside their shorthaired siblings first began to be noticed in the early to middle decades of the twentieth century. In the late 1940s, some breeders became taken with these beautiful longhaired versions, and steps were taken to consolidate and actively produce these cats. Their development can be largely attributed to a handful of the earliest breeders and

their enormous dedication. These were Mrs. Marion Dorsey of the Rai-Mar Cattery in California and Mrs. Helen Smith of Merry Mews Cattery in New York. Both these Siamese breeders found longhaired kittens in their litters and were captivated. The Balinese owes its exotic name to Helen Smith whose graceful, lithe cats reminded her of traditional dancers from Bali. Helen and Marion worked together during the 1950s and 1960s to increase breeding stock and to earn the fledgling breed official recognition. Helen was the first to exhibit Balinese at the Cat Fanciers' Association (CFA) Empire Cat Show in New York, entering them in the any other variety class, while Marion showed her Balinese at a CFF show in Glendale, California in 1956.

In 1958 Englishwoman and Siamese breeder Sylvia Holland of Holland's Farm Cattery in California acquired her first Balinese, Rai-Mar's Sputnik of Holland's Farm, from Marion. In 1965 she bought Marion's Rai-Mar Cattery and went on to dedicate the rest of her life to the Balinese. She managed to bring all the Balinese breeders together to work toward the same end goals—achieving official recognition for the breed, and its continual improvement. Her cats from Holland Farm feature in the majority of Balinese pedigrees. The Balinese Breeders and Fans of America (BBFA) was formed in the 1960s to support the breed; it was responsible for the first breed standard in 1965 with revisions in 1967 and 1970. The BBFA also wrote the Code of Ethics for the breed. Largely through Sylvia's efforts, the Balinese had been accepted by most of the registries by 1965, with the exception of the CFA. The CFA finally granted them provisional status in 1967 and in 1970 they were accepted for championship status. Sadly Sylvia had passed away by the time the first male grand champion was awarded in 1973–4, a male blue point called BW Gaynell's Spartacus. The first female grand champion was BW Gaynell's Tanisha of Die Lilo.

During the 1970s the breed became increasingly popular and successful in the show ring, but toward the end of the

decade a furor broke out among breeders. The Balinese was recognized in the same four pointed colors as the Siamese, but some breeders decided they wanted to breed their Balinese in the extended range of colors seen in the Colorpoint Shorthair, and began to cross their Balinese with the Colorpoint. This could potentially lead to the Balinese losing its status as a pure mutation of the Siamese. To overcome the issue these Balinese and Colorpoint Shorthair crossbred cats were given a new breed name, the Javanese, by the CFA in 1979. Not all associations recognize the Javanese and some accept the Balinese in a wider range of colors than the four traditional pointed colors.

Controversy over breeding continued to rage during the 1980s, this time based on conformation, particularly that of the head. Some Balinese resembled the more traditional Applehead Siamese, while others resembled the modern Siamese with its long, tapering, wedge-shaped head. At this time two breeders had great influence—Leslie Lamb, who concentrated on head shape in her breeding program, and Nellie Sparrow, who worked on improving the coat quality in the Balinese using Siamese that exhibited slightly longer coats than normal. Despite these efforts, there was still disparity among the breed and confusion as to what they should look like. This led to a lack of popularity in the show ring. The situation was partially rectified through the efforts of breeder Bobbie Short and her Balik Balinese cats, which earned great accolades in the show halls and started to put the breed back on the map. Today the Balinese is not as popular as it once was; however, as a breed they are finally more unified in their qualities.

Balinese cats did not arrive in England until early 1973 when breeder Sandra Birch imported the male blue point American Champion Verdes Blue Warrior of Davina and his daughter, Davina's Chocolate Gem. Gem was a shorthaired Balinese, the result of a cross between a Balinese and a Siamese—these crosses have been continually useful in establishing and maintaining type in the Balinese. Sandra was a driving force in England in promoting the breed in its early years, along with Margaret Manolson who produced the famous Cheldene line of Balinese. By 1986 the Governing Council of the Cat Fancy (GCCF) had recognized the Balinese and granted them championship status, and during the 1989/90 show season the first Balinese achieved grand champion status.

BURMESE

MODERN – UNITED STATES/BURMA – MODERATE

APPEARANCE

Muscular, compact, and sleek. Medium-sized, strong body with level back and rounded chest. Substantial bone structure and athletic musculature make it heavier than appearance suggests. Medium-length legs with rounded paws. Head rounded with a full face, broad, short muzzle, and rounded chin. Ears set well apart with slight forward tilt, broad at base and rounded at tip. Large, rounded eyes set well apart,

yellow to gold in color. Tail should be straight and medium length.

SIZE

Medium

COAT

Very short in length, glossy and satin-like in texture. Chiefly sable, champagne/chocolate, platinum/lilac, or blue in color, some registries allow further colors.

PERSONALITY

Highly intelligent, entertaining, playful, intensely loving, active

THE BURMESE MAKES A SUPERB COMPANION, second to none in terms of its affection and loyalty to its owner. In addition it can be extremely playful and interactive, nosy even. It is not as vocal as the Siamese, but does like a good chat in its unique, slightly raspy voice. Burmese tend to have enormous personalities and like to be the center of attention; life is never dull with a Burmese!

The modern history of this delightful and charming breed traces to the 1930s and to America, but its origins are far older than this. The Burmese cat has existed in Thailand, Burma, and Southeast Asia for many hundreds of years, having been first documented in the Thai *Cat Book Poems,* roughly dated to between 1350 and 1767. This manuscript contains illustrations of the Burmese, along with the Korat and Siamese, indicating that these three breeds have been clearly differentiated for many centuries.

Burmese cats had made their way to England by the end of the nineteenth century, coinciding with the rapid rise in cat fancy, but at this time they were largely considered to be dark brown Siamese and were not recognized as a breed in their own right. There was much crossbreeding between Burmese and Siamese, and eventually the Burmese as it is now known disappeared from England.

Their story began again in 1930 in the United States at the hands of the distinguished Navy medical officer,

Dr. Joseph Thompson. Thompson was an accomplished breeder of Siamese cats and had founded his own cattery, the Mau Tien Cattery, in around 1926. Here he bred Siamese cats of unusually large and robust frames and was active in promoting the breed. In 1930 Thompson imported a brown Burmese female called Wong Mau, having become enamored with these attractive cats during his travels in Asia. Breeders in the United States considered Wong Mau to be a dark Siamese, but Thompson was convinced of her difference and set about proving this through science; he also wanted to cement and preserve Wong Mau's special characteristics. Thompson later discovered that Wong Mau was actually a hybrid Siamese x Burmese, now known as a Tonkinese. He called on Billie Gerst and Mrs. Virginia Cobb, who were respected cat breeders and trained in genetics, along with the geneticist Dr. Clyde Keeler, and began a series of breeding experiments using Wong Mau.

Since there were no other male cats like Wong Mau, Thompson enlisted a male seal point Siamese called Tai Mau. In fact, at this time, the physical differences between the Burmese and the Siamese were less pronounced than they now are. The first litter from this cross produced a mixture of seal point kittens like their father and brown kittens like their mother. Wong Mau was then bred to one of her sons, Yen Yen Mau, to produce very dark brown kittens. These dark brown kittens were termed Burmese and found to breed true to type and in 1936 they were accepted for stud book registration by the Cat Fanciers' Association (CFA). Wong Mau herself continued to produce kittens with three different coat colors; brown, dark brown, and seal point. In April 1943 the results of the breeding experiments by Thompson and his colleagues were published in the *Journal of Heredity* in an article entitled "Genetics of the Burmese Cat." Other breeders had by this time imported Burmese directly from Burma to increase the gene pool, and the breed rapidly became popular among the cat fancy. This was detrimental at the time since supply could not match demand and there was some indiscriminate crossbreeding. As a result of the confusion caused by this, the CFA withdrew recognition of the Burmese in 1947, and it was not restored until 1953. In 1958 the United Burmese Cat Fanciers association developed a breed standard that was accepted by the CFA the following year; most other U.S. cat associations refer to this standard, which has remained essentially unchanged since. From the 1960s, and particularly in the 1970s, the breed became increasingly popular in the United States and was ranked third behind the Persian and Siamese for some time.

In England the breed developed more slowly and along another route; there is a difference in type now between the English and American Burmese with the English more Oriental in appearance and the American more rounded in body and head type. In 1949 a breeder of Siamese cats, Mrs. Lilian France, imported a male and female Burmese from the United States. She later imported another pair. These formed the basis for the development of the breed in the United Kingdom, and by 1952 three generations of kittens had been born. This was sufficient for the Governing Council of the Cat Fancy (GCCF) to grant the Burmese breed recognition, although the gene pool was very small. In 1955 the first blue Burmese kitten was born in England, bred by Vic Watson, who then tried to establish where this color gene had originated. Until this time most Burmese breeders had attempted to breed only for the dark sable coloring, despite champagne and blue kittens appearing sporadically. During the 1950s and 1960s there was great controversy over acceptable colors within the breed in both the United States and United Kingdom. Interestingly, Vic Watson's research eventually led back to Wong Mau as the probable carrier of the genes resulting in the blue and champagne coloring. Some U.K. breeders campaigned tirelessly for the blue, champagne, and platinum colors to be accepted. In the early 1960s a red tabby shorthaired cat bred to a Burmese by accident, resulting in a black tortie colored kitten. The breeder Robine Pocock decided to use this kitten to develop the color within the breed; since then, other colors have developed (not recognized by all associations), including the red, cream, and blue tortie, brown tortie, and a large number of color variations.

HIMALAYAN

MODERN – UNITED STATES – COMMON

APPEARANCE
Longhaired with pointed pattern, regal. Cobby build with substantial bone, massive through shoulders and rump, level back, short and heavy in leg with large, round paws. Head is round and massive with short, snub nose and broad jaws. Ears are small, tilt forward, and are set low on head. Eyes are large, round, set far apart, and blue in color. Tail is short in relation to body length.

SIZE
Large to medium

COAT
Long, thick, and stands away from body. Silky in texture with large ruff. All colors in pointed pattern.

PERSONALITY
Gentle, calm, even tempered, affectionate, loyal, playful

THE HIMALAYAN POSSESSES the luxurious coat and cobby physique of the Persian cat, with the pointed color pattern of the Siamese, and was developed by crossbreeding the two breeds during the first half of the twentieth century. The resulting cat has proved extremely popular both in the show ring and the pet market. The Himalayan requires substantial grooming and is suitable only for people who have the time to devote to its care. Its long coat needs daily maintenance to prevent matting. It likes to be the center of its owner's attention and in the middle of any activity. Himalayans are docile and gentle, but enjoy a good play; they also generally get along with other pets and children.

The first documented deliberate breeding of Siamese to Persian was by a Swedish geneticist in 1924. The next experiments began in the 1930s when Harvard medical employee Dr. Keeler and Viriginia Cobb of the Newton Cattery crossed a Siamese female with a black Persian male, producing a litter of shorthaired black kittens. Next they bred a Siamese male to a black Persian female with the same result. Then they bred a female from the second litter to a male from the first, producing a kitten of Siamese body type and coloring but with the Persian long hair. This kitten was Newton's Debutante and is referred to as the first Himalayan, although at this point she was very different in type to what the breed would become. Genetically, the coveted Siamese pointed color pattern and blue eyes is based on a single recessive gene in the albino series, so both parents must possess the gene to produce the traits in the offspring. It would take many years of intensive breeding to produce the desired results. Chiefly, the longhaired pointed progeny (still of Siamese body type) were bred back to Persians and the progeny of these interbred to work toward producing the correct color pattern and body type.

Experiments in such breeding were taking place almost at the same time in England by Brian Stirling-Webb of the Briarry Cattery and Mrs. Manton Harding of the Mingchiu Cattery. The first Himalayan produced in England was Bubastis Georgina, a seal point female from the Briarry Cattery. After about ten years of breeding Brian Stirling-Webb approached the Governing Council of the Cat Fancy (GCCF) to request recognition for the new variety of longhaired cat. The GCCF accepted the cat and in Britain it is recognized as the Longhaired Colorpoint.

In North America breeders of the cats, led by Mrs. Goforth, applied to the Cat Fanciers' Association (CFA) for breed recognition. In 1957 the CFA granted them recognition as Himalayans and as a separate breed from the Persian. The name Himalayan was based on the color pattern found in other animals such as the Himalayan rabbit. By 1961 all the major U.S. cat associations had accepted the Himalayan for registration as a separate breed. They became increasingly popular during the 1960s, although because of widespread uninformed breeding there was a deterioration in body type. In the 1970s breeders agreed to greater use of solid-colored Persians. Their efforts were successful and the Himalayan became increasingly similar to the Persian body type while keeping the Siamese coloring. In 1984 the CFA classified the Himalayan as a division of the Persian breed. The International Cat Association (TICA) still classes the Himalayan as a separate breed.

Today these cats are known as Himalayans only in the United States; elsewhere they are referred to as Longhaired Colorpoints or Colorpoint Persians.

COLORPOINT SHORTHAIR

MODERN – UNITED STATES/BRITAIN – UNCOMMON

APPEARANCE
Long, lithe, and elegant. Long, tubular, hard body with firm muscles and fine bone structure. Legs are long and slender, hind legs longer than front, and paws neat and oval. Head is long and wedge shaped with long, straight nose and distinctively large ears, wide at base and pointed at tip. Eyes are medium sized, almond shaped and deep, vivid blue. Tail is long and tapers to point.
SIZE
Medium
COAT
Short and lies close to body, glossy. Sixteen different pointed colors recognized including red, cream, tortoiseshell, and lynx.
PERSONALITY
Extrovert, lively, highly intelligent, interactive, playful, vociferous, very affectionate

THE COLORPOINT SHORTHAIR IS A MAN-MADE BREED very closely related to the Siamese. It is an extremely rewarding cat and makes a fantastic family pet. It has an enormous personality and will insist on being involved in its owner's life at all levels. Such is its affiliation with its owner that it is very sensitive to changes in mood and atmosphere, and will always be the first to console in times of sadness, or share in fun. Like the Siamese, the Colorpoint Shorthair is very vocal and enjoys a lively chat; it is persistent in its talking and will eventually engage even the most reluctant admirer. Known for its outgoing nature and sense of humor, the Colorpoint Shorthair makes an enviable addition to any home.

Ambition for color variety was the impetus behind the development of the Colorpoint Shorthair. In the years following World War II, breeders in both the United Kingdom and the United States started to experiment with breeding the Siamese for different colors other than the four traditional Siamese colors of seal, chocolate, blue, and lilac point. They started by crossing Siamese with Abyssinian and red domestic shorthair cats. The initial goal was to produce Siamese-type cats that had red coloration, but this was found to be extremely difficult because of the associated genetics. Finally, once breeders had managed to fix the color, there was found to be a loss of body type, so further Siamese crosses were introduced to reestablish the desired Siamese appearance and nature.

Through the extensive influence of Siamese blood in its breeding, the Colorpoint Shorthair is now predominantly Siamese in its makeup while retaining its own unusual color range.

The breed status of the Colorpoint Shorthair is the subject of some debate, with many cat associations worldwide considering them a color division of the Siamese. A number of dedicated breeders of the Colorpoint Shorthair have worked extremely hard to gain their breed recognition, and the Cat Fanciers' Association (CFA) has acknowledged this, although it remains the only organization to recognize them as a separate breed. The red points were the first to be accepted by the CFA in the late 1950s, and by the early 1960s they were granted championship status. In 1969 lynx points and torties were accepted, and in 1974 additional colors were also accepted. Today the Colorpoint Shorthair can be one of sixteen different, gorgeous colors. They are sometimes described as Siamese cats wearing colorful coats, which is apt. To all intents and purposes the Colorpoint Shorthair is identical to the Siamese in appearance and shares very similar characteristics and personality; it differs only in its range of colors. Its status continues to be controversial among some Siamese breeders, who feel that the Colorpoint Shorthair is not pure Siamese and therefore should not be shown in Siamese categories.

According to the CFA classification, the longhaired variety of the Colorpoint Shorthair is called the Javanese. The Javanese was developed in the United States and is not named after the island of Java—the name was chosen simply because of its exotic associations. The Javanese shares a great deal in common with the Balinese, which is the longhaired Siamese, and was created through crossbreeding Balinese with the Colorpoint Shorthair. Other than its coat length and range of colors, the Javanese shares the same characteristics in body shape and temperament as the Siamese.

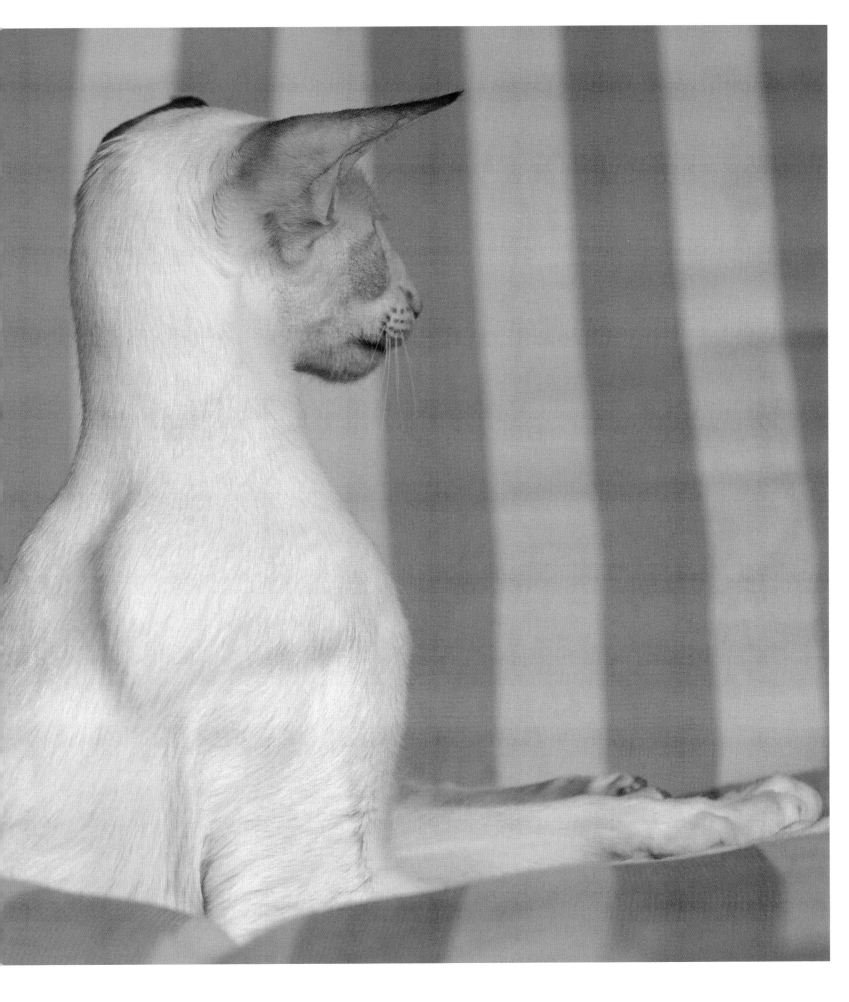

ORIENTAL
MODERN – BRITAIN – MODERATE

APPEARANCE
Slender and long in body with strikingly large ears. Svelte, lithe, and muscular through the body, which is firm to the touch. Frame is slender, legs long and slim, with small, neat, oval paws. Head is a long, tapering, wedge shape with a long, straight nose and large pointed ears that are wide at the base and follow the lines of the wedge. Eyes are medium sized, slanted, and almond shaped. They are green, but white Orientals may

have blue, odd, or green eyes. Tail is long, thin and tapering.
SIZE
Medium
COAT
Shorthaired, close lying, short, smooth, and glossy; longhaired, medium length fine, silky, no downy undercoat. Orientals come in over 300 colors and patterns.
PERSONALITY
Highly intelligent, lively, playful, devoted and loyal, interactive, vocal, extroverted

THE ORIENTAL is another breed within the Siamese family, much like the Colorpoint, and is only truly differentiated through the extensive range of coat colors. While the Siamese is recognized in four main pointed colors (this may vary slightly between associations and countries), and the Colorpoint in sixteen pointed colors, the Oriental can be found exhibiting an astonishing range of 300 different colors and patterns, including solids, smoke, shaded, tabby, bicolor, and parti-color. In all other respects the Oriental displays the same body conformation associated with the Siamese and very similar characteristics and temperament.

Like the other members of the Siamese entourage, the Oriental Shorthair and Longhair make loving, entertaining companions. They are highly intelligent cats that have an uncanny ability to access all areas, and are most happy in the company of loved ones and family. Personality and charisma define these beautiful cats who are equally at home in the show ring as they are keeping one's lap warm.

The first cats that were imported to England from Thailand during the nineteenth century were a variety of colors including solid and bicolors, and it was not until the end of the 1920s that the British Siamese Cat Club decreed that only blue-eyed pointed cats could be registered as Siamese. Therefore there was a history of solid-colored and parti-colored cats of Siamese type in England, and these

contributed towards the development of the Oriental. Following World War II—a time when purebred breed numbers were down—breeders crossed Siamese cats with Russian Blues and domestic shorthairs, with the first Orientals being solid colors (self-colored). The efforts of Brian Stirling-Webb, Mrs. Armitage Hargreaves, and Baroness Edit von Ullmann produced a cat in a chocolate-brown color. This kitten was born in 1952 and was called Elmtower Bronze Idol; its color came to be called Havana (first called the Chestnut Foreign Shorthair). In the 1950s the Havana Group, later the Havana and Oriental Lilac Cat Club, was formed. As the cats became popular with people breeding for the brown coloring rather than body type, there was quite a divergence of conformation. In the United Kingdom, following the Havana, a pure white Oriental type was developed and called the Foreign White.

In the late 1960s, Mrs. Pat Newton bred a chocolate-brown kitten of Oriental body type, Ch Scintilla Copper Beech, and she went on to appear in many of the pedigrees of today's Orientals. Pat Newton became a driving force in the development of the Oriental breed in England and, through exported cats, across much of the world. At the same time, the Lavender Oriental became very popular in England, Ch Burdach Cartagena being an early champion. By the 1970s in addition to the chocolate-brown, white, and lavender Orientals, there were black and blue, followed by tabby-patterned, creams, reds, and torties.

At first, as each variety emerged, it was categorized by its color in the United Kingdom; this changed in the 1980s when the many different color and pattern varieties of essentially the same cat were grouped under the name Oriental, while the self-colored cats were termed Foreign. In 1991 the Governing Council of the Cat Fancy (GCCF) made a further change and all varieties of colors and patterns were termed Oriental, except for the Havana and Foreign White. Today in England the GCCF divides Oriental Shorthairs into three main divisions: Oriental

Selfs, which includes the solid colors such as Havana, Black, Blue, Lilac, and so on; Oriental Non-Selfs, which includes Torties, Smokes, and Shaded; and Oriental Tabbies, which includes the four tabby patterns.

In the mid-1950s, the first British Havanas were imported into the United States. From these the American Havana Brown developed, becoming eventually an entirely different breed from the Oriental. By 1968 Mrs. Ann Billheimer of Florida was developing lavender and chestnut cats of Siamese body type. Mrs. Billheimer and another breeder, Mrs. Hackett, were the first to petition for recognition of the lavenders by the Cat Fanciers' Association (CFA) in 1972, although they were unsuccessful at this attempt.

Also in 1972, two Siamese cat breeders of note, Peter and Vicky Markstein, who established their Petmark Cattery in 1967, traveled to England to look for new Siamese lines to add to their breeding program. Instead they came across the Oriental Shorthair at Mary Dunnill's Sumfun Cattery and Angela Sayer's Solitaire Cattery. The Marksteins were greatly impressed with these cats and returned to the United States determined to try and create breed recognition and a market for them. They contacted other enthusiastic breeders, and arranged to import several Orientals. The breeders Pauline and Sid Thompson had also imported two cats: Solitaire Tongan Princess and Alice's Sakura. Several of the newly imported Orientals were exhibited at the Westchester Cat Club Show in 1974 and caused an immediate sensation—clearly there would be enthusiasm for the breed.

In 1974 the Governing Council of the Cat Fancy (GCCF) accepted the Oriental Shorthair for registration and they were granted championship status in 1977. The rapidity with which the Oriental was accepted and advanced to championship level is largely thought to be a direct result of the cooperation among the early U.S. and U.K. breeders and experts, and the enthusiasm with which the cat fancy world adopted this special breed.

In the late 1970s the Oriental Longhair was developed using the Oriental Shorthair crossed with the Balinese, which is the longhaired variety of the Siamese. In the United States, the Oriental Longhair was accepted by The International Cat Association (TICA) in 1985 and by the CFA in 1988—in 1996 the CFA combined the Oriental Shorthair and Longhair into one breed division.

HAVANA BROWN

MODERN – UNITED STATES – RARE

APPEARANCE

Luxurious, brown colored, alert, with distinctive-shaped head. Body type is midway between cobby and svelte with good muscle tone and heavier in weight than it might appear. Legs are relatively long with hind legs slightly longer than the front; paws are neat and oval. Head is longer than it is wide with full whisker pads and a prominent, broad nose with distinct stop at the eyes; muzzle has a rounded appearance. The eyes are set well apart, medium sized, oval, and vivid green. Ears are large, round tipped, and tilted forward. Tail is medium length, slender, and tapers to the end.

SIZE

Medium

COAT

Medium length, close lying, smooth, lustrous. Rich, mahogany-brown color.

PERSONALITY

Charming, playful, devoted, quiet, gentle, interactive, intelligent

THE HAVANA BROWN, OR HAVANA, is an inquisitive and intelligent cat that often investigates with its paws. It is extremely affectionate and likes to be right in the middle of whatever its owner is doing, but is vocally quiet. The Havana Brown thrives on company and will return any affection with great enthusiasm.

First developed in England in the 1950s, the Havana Brown is a created breed that has since established its own unique identity in the United States. Despite its relatively short history, the breed has ties dating back several centuries to Thailand. Here, dark brown cats were greatly admired for their exotic looks, and were thought to ward off evil spirits. Dark brown cats were some of the first to be imported from Thailand into England during the 1800s; they were shown in early cat shows toward the end of the nineteenth century and were occasionally referred to as Swiss Mountain cats. They continued to be popular until the late 1920s when the British Siamese Cat Club decided that only pointed blue-eyed cats could be registered. Shortly afterwards the brown cats became unfashionable.

In the early 1950s a circle of British breeders led by Mrs. Armitage Hargreaves, Baroness Edit von Ullmann, Mrs. Munroe-Smith, Mrs. Judd, and Mrs. Fisher reignited interest in brown self-colored cats with the foreign body type. They bred chocolate point and seal point Siamese with solid black domestic shorthairs and Russian Blues to achieve the solid brown color. The first registered kitten was Elmtower Bronze Idol, followed closely by Praha Gypka and Elmtower Brown Prior. By 1953 the first female Havana had been born, Elmtower Brown Study, meaning there were now a total of four of these cats in the world. The new breed was recognized by the Governing Council of the Cat Fancy (GCCF) in 1958 as the Chestnut Foreign Shorthair, with its name being changed to Havana in 1970. The name Havana has two sources, one being the rich brown cigars of the same name, and the other the Havana rabbit, which can have a chocolate-colored coat.

In the mid-1950s Mrs. Elsie Quinn from California imported the first Havana Brown from the United Kingdom, a female called Roofspringer Mahogany Quinn. This female was later bred to another imported Havana Brown to produce the first American grand champion, Quinn's Brown Satin of Sidlo. Today all American Havana Browns trace back to this important foundation cat.

In the United Kingdom the Havana Brown was bred specifically along Siamese lines to reinforce the foreign body type, whereas in the United States the cats remained more like the original ones imported. These were slightly heavier in build than the Siamese and now have a very distinctive appearance, particular in the conformation of their heads. Today the Havana Brown is a purely American breed and has little in common with the British Havana. The British Havana falls within the Oriental division in the United Kingdom. In the United States the Cat Fanciers' Association (CFA) only recognizes the rich brown coloring of this breed, whereas since 1983 The International Cat Association (TICA) has also accepted Lilac Havanas for championship status.

The gene pool for this breed had become relatively small by the late 1990s. Approved outcrossings were made and have resulted in some outstanding stock. Despite this, the Havana Brown is rare and numbers remain low.

SOMALI

MODERN – UNITED STATES – UNCOMMON

APPEARANCE

Athletic, graceful, distinctive ticked coat. Muscular and strong through the body, which is between cobby and svelte. Proportionate legs, compact, oval feet with tufts of hair between the toes. The head is a modified, slightly rounded wedge shape with rise from bridge of nose to forehead. Large, slightly pointed ears are broad and cupped at base with tufty hair in the inner ear. The eyes are large, expressive, and almond shaped, from copper and gold to green in color with a dark line to the outside. Tail is thick at base and tapers to end with a full brush.

SIZE

Medium to large

COAT

Medium length, soft, double coated, can be shorter over shoulders; ruff and britches desired. Colors can be ruddy, red, blue, and fawn, some accept silver, tortie, chocolate, and lilac.

PERSONALITY

Curious, active, determined, affectionate, intelligent

THE BEAUTIFUL SOMALI BREED is the longhaired Abyssinian. Somalis are extroverts, playful, and active, with a pronounced sense of humor and an affectionate nature. They are extremely interactive with their owners and enjoy serious playtime, extending to games such as fetch, but generally on their own terms! These cats are exquisite in appearance, with an almost fox-like look that is emphasized in the ruddy or red colors; accepted colors for the Somali vary between different associations and different countries. Somalis have full, brush tails and a silky medium-long coat that needs relatively little management.

Somalis have only been recognized in the cat fancy relatively recently. There is little evidence about their origins. Some believe that their long hair was the result of a natural mutation within the Abyssinian breed; if this is the case, it is likely that Somalis (or longhaired Abyssinians) have been around for a very long time. Another more recent school of thought is that the Somali was the result of an unknown longhaired interloper into the breed. This is most commonly traced to England and the early years of the twentieth century, when breed numbers of Abyssinians were very low; in order to bolster numbers, British breeders are thought to have crossbred to other stock, which might have carried the recessive longhair gene.

An important cat in the development of the Somali was Raby Chuffa of Selene, a male Abyssinian who was imported to the United States from England in 1953; he features in many of the American Abyssinian pedigrees as well as those of the Somali. Raby Chuffa traced his pedigree back to the British female Abyssinian Roverdale Purrkins, whose own mother, Mrs. Mew, was of unknown parentage but is thought to have carried the longhair gene. Roverdale Purrkins was a founder of the Roverdale cattery, and from here Abyssinians were exported to America, Australia, New Zealand, Canada, and Europe. The Abyssinian Bruerne Achilles from Australia was also identified as a carrier of the longhair gene and appears often in Somali pedigrees.

It was not until the 1960s that longhaired Abyssinians began to attract a dedicated following, and it was at this time that breeders began to consolidate them into a separate breed. One of the most influential breeders in this respect was the American Evelyn Mague, who was also responsible for suggesting the name "Somali"; it was perhaps a natural choice, with Somalia bordering Ethiopia (formerly Abyssinia). Mague had an Abyssinian, Lynn-Lee's Lord Dublin, whom she bred to a female, Lo-Mi-R's Trill-By, and in the subsequent litter there was a small, fuzzy, dark kitten that they named George. George had a checkered early life and passed through five different homes before arriving, by chance, back with Mague. Angry that this cat of such good breeding had been shunned by the cat fancy world, Mague was spurred into developing the longhaired Abyssinian as a recognized breed. Her efforts were eventually rewarded, aided by breeders in Canada; Mague founded the Somali Cat Club of America in 1972 and in 1975 the Cat Fanciers' Association's International Somali Cat Club was established.

The first Somalis in England were Foxtail's Belle Starr and Ch Naphrani's Omar Khayyam, imported in 1980. Black Iron Vagabond and Black Iron Venus were imported in 1981 by Peter and Margaret Frayne; Black Iron Vagabond is now considered the foundation cat of the breed in England.

CORNISH REX

MODERN – BRITAIN – RARE

APPEARANCE

Slender, racy, athletic, wavy coat. Svelte in appearance with fine boning, standing tall on long legs with a tuck up. Long, narrow torso, back slightly arched, and muscular through body. Head is relatively small and about one-third longer than its width. High cheekbones, Roman nose with prominent bridge. Eyes are medium to large, oval, and a clear, vivid color—dependent on coat color. Ears are large and set reasonably high on head. Tail is long and slender, paws are small, slightly oval, and neat.

SIZE

Small to medium

COAT

Wavy, dense coat, soft and silky in texture and free of guard hairs. All colors and patterns.

PERSONALITY

Very active, outgoing, intelligent, playful, affectionate, humorous

THERE IS SOMETHING MAGICAL about the Cornish Rex. This is in no small measure due to its amazing temperament in addition to its elegant appearance. The Cornish Rex is full to bursting with personality, energy, vigor, and affection. It is a lively, playful, and highly interactive cat with a pronounced sense of humor and clownish tendencies. It is extremely sociable and loving, and highly intelligent—nothing is out of reach or safe from a Cornish Rex. It is virtually guaranteed to bring endless laughter and enjoyment to any home.

The history of the Cornish Rex is quite extraordinary; the breed was "discovered" by chance—and an awful lot of dedicated hard work by early breeders. Its origins, unusually, can be traced to an exact day, July 21, 1950. In a farmhouse on Bodmin Moor, Cornwall, in southwest England, a tortoiseshell cat called Serena, belonging to Mrs. Ennismore, gave birth to a litter of five kittens. Among the kittens, one stood out. He was red and white in color and appeared to have a curly coat—he was also notably different in body shape to his litter mates, being "foreign" in type, meaning slender and athletic with a wedge-shaped head. Mrs. Ennismore realized the importance of this little kitten and that he had derived through a genetic mutation. She decided to keep him and named him Kallibunker. Kallibunker eventually became the first Rex cat to be registered in the United Kingdom;

the term "rex" was taken from the Rex rabbit, which shares a similar coat. Mrs. Ennismore's veterinarian put her in contact with a genetics specialist, A. C. Jude, who advised her to breed Kallibunker back to his mother to try and fix his characteristics in his progeny. In 1952 Kallibunker and his dam Serena produced a litter of three kittens, of which two had curly coats. One of these died very young, but the remaining kitten, a male called Poldhu, survived. Kallibunker and Poldhu were bred to Burmese, Siamese, and British Shorthairs as well as back to their own curly-coated progeny. It was discovered that the curly coat was caused by a recessive gene, so two curly-coated cats bred together would result in all curly kittens.

In 1956 *Life* magazine published an article about Kallibunker (who died the same year) and some photographs of the new breed. The article brought these little-heard-of cats to international attention and in 1957 Frances Blancheri, a Californian cat breeder, imported two Rex cats from Mrs. Ennismore. The female, Lamorna Cove, had been bred to her father Poldhu before setting off, and produced a litter of four kittens. Two of these, the male Marmaduke of Daz-Zling (owned by Helen Weiss) and the female Diamond Lil of Fan-T-Cee (owned by Mrs. Galvin) became the foundation cats for the Cornish Rex breed in the United States.

Back in England in 1958, renowned cat breeder Brian Stirling-Webb purchased Poldhu. Accounts describe Poldhu as a tortoiseshell, which is highly unusual because most male tortoiseshells are sterile, and Poldhu had already sired several litters. Very sadly, his veterinary surgeon took a tissue sample from the cat to examine the genetics and, in so doing—with no small measure of irony—rendered him infertile. The sample was also lost. By this time in the United Kingdom the number of Rex cats was severely limited. Following Poldhu's infertility there was just one remaining male, Champagne Chas, who was another son of Kallibunker. Brian Stirling-Webb borrowed Chas and bred

him to Burmese and British Shorthairs. The resulting progeny were straight coated, but when bred back to Chas or to each other, they produced Rex kittens. The gene pool was incredibly small, and with consistent inbreeding, problems began to occur. To combat this, a blue male called Riovista Kismet was imported from Calgary, Canada, and used to broaden the breeding stock in the United Kingdom—Riovista Kismet was actually a great-great-great grandson of Kallibunker. By 1965 the Cornish Rex was established enough to be granted provisional approval by the Governing Council of the Cat Fancy (GCCF), and this was extended to championship status in 1967. The first British female champion was Noend Crinkle, and the first male champion Lohteyn Golden Peach.

Back in the United States, the Rex were initially crossbred with Siamese, American Shorthairs, Havana Browns, and Burmese. At first this led to a slight loss of body type, but it did serve to increase the gene pool, which was crucial for sustaining optimum health and well-being in the breed. Another step for the Cornish Rex in the United States was when an odd-eyed calico with a curly coat arrived in a California animal shelter. Bob and Dell Smith of the Rodell Cattery adopted the cat and named her Mystery Lady of Rodell. She was bred to Fan-T-Cee Blue Boy, the son of Diamond Lil of Fan-T-Cee, who was the first Rex cat born in the United States. Although Mystery Lady's first litter of kittens were straight coated, when these were bred back to her, she produced curly-coated kittens. The major cat associations began to accept the Cornish Rex during the 1960s, with Marmaduke of Daz-Zling being the first registered by the Cat Fanciers' Association (CFA) in 1962; they were first accepted into The International Cat Association (TICA) in 1979. Since that time, the Cornish Rex has achieved numerous accolades in the show ring and is supported by a small but devoted following.

As a final word on this breed, they can also be suitable for people who are allergic to other breeds. Allergic reactions to cats are caused by an allergenic protein secreted via saliva. When cats groom themselves this protein is spread onto the coat and, when the cat sheds, is spread across the house. Cornish Rex simply do not shed as much as other breeds, so less of the allergenic protein is present, making them more suitable for those with allergies.

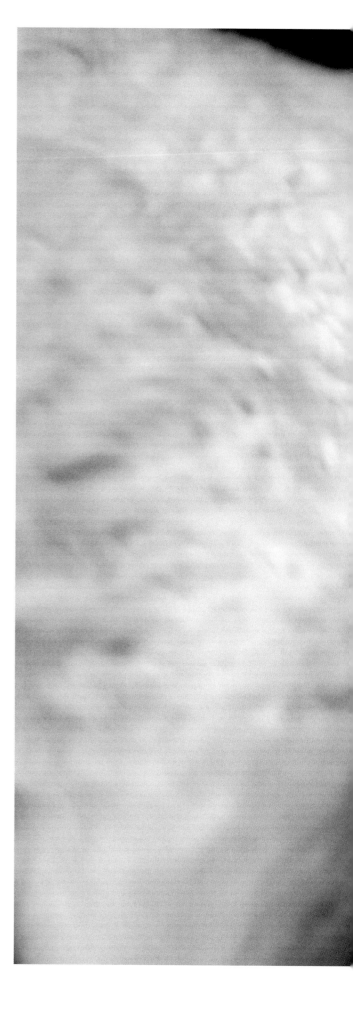

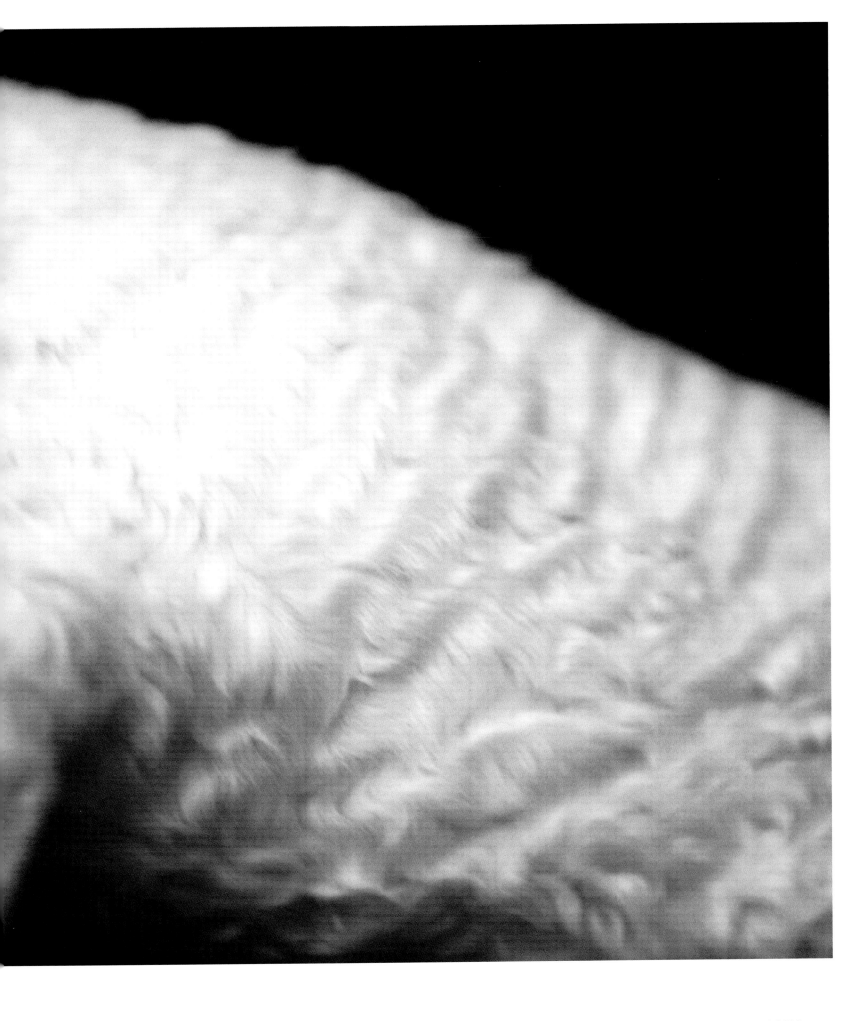

BOMBAY

MODERN – UNITED STATES – UNCOMMON

APPEARANCE
Glistening black and beautifully proportioned. A muscular, athletic build that is neither cobby nor rangy, deceptively heavy for its size. Medium-sized body with legs and tail in proportion and round paws. The head is rounded with a full face and a broad muzzle. Eyes are rounded and range in color from gold to copper (copper preferred), ears are medium sized, set well apart, and slightly tilted forward.

SIZE
Medium

COAT
Short, sleek, and shiny, always black to the roots.

PERSONALITY
Very affectionate, curious, playful, intelligent, outgoing, easy-going

WITH ITS JET-BLACK, SHINING COAT and large copper-colored eyes, the Bombay is like a mini black panther in appearance, which is exactly what the breed was developed to resemble. Easy-going and highly affectionate, the Bombay makes the perfect family cat. Rather than bonding with one person, it tends to devote itself to its entire human family, but is noted for being particularly patient and playful with children and delights in a game of fetch. The Bombay thrives on company and is happiest when sharing its owner's space. It is not overly demanding, however, and is polite and gentle in its quest for attention.

The breed owes its existence to the dedication of Nikki Horner and her Shawnee Cattery in Louisville, Kentucky. Nikki wanted to create a breed with the appearance of the Burmese but with a sleek, black coat and copper eyes, like the black panther. She named the breed Bombay after the large black wildcats of India. She began in the early 1950s by breeding Burmese to black American Shorthairs, at first with disappointing results. She continued her efforts, choosing her breeding stock with great care, and over time began to achieve the results she wanted. The foundation cats for the Bombay were eventually recognized as the male Burmese cats Shawnee Cassius Clay, Shawnee Col. Casey, and Shawnee Little Brown Jug, and the male black American Shorthairs Shawnee Shot in the Dark and David Copperfield. The females included David's Black Onyx, Shawnee Obsidian, and Esquire Escapade.

Despite the success of the Nikki's breeding programs there was considerable antipathy toward the new breed, particularly from Burmese breeders. Nikki continued to exhibit her cats at many shows to gather support and in 1970 the breed was acknowledged by the Cat Fanciers' Association (CFA) on a provisional basis. In 1976 it was granted championship status by the CFA. The International Cat Association (TICA) recognized it in 1979. Suzanne and Herb Zwecker were also influential breeders with their Road to Fame Cattery. In the late 1980s a pair of Bombay cats from Ron and Wendy Klamm's Katsnklamms Cattery were exported to Pascal Portales in France and founded the Bombay in continental Europe. European Bombays are very similar to their American relatives.

The story is a little different in the United Kingdom. Several Burmese breeders in the United Kingdom had bred litters of all-black kittens during the 1960s and exhibited them in the north of England, causing quite a sensation. It was not until the 1980s that there was a concerted effort by several breeders to develop these all-black cats. The earliest Bombay breeding was actually a happy accident when Ms. Billie Oliver's Burmese female Lochibank Blue Viola was bred by an unregistered shorthaired black male. The resulting kitten was a beautiful shorthaired black female of Burmese appearance called Lochibank Princess. Lochibank Blue Viola had another unplanned match with an unregistered male to produce Black Midget. Lochibank Princess was bred to Cataumet der Rosenkavalier to produce Adreesh Piyada; Piyada went on to be an important cat in the foundation of the British Bombay. British breeders continued to consistently breed for color and conformation, and after some years the British Bombay had appeared. In the United Kingdom the Bombay is not recognized as a separate breed, but is grouped under the Asian Group of cats. In Australia and New Zealand the breed was developed along slightly different lines with breeders using British Shorthairs and Burmese in their breeding programs.

CHAPTER 4
1960 TO 1969

The 1960s was a decade of profound global change in many spheres—politically, culturally, economically, spiritually, and in the world of cats. There have been few decades through the course of history that have retained such a firm identity, often reviewed with great nostalgia. It was also a time of momentous events, one of the most memorable being the landing of the first man on the moon in 1969. Rather less celebrated was the journey of the first cat into space, which took place on October 18th, 1963, although Félicette, as the cat was called, did not make it to the moon. The French government was behind the "cat in space" program and trained a number of cats for the trip. It is said that ten of the trainee cats were thrown off the program for eating too much! Leading the candidates was a French stray called Felix, who had been designated to make the trip. However, Felix escaped the day before the launch, and the female Félicette was swiftly drafted in to take his place. She had electrodes fitted to her head, which transmitted neural impulses back to base throughout her short, 15-minute flight. Félicette never made it into orbit,

but did journey approximately 100 miles into space. She landed safely back on earth, although a second attempt using a different cat ended less successfully. Some years later, several postage stamps were illustrated to commemorate animals in space, and Félicette was among them. So far as it is known, there have not been any other cats in space of any nationality.

By the 1960s cats had become firmly entrenched as pets and although there were still many nonpedigreed cats, as there are today, there was also an increasing interest in purebred breeds and cat shows. There was a passion for exotic animals, which included cats, and this was part of the impetus behind a number of breeds developed during this period. In addition there were also huge advances in science, leading to an even greater understanding of genetics. Within the context of the cat fancy world this had significant impact on the development of new breeds through combining existing breeds (hybridization) and the establishment of different coat colors and patterns within breeds, plus the manipulation of spontaneous genetic

mutations. Cat ownership was on the increase and the older breeds such as the Siamese and Abyssinian, for example, that had suffered greatly in numbers during the war years were by now reestablished.

Breeders began to look toward wildcats, being particularly attracted to their appearance. This led to the early development of two hybrid breeds, the Bengal and the Chausie, both of which did not receive official recognition from the various cat associations for many decades. The Bengal has domestic shorthair crossed with the wild Asian Leopard cat (*Prionailurus bengalensis*) at its root, while the Chausie has domestic breeds such as the American Shorthair and Abyssinian crossed with the wild Jungle Cat (*Felis chaus*) behind its development. As with any breed creation, it took enormous dedication and knowledge from breeders to establish these breeds and in particular to stabilize their wild looks while maintaining the superb temperament for which they are now known.

Work on developing another very exotic breed, the Ocicat, also began during this decade. The Ocicat is again noted for its wild look, which reflects the appearance of the wild Ocelot, but unlike the Bengal and Chausie, there is no wild blood in the Ocicat. Instead, the breed actually originated as something of an accident, when noted Siamese breeder Virginia Daly was attempting to breed a pointed Siamese with Abyssinian coloring. One of the kittens in her litter of Siamese and Abyssinian crosses was an unexpected ivory color with golden spots and had the appearance of the wild Ocelot. The beauty of this kitten inspired Daly to try and reproduce its appearance, eventually leading to the Ocicat.

Yet another wild-looking cat that emerged during this same period is the American Bobtail. Unlike the three exotic-looking breeds, though, the American Bobtail was a naturally occurring cat that developed its particular bobtail appearance through a spontaneous genetic mutation. Breeders discovered feral cats of wildcat appearance with bobtails in many different regions of the United States and began to breed them to establish their characteristics.

Spontaneous genetic mutations also account for a large number of the distinctive characteristics seen in many of the new breeds in particular. With increasing understanding of the science behind the mutations, breeders and scientists were better able to fix new traits. The gene responsible for a trait is either dominant or recessive. The Scottish Fold with its forward-folded ears is a good example. A kitten exhibiting this trait was discovered in 1961 on a farm in Scotland and a year later gave birth to two kittens also displaying folded ears. A geneticist was taken on board and the cats were bred to try to establish the characteristic. It was discovered that the folded ear was caused by a dominant gene that affects the cartilage in the ear, causing it to fold forward. Because this is caused by a dominant gene, at least one parent must exhibit the characteristic to reproduce it. When a cat with the dominant gene is bred to a cat without, approximately half of the progeny will exhibit the characteristic. If two parents exhibiting the dominant gene are bred together, the percentage of progeny exhibiting the trait increases, but so too do congenital problems. Other breeds that began to be developed during the 1960s and also derived from spontaneous genetic mutation include the American Wirehair, the Devon Rex, and the distinctive Sphynx. The Sphynx's lack of coat is caused by a recessive gene. With recessive genes it takes two copies of the gene for the trait to be exhibited, so if each parent only has one copy of the gene only about one in four of the kittens will show the trait. Breeding to stabilize a genetic mutation to form a new breed while ensuring that the breed is robust and the gene pool large enough is a painstaking process.

Other cat breeds that were developed by breeders during this decade include the Tonkinese, the Ragdoll, and the Snowshoe. The Tonkinese was bred as a cross between Siamese and Burmese. The Ragdoll and Snowshoe, however, both arose partly by chance, when breeders noticed a kitten in a litter with interesting markings or temperament, and then started a breeding program to reproduce the same characteristics.

Other changes were afoot that affected cats, pedigreed or not, during the 1960s. First was the development of the clay-based cat litter, trademarked Tidy Cats. American Ed Lowe had first come up with the idea in 1947, and had begun to sell paper bags full of the clay litter, calling it Kitty Litter. He did the circuit of the cat shows with his new product to spark interest among the cat fancy. It was in 1964, though, when Ed trademarked his litter Tidy Cats that it really took off. Until then the few people that kept their cats indoors did so using earth, sand, ash, or shredded paper in their trays, but the super-absorbent clay pellets made an enormous difference. This clay-based litter also allowed many people who had not kept cats before due to worries over their location, to keep cats hygienically indoors. Also, because of the high price of pedigreed cats, it gave breeders and owners the opportunity to protect their cats by keeping them inside if they wished to.

Within the same time frame the British Cats Protection League (now known simply as Cats Protection), which was formed in 1927, was actively lobbying for changes in legislation to improve cat welfare. In 1960 the Abandonment of Animals Act was brought into force in the United Kingdom, making it an offense for any person to abandon an animal (including a cat) in a way that might "cause the animal any unnecessary suffering." Then in 1963 the Animal Boarding Establishments Act was introduced and required all boarding establishments, including catteries, to be inspected and licensed; it should be noted, however, that some places that apparently met the criteria were far from salubrious. Other U.K. legislation was brought in during the decade that extended to all domestic animals and included deliberate poisoning becoming an offense, as well as performing surgery on a domestic animal without "due care and humanity." Neutering and spaying of cats had only started to become more common during the late 1940s. Until that time if male cats were neutered it was using barbaric methods, and females were left to breed repeatedly. This in itself had health issues for the female and resulted in unwanted kittens that were routinely disposed of. The introduction of spaying and neutering under surgical conditions and by professionals was a giant step forward. The Theft Act of 1968 made it clear that all domestic animals including cats were capable of being stolen if taken from the owners unlawfully.

In the United States the Animal Welfare Act was introduced in 1966 to protect the welfare of animals, including cats, and has been updated numerous times in the intervening years. American presidents have famously enjoyed keeping cats at the White House. During the 1960s there was one special cat called Tom Kitten who made an appearance, albeit briefly. Tom Kitten, named after the character in the Beatrix Potter books, belonged to Caroline Kennedy, John F. Kennedy's daughter. The cat lived in the White House for around a year before it was discovered that J. F. Kennedy was allergic to him, and to dogs. Sadly Tom Kitten went to live with friends, but he had obviously made his mark with the presidential family because on his death in 1962 an obituary for him appeared in a Washington newspaper.

On the other side of the Atlantic there was another particularly notable cat enthusiast, namely Winston Churchill (1874–1965). Churchill adored cats and always had at least one or two in his private and official residences, with the most famous being the cats at Chartwell, his family home in Kent. One of his Chartwell cats was a large tabby called Mickey. Once, when Churchill was on the telephone to the Lord Chancellor, Mickey began to play with phone line and Churchill bellowed, "get off the line, you fool." He hastily had to explain to the Lord Chancellor that this was not directed at him, but at his cat. Another was a marmalade colored cat called Tango to whom Churchill was particularly devoted. Tango would sit in a chair next to him during dinner and received most of his master's attention and some of his food as well. Nelson was a large gray cat named for his bravery and fighting skills, who Churchill owned during the war years. In 1940 when he was voted in as Prime Minister, Churchill moved to 10 Downing Street, taking Nelson with him. When they arrived, his predecessor's cat, referred to as the "Munich Mouser," was in residence and there was some debate over how Nelson and MM would get along. Nelson, it is said, usurped MM with ruthless efficiency.

Many stories surround Churchill and his numerous cats, but perhaps none are so moving as that relating to his last cat, Jock. Jock was a handsome ginger cat with a white bib and paws who was given to Churchill on his 88th birthday in 1962. Churchill and Jock became devoted companions, with the cat traveling with Churchill between Chartwell and his London residence at Hyde Park Gate. Jock was even present on the occasion of Churchill's last visit to the House of Commons in 1964 and appears in a photograph taken as the former prime minister left his home. When Churchill died, Chartwell was turned over to the National Trust, but with one proviso—that Jock should live out his days there and that there should always be a ginger cat called Jock kept at the house in honor of Churchill's love for his pet. In accordance, Jock stayed at Chartwell until his death in 1975, and now the fifth Jock is in residence, a charming and handsome ginger fellow.

During the 1960s cats also began to hit the small and big screens, appearing in a variety of commercials on television and also featuring in films and cartoons. One of the first feline television stars in the United States was a large ginger tom cat called Lucky, who was discovered in an animal shelter in Chicago in 1968 by animal handler Bob Martwick. He was quickly renamed Morris and was employed to advertise 9-Lives cat food. Morris starred in numerous commercials and was known as being "easy to work with" due to his sweet, quiet nature, although he was said to be a picky eater; naturally he preferred 9-Lives food. He amassed a huge fan base, receiving sacks of mail from all over the world, and reputedly lived a particularly lavish lifestyle, including being driven around Hollywood in a limousine and using a litter tray designed by Louis Vuitton! He also enjoyed a turn on the big screen, starring in the movie *Shamus* with Burt Reynolds. Morris represented one of the most successful advertising campaigns of the time and, following his death in 1978, he was replaced with another Morris, and then another, both also rescued from animal shelters. The current Morris, who lives in Los Angeles, is still the face of the company.

In the United Kingdom a white cat called Arthur took the world of advertising by storm in the 1960s and early 1970s. He had the particular gift of being able to help himself to cat food out of a can by using his paw, and this earned him a job with the British pet food company Spillers. He appeared in hundreds of commercials for the company, with his fame extending beyond the simple sales of cat food. His face appeared on everything from tea towels to T-shirts and he even had his autobiography ghost written for him by John Montgomery. Arthur eventually died in 1976 at the grand old age of 16.

Other famous cats of the decade include Orangey, who appeared as Cat in *Breakfast at Tiffany's* with Audrey Hepburn in 1961, having previously starred in *Rhubarb* in 1951. Orangey was allegedly temperamental when not filming, although this did nothing to diminish his image with the public, who adored him.

The 1960s was also a time when cartoon animals were building on their popularity. Previous decades had seen the creation of Felix the Cat, an animated cat who started life as a silent movie star for Paramount Pictures; Tom and Jerry by Fred Quimby, William Hanna, and Joseph Barbera; and Sylvester by Warner Brothers. In 1961 Hanna Barbera produced *Top Cat,* a television series about the smart-talking leader of a gang of alley cats on the streets of Manhattan, which became an instant success. This was followed in 1965 by the less commercially viable *Fritz the Cat,* created by Robert Crumb. Fritz was a subversive comic-strip cat who acquired a huge cult following.

DEVON REX

MODERN – BRITAIN – RARE

APPEARANCE

Elfin look with very large ears and large, luminous eyes. Slender, muscular, and body with broad chest. Legs long and of medium bone with hind legs longer than front; paws small and oval. Tail is long and tapers to end, covered with short fur. Comparatively small head appears broad, but is slightly longer than wide. Has very pronounced cheekbones, full cheeks, and prominent whisker pads. Muzzle is short and in profile has clear stop. Ears are large, low set, and wide at base, covered in fine fur. Eyes are oval, large and wide set, they can be any color.

SIZE

Medium

COAT

Coat is fine and wavy and most dense along the back, sides, tail, legs, face, and ears. Can be less dense, softer, and downy on the underparts and top of head. Whiskers may be short or missing. Can be any color or pattern.

PERSONALITY

Extremely vivacious, friendly, very athletic and energetic, highly intelligent, playful, interactive, loyal, and devoted

ALL PRECONCEIVED IDEAS about what a cat should look like need to be put firmly to one side when encountering a Devon Rex for the first time. This cat has a truly unique appearance and is often described as "elfin-like," "pixie of the cat world," "alien-like," and occasionally as a "poodle cat." The Devon Rex also has a particularly endearing and captivating character that far outshines its elegant, other-worldly looks. This is a very people-oriented cat that likes to share its owner's space as much as possible. When not eating, which it does with great enthusiasm, or napping, the Devon Rex is also extremely active and agile. It is a great jumper and can normally access the most remote ledge or shelf; in addition it has bags of energy. It seems to have a real sense of humor and often actively engages in an activity that seems designed to entertain.

The Devon Rex traces its origins to 1959 and an illicit union between two stray non-pedigree cats living in Buckfastleigh, Devon, in southwest England. The male was a large, black tomcat, with an unusually curly coat, while the female was tortoiseshell and white, and may have also been his daughter. The female produced a litter of kittens on July 15, 1959 in the backyard of Mrs. Beryl Cox. One of the kittens was a beautiful dark brown male covered with long curls and ringlets, which extended along his tail. Mrs. Cox was instantly taken with the unusual kitten and took him into her home, naming him Kirlee.

Some months later Mrs Cox saw an article in a national newspaper about the forthcoming Kensington Kitten and Neuter Show that featured a photograph of a kitten, Du-Bu Lambtex. Du-Bu Lambtex was described as incredibly rare and the only curly coated cat in the country; he was to be exhibited at the show. On seeing this Mrs. Cox realized that Kirlee might be even more special than she had thought. Almost exactly ten years previously a curly coated kitten had been discovered in Cornwall and called Kallibunker. He went on to found the Cornish Rex and, since the counties of Cornwall and Devon are next door to one another, it was thought that Kallibunker and Kirlee must have been distantly related and shared the same genetic mutation. Interestingly both the Cornish Rex and the Devon Rex emerged as the result of a tortoiseshell-and-white female breeding to a feral male and producing a litter of straight-coated kittens with just one curly coated.

Given that the Cornish Rex was struggling with low breed numbers and a tiny gene pool, British breeders were thrilled to hear about Kirlee, whom they hoped would boost the Cornish breeding program. At this time the cats were simply called Rex cats. The noted breeder and judge Mr. Brian Stirling-Webb and Mrs. Agnes Watts, who had bred Du-Bu Lambtex, encouraged Mrs. Cox to sell Kirlee so he could be used in the breeding program. Kirlee was bought by Brian and went to live with Agnes where he was bred to several (Cornish) Rex females. After great anticipation the kittens were born, but all turned out to be straight coated. This indicated that Kirlee was the result of a completely separate genetic mutation. At this point breeders began to distinguish between the two different Rex-coated cats by referring to them as (Cornish) Gene I Rex and (Devon) Gene II Rex, and set about trying to establish them as different breeds.

Some Devons began to exhibit a neurological condition causing muscle spasms because of too much inbreeding, and so it was necessary to increase outcrossing. Initially a number of different breeds were introduced and The International Cat Association (TICA) allows Siamese, Burmese, Bombay, Sphynx, American Shorthair, and British Shorthair. Other associations allow just British and American Shorthair, and these are the two breeds most often used today. The Rex gene is a simple recessive, meaning all kittens born from a Devon Rex and an outcross breed will be straight haired. When those first-generation cats are bred back to Devon Rex cats they produce on average half straight and half curly haired kittens. As a result, it is a long, slow process to bolster Devon Rex breed numbers. The Devon Rex breeder faces a further serious problem. These cats carry two different blood types, type A and type B. When type A males are bred to type B females the mother's milk contains antibodies that work against the kittens' blood and results in their death. Now all breeding Devon Rex cats are blood typed to avoid this situation. The Devon Rex was recognized by the Governing Council of the Cat Fancy (GCCF) by 1967, with the first champion being Ch Amharic Kurly Katie.

The first two Devon Rex cats to cross the Atlantic were imported by Mary Carroll to Canada. In 1968 Marion and Anita White returned from a military posting in England to America taking two Devon Rex cats with them. The following year breeder Shirley Lambert imported two pointed Devons. The Whites and Shirley Lambert worked together and were very influential in establishing the breed in the United States. The U.S. gene pool was greatly added to in 1978 when British breeders Roma and Lajla Lund of Homeacres Cattery emigrated to the United States, taking over a dozen of their breeding stock Devons with them.

The American Cat Fanciers Association (ACFA) was the first U.S. association to recognize the Devon Rex as a separate breed, accepting them for championship status in 1972; TICA accepted them in 1979. The Cat Fanciers' Association (CFA) initially did not differentiate between the Devon and Cornish, embracing all curly coated cats as the same breed—Rex cats. Despite this, the Cornish and Devon breeders maintained their separate breeding policies. In 1979 the two breeds were recognized separately; the Devon was granted championship status in 1983.

SCOTTISH FOLD

MODERN – BRITAIN – RARE

APPEARANCE

Rounded, solid, ears folded forward. Medium-boned cat that is well padded and feels solid. Distinctive head with small ears, tightly folded forward. Head is rounded with short nose and prominent cheeks. Eyes are large and rounded with gentle expression. Tail is medium to long, tapers to end, and flexible.

SIZE

Medium

COAT

Can be medium short with dense hair that stands out from body, or medium long with tufts, britches, and ruff. Any color or pattern.

PERSONALITY

Loyal to owner, affectionate, curious, intelligent, playful, easygoing, vocally quiet

THE SCOTTISH FOLD is most obviously distinguished through the conformation of its ears, which are folded tightly forward, giving its head a very round appearance. It is a laid-back cat with a very placid temperament. Devoted to its family, it loves affection but is not overdemanding. It lives happily with other animals and children.

The documented story of these unusual-looking cats starts in Scotland in 1961, although it is entirely possible that they have a much longer and more far-flung history. Sources indicate that there were folded-ear cats in China during the eighteenth century, to which Howard Loxton makes reference in his *Guide to the Cats of the World* (1975). According to Loxton these folded-ear cats had been described in around 1796 as being native to China and with "hanging ears." A century later a sailor is said to have returned from China with one of these drop-eared cats, a breed that he described as being reared for meat.

To date it has not been proven whether the folded-ear trait originated from China. It is entirely likely that the condition also occurred among feral cats in Scotland as a spontaneous genetic mutation, and that there might have been feral cats carrying this trait for many years, but they had simply gone unnoticed. What is known is that the earliest such cats discovered in Scotland were white and medium longhaired. The first recorded folded-ear cat was discovered in 1961 by William Ross at the farm of his friends the McRaes near Coupar Angus in the Tayside region (now Perth and Kinross). The white folded-ear cat,

who was called Susie, was a barn cat of no recognized pedigree; her mother was a straight-eared white and her father unknown. Susie is said to have had a male litter-mate who also had folded ears, but nothing more is known about him. A little over a year later, Susie had her own litter of kittens with two exhibiting folded ears. The Rosses, who also bred British Shorthairs, chose a white one and named her Snooks. In order to help establish the breed the Rosses enlisted the help of the English geneticist Peter Dyte and set up a breeding program to replicate what they originally referred to as "lop-eared" cats. They used British Shorthairs and farm cats, first breeding Snooks to an unregistered red tabby cat to produce a male called Snowball. Snowball was bred to a white British Shorthair called Lady May, and she produced a litter of five folded-ear kittens. Snooks had another litter of kittens at the end of the decade to produce two folded-ear kittens, Denisla Hester and Denisla Hector. These cats bred by the Rosses formed the foundation for the breed.

Establishing the breed was no easy task. Scottish Fold kittens do not exhibit the folded-ear trait until they are around three weeks old, keeping their breeders guessing. The folded ear is caused by a dominant gene that affects the cartilage in the ear, causing it to fold forward. Because it is a dominant gene, at least one of the parents must exhibit the trait to reproduce it in their progeny. If a folded-ear cat is bred to a straight-eared cat then the progeny will be roughly half folded-ear kittens and half straight-ear kittens. If two folded-ear cats are bred together, the percentage of folded-ear kittens rises, but there is also a much greater risk of congenital problems, such as osteodystrophy, a very painful condition that affects the bones. Dr. Oliphant Jackson, an English geneticist, published a report in the early 1970s about this bone condition and indicated that it was vital to outcross the breed in order to combat the problem. It was felt that the condition was more likely a result of too much inbreeding than being related to the folded-ear gene.

The Rosses began to exhibit their folded-ear cats in the 1960s and in 1966 the Governing Council of the Cat Fancy (GCCF) recognized the breed and named it Scottish Fold. The breed enjoyed a brief period of popularity before the GCCF stopped registering the cats in the early 1970s due to concern over congenital health issues, and problems with ear mites and deafness; the latter two were later proved unfounded. The breed rapidly fell out of fashion in England but luckily it was taken up by the Americans.

An American geneticist, Dr. Neil Todd, acquired three Scottish Folds, Denisla Judy, Denisla Joey, and Denisla Hester in 1970 to use as part of a study he was undertaking on genetic mutations at the Carnivore Genetics Research Center, Newtonville, Massachusetts. As it happened, the study was never completed and Todd rehomed all the cats, but not before Joey and Judy had produced two litters. Hester was acquired by Salle Wolf Peters, a noted Manx breeder, who went on to become influential in establishing the Scottish Fold in the United States. Another important early breeder was Karen Votava, who founded the Bryric Cattery with the cats Mr. Morgan LeFaye and Doonie Lugs;

the Bryric Cattery features in the early pedigrees of many Scottish Folds in the United States. In 1974 Karen Votava, Salle Wolf Peters, Bobbie Graham, and a number of others set about trying to win recognition for the breed. Driven by the reports on congenital problems and on the advice of Dr. Rosemond Peltz, a genetic consultant for the American Scottish Fold Breeders, the stud book was closed to all outcrosses except American Shorthair or British Shorthair. The Cat Fanciers' Association (CFA) finally awarded championship status to the breed in 1978. The Scottish Fold is now recognized by all the main associations including The International Cat Association (TICA), which also allows outcrosses to American Shorthairs and British Shorthairs. The Longhaired Scottish Fold is also now recognized by all the major associations and differs only in the length of its coat.

No account of the Scottish Fold is complete without a mention of Norton, the famous Scottish Fold who belonged to author Peter Gethers, and about whom Gethers wrote the books *The Cat Who Went to Paris* (1990), followed by *A Cat Abroad* (1993), and *The Cat Who'll Live Forever* (2001).

RAGDOLL

MODERN – UNITED STATES – MODERATE

APPEARANCE
Large and substantial, semi-longhaired. Powerful, heavy cat, long in the body and muscular with heavy bones. Hindquarters are slightly higher than the shoulder, legs medium length and solidly boned, hind legs slightly heavier than front legs. Paws are large, round, and tufted. Head is a broad modified wedge, ears tilt forward slightly and are broad at base. Eyes have a sweet expression and are large, oval, and a striking blue color. Long, full, plumelike tail tapers to tip.

SIZE
Large

COAT
Medium length, soft, and silky, no excessive shedding or matting. Colors vary for different associations; patterns include colorpoint, bicolor, and mitted; seal and blue most popular.

PERSONALITY
Easygoing, affectionate, people oriented, vocally quiet, charming

THIS IS A CAT THAT ATTRACTS CONTROVERSY, which is ironic given the laid-back nature of the Ragdoll. A truly lovely cat, the Ragdoll is an excellent companion. It has a quiet, amiable disposition, making it highly suited to indoor living. The Ragdoll is one of the largest of the cat breeds and is surprisingly heavy to pick up; when it is held in one's arms it has a tendency to go completely limp, hence its name. As a breed it is very affectionate and people oriented, but is not excessively demanding and does not vocalize very often. Although it enjoys a play session, it is quick to settle back down to some serious napping. A perfect family cat, the Ragdoll generally gets along well with other pets and children.

There are some colorful accounts of the breed's history, all of which are either untrue or unproven. One of the stories surrounding its origins suggests that the breed is descended from a cat called Josephine (this much is true) who, following a car accident, suddenly began to have large kittens with quiet natures who would go limp when picked up. Another even more far-fetched tale recounts that Josephine had her genes altered at a research facility following her car accident, and that this intervention led to the Ragdoll kittens. What is true is that the breed owes its origins to Ann Baker of Riverside, California, a breeder of black Persians. In 1963 Baker bred one of her cats to

Josephine, a longhaired white cat sometimes described as a Turkish Angora-type, belonging to her neighbors. This union produced Daddy Warbucks. It appears that Josephine then had a number of litters, some by unknown fathers, so the pedigrees of these early progeny are not an exact science. She also produced a daughter called Buckwheat and another called Fugianna. Although these three cats were not Ragdolls as they are now recognized, they would give rise to the Ragdoll through their own progeny. In 1965 Baker bred Daddy Warbucks to Buckwheat (who was a very dark-colored cat) to produce two solid-colored kittens called Gueber and Mitts and two pointed kittens called Kyoto and Tiki; the latter two became the first to be registered as Ragdolls with the National Cat Fanciers Association (NCFA) in 1966.

At the end of the 1960s Denny and Laura Dayton purchased a pair of Ragdolls, Buddy and Rosie, from Baker and began their own breeding program. The Daytons' unrelenting enthusiasm for the breed and huge effort became fundamental to the breed's unilateral recognition. The Daytons named their cattery Blossom-Time and began to create a chart to document the genetics of as many Ragdolls as they could; they also went on to form the Ragdoll Fanciers Club and worked tirelessly to get the breed recognized by the other major cat associations. Another early breeder of note was Blanche Herman (Ragtime Cattery), who worked with the Daytons in getting the breed accepted, and had great success in the show ring.

In 1971 Ann Baker established her own registry for the new breed, the International Ragdoll Cat Association (IRCA), and attempted to franchise and trademark the Ragdoll name. She also required all "her" breeders to register only with her registry. This proved extremely unpopular with other Ragdoll breeders and there was a split within the breed. The extent of this split and the depth of feeling it generated almost certainly contributed toward the reluctance of some of the major cat associations to

recognize the breed. The Daytons continued their breeding program at Blossom-Time Cattery, which at its height had eighteen Ragdolls; Blanche Herman and many other breeders joined with the Daytons and together they established the first Ragdoll Society in 1975.

The process of gaining the Ragdoll recognition by the main cat associations began in the 1970s through the continued efforts of the Daytons, Herman, and other breeders, who exhibited their cats at shows to bring them to the public awareness. Herman in particular exhibited her Ragdolls widely in the Chicago area and by the end of the decade it was felt that the Cat Fanciers' Association (CFA) should be approached to register the breed. In 1981 the application was made by Denny Dayton, and he was advised that the breed standard would need to be rewritten to accord with the CFA. Despite rewriting the standard, the application was rejected, and it would take another twelve years before the Ragdoll would earn its place in the largest cat association in the United States. When what is now the second-largest registry, The International Cat Association (TICA), was established in 1979 they welcomed the Ragdoll immediately. That same year the Ragdoll Fanciers Club organized a genetic seminar on the breed led by the genetics specialist Dr. Pflueger. The results dispelled any lingering myths definitively and underlined that the cats were an established breed that bred true to type.

The first Ragdolls in the United Kingdom were imported by Lulu Rowley of the Petil-Lu Cattery near Norwich, and her friend Pat Brownsell of the Patriarca Cattery. Both had sourced their Ragdolls from Denny and Laura Dayton's Blossom-Time Cattery. Rowley had purchased Lad and Lass, who produced a litter of three kittens while living out their six-month quarantine in England, while Brownsell was the proud new owner of the pair Prim and Proper. The two enthusiasts quickly added to the gene pool of the fledgling breed in the United Kingdom by importing eight more Ragdolls within the year. The cats rapidly became extremely popular and in great demand across Europe and even Australia. Another important early British breeder was Sue Ward-Smith and her Pandapaws Cattery. Sue, along with other breeders, was instrumental in founding the British Ragdoll Cat Club in 1987 and helped to get the breed accepted by the Governing Council of the Cat Fancy (GCCF); this was eventually achieved in 1990.

EXOTIC SHORTHAIR

MODERN – UNITED STATES – MODERATE

APPEARANCE
Solid and cobby with dense coat. Heavy boned with solid body and short, thick legs; paws are large and round. As massive through the shoulders as rump, chest broad and deep, and back level. Head is massive and round with short, broad snub nose and full cheeks. Ears are small and tilt forward, and eyes are large, round, and set far apart; color depends on coat color.

Tail is short but in proportion to length of body.
SIZE
Large or medium
COAT
Dense and soft, medium length, and stands out from body, has thick undercoat. All patterns and colors found in Persian and the pointed pattern of the Himalayan.
PERSONALITY
Sweet, quiet, gentle, playful, very affectionate, easygoing

THE BEAUTIFUL EXOTIC SHORTHAIR is in essence a shorthaired Persian. These cats have the appearance of the Persian, and the breed standard for the Exotic is identical to that for the Persian in all respects apart from the coat. In terms of temperament, the Exotic exhibits the same sweet disposition and naturally gentle nature as the Persian. The Exotic is extremely affectionate and reasonably active. Being particularly easygoing, it will rub along well with other domestic pets and children. It is a quiet cat and vocalizes with a soft, almost silent, meow. Its coat, being shorter than the Persian's, requires less time grooming.

The breed was developed in the early 1960s when American Shorthair breeders began to introduce Persian blood to their cats to try to achieve the silver Persian color with green eyes. The resulting kittens were very attractive, but did not look like American Shorthairs. Continued introduction of Persian blood to American Shorthairs began to alter the body type to resemble the Persian. This signified a loss of type within the breed, which was a serious worry to a number of American Shorthair breeders. Eventually, noted Cat Fanciers' Association (CFA) judge Jane Martinke realized the potential damage to the American Shorthair, but also the qualities of the developing crossbred hybrid. In 1966 Martinke proposed that the hybrid cats be recognized as a new breed and in 1967 the CFA recognized them for championship status. At first the cats were referred to as Sterlings due to the silver color of their coats, but this was changed to Exotic Shorthair to make way for different color and pattern varieties.

Initially the breed standard for the Exotic was based on that for the Persian with the only differences being the length of coat, and no requirement for a nose break. Early breeders of Exotics mainly crossed American Shorthair with Persian, but occasionally used other breeds including Burmese, Russian Blue, and Himalayan. The American Shorthair and other shorthaired breeds were used only to introduce the shorthair genes; the progeny were then crossed back to Persians to maintain the Persian body type.

The early success of the Exotic was down to the hard work of breeders, often against opposition from purebred Persian and American Shorthair circles. Such breeders include Doris Walkingstick, who bred the first Exotic grand champion at her Grayfire Cattery, and Carolyn Bussey of New Dawn Cattery. Carolyn began her breeding program based on an outcross to a Burmese and went on to have twenty-four grand champions.

Because the standard for the Exotic matched that for the Persian, the two standards have been updated together. In 1973 the Exotic standard was changed to add the words "with break" to the nose conformation. This brought their standard in line with that of the Persian except for the coat. The allowable outcrosses at the time were to the Persian and American Shorthair; this was updated in 1987 to prevent outcrosses to the American Shorthair, so from this time on the only allowable outcross has been to the Persian.

Litters of Exotics invariably contain longhaired kittens. These can be bred to Exotic Shorthairs and will then produce shorthaired kittens. The longhaired kittens are themselves, however, beautiful cats: a detail of one appears on the following page. Each association has slightly varying opinions on the Exotic Longhair; the CFA has granted them championship status since 2009, while The International Cat Association (TICA) accepts them in the Persian classes.

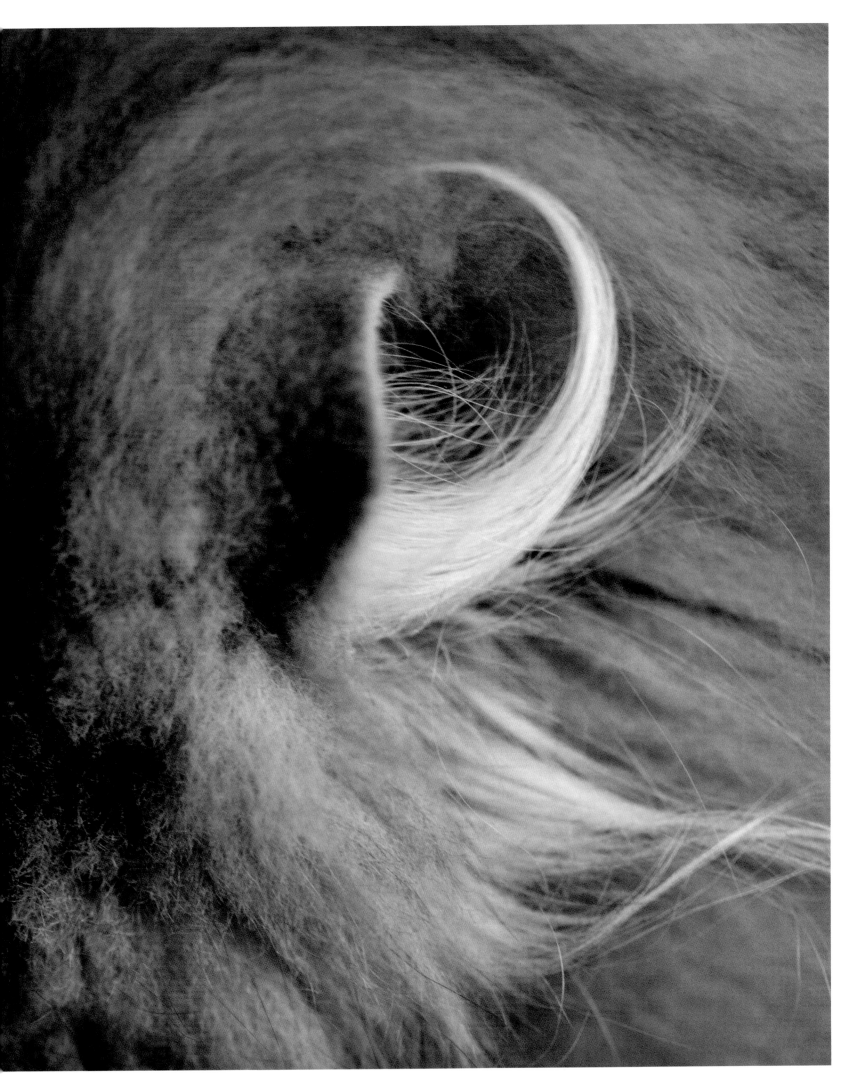

1960 TO 1969

SNOWSHOE

MODERN – UNITED STATES – RARE

APPEARANCE

Elegant, athletic, distinctive white markings and blue eyes. Semi-foreign build, neither lithe nor cobby. Moderately long, balanced, and well proportioned. Head is broad modified wedge with high cheekbones. Ears are medium, broad at base with slightly rounded tips; eyes are oval and can be any shade of blue. Legs are of good length with medium boning. Tail is in proportion to body and gently tapers to end.

SIZE

Medium

COAT

Short to medium-smooth, smooth to touch, single layer. All pointed colors and mitted or bicolor patterns.

PERSONALITY

Loyal to owner, affectionate, fairly demanding, self-possessed, vocal, intelligent, extrovert, playful

THE BEAUTIFUL SNOWSHOE CAT has both Siamese and American Shorthair in its heritage and combines the best qualities from both breeds. The Snowshoe is an interesting breed that has a very distinct personality, and is not afraid to share its wishes with its family, sometimes quite vocally. This communicative nature is certainly reflective of its Siamese heritage, although its voice tends to be neither as loud nor as raspy as the Siamese. It can, however, be persistent; given its intelligence, the Snowshoe will often believe that it is in charge of the household and all the goings on. It also has an uncanny ability for problem solving, such as opening doors. The Snowshoe makes a perfect companion for someone who has time to devote to it. A particularly attractive cat, it has a body type somewhere between the Siamese and the American Shorthair, and very distinctive markings. It is in essence the markings and patterns of the breed that distinguish it, and these have been extremely hard to fix and reproduce. The Snowshoe is currently a fairly rare breed and this is partly due to the issues in reproducing the coat pattern.

A relatively young breed, the Snowshoe was developed in the early 1960s. As with several other breeds at this time, the Snowshoe came into being partly by chance. A Siamese breeder in the United States called Dorothy Hinds Daugherty, from Philadelphia, Pennsylvania, noticed three unusual kittens in one of her Siamese litters. All three kittens had very distinctive white socks on all four paws—far from ideal for a Siamese, but Dorothy liked the combination of the Siamese pointed coloring with the four white socks. She decided to try and recreate this pattern and work towards developing a new breed. Initially she referred to these cats as "Silver Laces," and set about breeding the three kittens to an American Shorthair with white tuxedo markings. These crosses eventually led to the distinctive inverted V-shaped facial marking.

The addition of the American Shorthair to the mix was fundamental in establishing the body type of what would become the Snowshoe since it contributed to a heavier frame and rounder aspect than is seen in the Siamese. Sadly, many breeding records at the foundation of this breed have been lost, although it is known that some unregistered Siamese and unusually marked Siamese were also used. Dorothy eventually scaled down her breeding program and handed over to another breeder, Vikki Olander of the Furr-Lo Cattery in Norfolk, Virginia. Vikki wrote the first standard for the breed and managed to obtain experimental breed status with both the Cat Fanciers' Federation (CFF) and the American Cat Association (ACA) in 1974. Despite this, there were still very few people breeding Snowshoes and by 1977 Vikki was thought to be one of the only breeders left.

Quite by chance, that same year, Jim Hoffman of the Sujym Cattery in Defiance, Ohio, and Georgia Kuhnell of Cincinnati contacted the CFF for information on other Snowshoe breeders. The three enthusiasts were put in touch and together were able to once again start promoting the breed. New people were encouraged to start breeding these lovely cats, and several years later the CFF upgraded the breed from experimental to provisional. The Snowshoe was awarded championship status with the CFF in 1982. That same year, several articles about the Snowshoe appeared in cat fancy magazines, which increased public interest and encouraged more people to support the breed.

The Snowshoe was accepted into The International Cat Association (TICA) in 1982 and awarded championship status in 1993. Breeders such as Phyllis Thompson, President of the Snowshoe Club, Maia Sorenson, Mary Schlagle, Judi Dupont, and Margot Scott were also influential. Snowshoes have yet to be recognized by the Cat Fanciers' Association (CFA).

The noted British cat breeder and judge Pat Turner was very taken with the Snowshoe breed at the annual cat show at Madison Square Garden, New York, in the early 1980s; she decided to try and start breeding Snowshoes herself in England. She based her breeding program around the use of the piebald spotting gene in cats—this gene gives rise to the white markings seen in the Snowshoe—and got together with several other breeders in England who were working along similar lines. Together this core group established a breed club, Snowshoes UK, which was affiliated to the U.K. branch of the Fédération Internationale Féline (FIFe). FIFe accepted Snowshoes as an experimental breed. As in the United States, after initial enthusiasm for the Snowshoe, interest in the breed dwindled in the United Kingdom, and by 1998 Maureen Shackell was the only breeder left. By luck, another noted cat breeder, Mollie Southall, contacted Maureen and the two decided to try and renew interest in the Snowshoe. Between them they had only five cats—a stud cat, two females, and two female kittens—on which to base the resurrection of the breed. Maureen and Mollie formed the Coldenufforsnow Cattery and initially crossbred to other cats to bolster the tiny gene pool. These included a blue tabby mitted female (Emerisle Blue Cinders) and a lilac tabby bicolor (Emerisle Snowitch), both of which were Ragdoll/Oriental cross. Mollie contacted two Snowshoe breeders in Germany, Gunter and Renata Noetzig, who offered her an exquisite male seal point Snowshoe (who had 100 percent American bloodlines) called Ferry vom Friedewald. Ferry became extremely influential on the breed in the United Kingdom and went on to become the first FIFe champion male; his daughter Coldenufforsnow Pila became the first female champion. The Snowshoe was given preliminary recognition by the GCCF in 2004 and is now supported by a number of new enthusiasts as well as the Snowshoe Cat Club and Snowshoe Cat Society. The Snowshoe also has championship status with Australian National Cats (ANCATS).

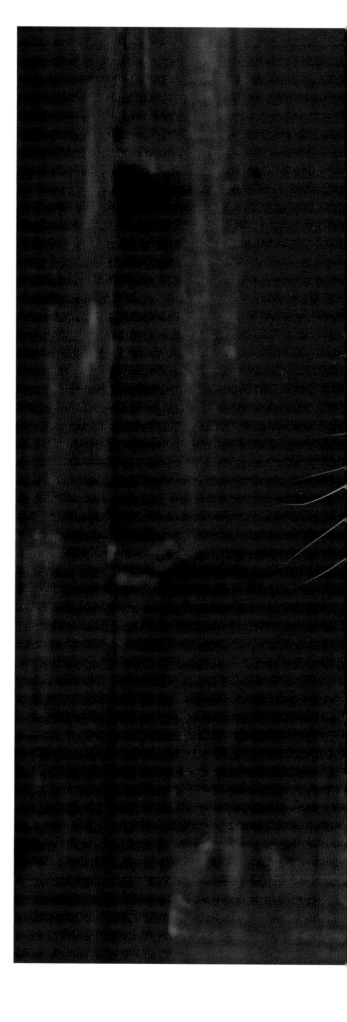

OCICAT

MODERN – UNITED STATES – UNCOMMON

APPEARANCE

Powerful and "wild" looking. Long in the body, hard, solid, muscular, and athletic in appearance with substantial bone. Legs are medium long and powerful, and the paws compact and oval. The head is a modified wedge with a wide, slightly square muzzle. Ears are preferably tufted and moderately large; eyes are large and almond shaped with all colors except blue accepted. Tail is fairly long and fairly slender with a dark-colored tip.

SIZE
Medium to large
COAT
Short, sleek, and close lying with a lustrous sheen. All the hairs have agouti banding. The Ocicat is a spotted tabby found in twelve colors including black (called tawny in most associations for the background color), chocolate, cinnamon, blue, lavender, fawn, and the same six colors on silver.
PERSONALITY
Outgoing, sociable, lively, active, playful, devoted

THE OCICAT COMBINES A WILD APPEARANCE with an utterly charming personality. This cat has a wonderful, if lively, temperament and is extremely loyal and devoted. The Ocicat has a high energy and activity level and is a natural athlete. It also has great intelligence and excellent problem-solving abilities, making it an entertaining and very interactive companion. It loves to settle on the warmest, most comfortable lap, and has a tendency to chat gently and harmoniously. Ocicats do not do well on their own for long periods of time and are most happy when with their family and preferably basking in the limelight.

The inspiration for this created breed came about by accident and was driven by Virginia Daly of the Dalai Cattery, Berkley, Michigan, a noted Siamese breeder. The Ocicat first appeared when Daly was trying to breed a pointed Siamese with Abyssinian coloring in 1964. She began by breeding a ruddy Abyssinian male called Dalai Deta Tim of Selene to a seal point Siamese called Dalai Tomboy Patter. Tim was the son of an imported Abyssinian champion called Raby Chuffa of Selene, and Raby had featured largely in the development of the Somali breed—the longhaired Abyssinian. The litter from Tim and Patter's union all had the appearance of Abyssinians, and Daly kept one of the kittens, a ruddy-colored female called Dalai She. She was then bred to a champion chocolate point Siamese called Whitehead Elegante Sun. This union and others produced what Mrs. Daly was after—Abyssinian pointed Siamese—but in the second litter she also had a surprise, a beautiful ivory-colored kitten with golden spots. Daly's daughter remarked that the kitten looked just like an Ocelot, the small wildcat of South America. She suggested they called this new spotted wonder an Ocicat, and gave him the name Tonga.

As lovely as Tonga was, he was not what Daly was trying to breed and she eventually sold him for a small sum to a medical student, with a neuter agreement in place. It seems the neutering did not happen, or at least not until Tonga had bred several litters of kittens, which according to Daly, in 1988 were all destroyed bar two. She later lost track of these two as well. So it seems the breed was almost lost before it had become established, except that Daly still owned both of Tonga's parents.

At this time Daly was still not concerned with breeding the spotted cat, but this all changed when she began corresponding about her cats with a geneticist, Dr. Clyde Keeler, of Georgia University. Quite in passing she mentioned Tonga to him and he expressed immediate interest in finding breeders who would be willing to try and establish this spotted cat. In particular, Dr. Keeler wanted to create a cat with a look similar to the extinct Egyptian Spotted Fishing Cat. Tonga had by now been neutered, but Daly's interest was sparked and she set about trying to breed more spotted kittens. First Daly bred Tonga's mother, Dalai She back to his father, Sunny, to produce a male spotted tawny called Dalai Dotson, who became important in establishing the fledgling breed. Other breeders became interested in the Ocicat, and the gene pool and network of breeding programs was expanded; this included the Aruby Cattery, Darwin Cattery, and Jobecua Cattery, which all worked together to promote the breed.

The development of the breed suffered a slight setback when Daly scaled back her breeding program in 1966 due to family commitments. In 1984 the Ocicat Breed Club was formed. Mrs. Daly had again become active in the breed and in 1986 the Ocicat was granted provisional status by the Cat Fanciers' Association (CFA), being advanced to championship the following year. With this "seal of approval" by the CFA, the breed became rapidly popular, with many more breeders and exhibitors supporting them. In 1986 the Ocicat registry was closed to Siamese and American Shorthair outcrossing, although Abyssinian outcrosses are allowed until 2015. Ocicats have become increasingly popular as companions since the 1980s and are in the top twenty most popular cat breeds in the United States; they are also found across much of the world.

The breed first arrived in England in 1988 when a pair was imported from the Catoninetail Cattery, Indiana. The cats had to spend six months in quarantine where they were looked after by Rosemary Caunter, who went on to establish the Thickthorn Cattery in Hampshire. She fell in love with the breed and quickly acquired three Ocicats of her own, a tawny male, a cinnamon female, and a chocolate silver female. These were followed by grand champion Catoninetail Kanaka and L'Belle Tiger Lily. By 1993 there were twenty-seven Ocicats registered with the Governing Council of the Cat Fancy (GCCF) and in 1994 a number of breeders, led by Rosemary, established the Ocicat Club. In 1997 the GCCF granted the breed preliminary status and that same year around fifty new Ocicats were registered. The GCCF awarded the breed championship status in 2004. Since then one hundred or more Ocicats have been registered annually.

Breeders such as Rosemary have added to the gene pool by importing cats from United States. Outcrossing to Abyssinians is permitted in the United Kingdom, which has also contributed to the robust health of the cats and to the rich variety of colors found. In the United Kingdom the Ocicat Classic is bred and there is currently a move to have this variation on the Ocicat recognized as a separate breed. The Ocicat Classic differs from the Ocicat only in its classic tabby coat pattern, which includes an M-shaped mark on the forehead, ringed tail, stripes along the back, and oyster-shaped patches on the flanks surrounded by one or more unbroken rings.

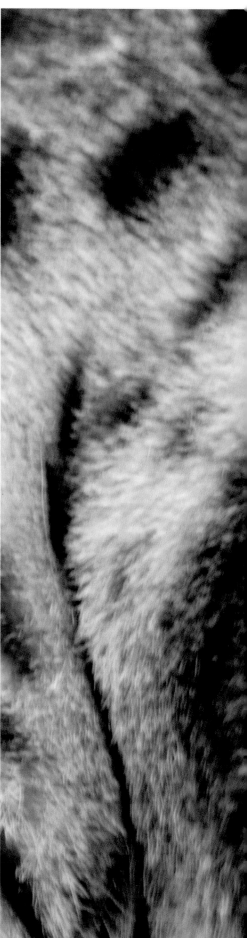

1960 TO 1969

AMERICAN BOBTAIL

MODERN — UNITED STATES — UNCOMMON

APPEARANCE

Solid, athletic, graceful with short tail and "look of the wild." Substantial, rectangular body. Hind legs slightly longer than front, legs heavily boned, paws have toe tufts. Tail is short and carried above the back when alert. Head is a broad, modified wedge shape with prominent brow. Eyes are large, almost almond shaped, color dependent on coat color. Ears are wide at base with rounded tips, preferably with tufts, and set as much on the side as the top of the head.

SIZE

Medium large to large

COAT

Two coat lengths: medium-short, dense, plush all-weather coat with undercoat; or medium-long, slightly shaggy with longer hair on ruff and britches, not very dense, has undercoat. Can be any color.

PERSONALITY

Very affectionate, intelligent, quite active, loyal, easygoing

THE CHARISMATIC AMERICAN BOBTAIL, or AB, is recognized as a relatively "new" breed, although it has been around for many years. On first glance, the AB has all the magnificent appearance of a wildcat that has strolled in from the wilderness. Its temperament, however, could not be further removed; it is among the most affectionate, charming, engaging cats around. The AB devotes itself to its entire family, not just a single member, and is (generally) excellent with children, dogs, and other pets. It is fairly active, with a keen sense of play, and is very intelligent, which it often uses to its advantage. It is not unheard of for ABs to be leash trained and to engage in a riotous game of "fetch." The other significant aspect of the AB is, of course, its short tail. The tail should not extend below the hock, but should be present and a minimum of one inch. Each tail is unique, and may be slightly knotted or curved, exhibit bumps, or be straight. The AB carries its tail proudly above its back when in motion, and may even gently wave it much like a dog wagging, when it is happy or concentrating hard.

The AB is recognized as a naturally occurring short-tailed breed, although it is also a product of the hard work by a number of early breeders, who consolidated and developed the natural traits. Interestingly, the breed is not believed to be linked to the Manx or the Japanese Bobtail, and both of these breeds have been kept out of the AB's

bloodlines. The AB's short tail is believed to be due to a dominant gene (like the Manx) that could have occurred as a spontaneous mutation. Most surprisingly, given their appearance, the AB is not believed to have originated through wild bobcat and domestic cat hybrids.

All accounts of the AB's development trace back to John and Brenda Sanders from Iowa. While on vacation in Arizona, the couple came across a short-tailed kitten, which they retrieved and took home. He was a brown tabby and they called him Yodie. Yodie took a shine to the Sanders' other cat, a female non-pedigree domestic colorpoint called Mishi, and Mishi produced a litter of short-tailed kittens. A friend of the Sanders, Mindy Schultz, saw the kittens and realized they might lead to a new breed. She took several and introduced a long-haired colorpoint cat to the breeding mix, as well as using other feral cats with naturally short tails—feral cats like this occur across the United States and Canada. Mindy Schultz wrote the first provisional standard for the breed in the early 1970s, but unfortunately these original cats were excessively inbred, leading to health issues, and this first breeding initiative was lost.

In the late 1970s another group of breeders began to re-establish the American Bobtail using naturally occurring bobtailed cats. In 1989 two breeders, Lisa Black Borman and Reaha Evans, submitted the AB to The International Cat Association (TICA) committee to seek recognition, and were accepted. Since then breeders have used domestic bobtails from across the United States and Canada to produce the AB and have thus kept the gene pool healthy, leading to the AB being a robust cat. Interestingly, although it is from an apparently fairly random, disparate breeding program, the AB always shows striking similarities and characteristics. Some breeders continue to use bobtail cats of unknown parentage in their breeding programs. The result is a breed that has no other recognized cat breed in its foundation and bears an uncanny resemblance to the wild bobtail cat.

SPHYNX

MODERN – CANADA/UNITED STATES – RARE

APPEARANCE
Appear hairless with large upstanding ears. Medium to medium long in the body and solid in stature. Broad almost barrel chest and rounded abdomen giving appearance of having eaten a large meal. Hind legs are slightly longer than front. Front legs set widely apart and well boned and muscular. Paws are oval with thicker paw pads than other breeds and long, prominent toes. Head is longer than wide with rounded contours and prominent cheekbones. Ears are large and upright; eyes are large with color relating to 'coat' color. Tail is in proportion to body and whip-like; a tuft of hair on tip is allowed.

SIZE
Medium to large

COAT
Appear hairless but may be covered in very fine, short down. Texture is akin to a chamois leather. Can be any color.

PERSONALITY
Extremely extrovert, highly intelligent, very playful, very affectionate, clownish

THE SPHYNX IS AN ARRESTING SIGHT with its slightly alien and not entirely catlike appearance, sometimes described as part cat with a little bit of monkey thrown in. The Sphynx is an utterly captivating breed with tremendous personality (and energy). It delights in launching itself off any vertiginous ledge with great acrobatic skills. One of the most intelligent breeds, it seems to have a real sense of humor; it is quite extraordinary to see a cat evaluate the effect it has on people with such perceptiveness. The Sphynx adores people and is happiest when it has the full attention of its owner, although it will generally also get along well with other cats and dogs. It might have an ulterior motive for being so easygoing—it is not unusual for a Sphynx to utilize the heat from others and curl up next to the family dog or find its way under the bedclothes.

With its lack of coat, this breed is most suitable for indoor living. It also needs to be bathed quite regularly to remove oily secretions from its skin. Normally this oil is absorbed by a cat's hair, but with the Sphynx it collects on the skin and can eventually cause skin problems. While Sphynx can be tolerated by some people who have cat allergies, they are not "non-allergenic" as some breeders may claim. Cat allergies are caused by an allergenic protein secreted via saliva and sebaceous glands. When cats clean themselves they transfer this allergen to their coat, and when they shed the allergen is spread throughout the house. The Sphynx still has the allergenic protein in its saliva, it just doesn't shed hair. In fact, the Sphynx is not necessarily totally "hairless"; it is often covered with very fine, short down.

Hairlessness in cats is caused by a natural, spontaneous mutation and could have been occurring for many years. The earliest documented cases date back about one hundred years, when hairless cats were described by Frances Simpson in *The Book of the Cat* (1903); they were referred to as "Mexican Hairless." Others occurred naturally through the first half of the twentieth century and in many different countries from Australia to France, Morocco, Canada, and the United States.

In 1966 in Canada, a black and white cat called Elizabeth produced a hairless kitten in her litter; Elizabeth and the father were domestic shorthairs. The kitten, who was male, was named Prune. Prune and Elizabeth were acquired by Yania Bawa, a cat breeder, and her son Ryadh, a college student with an interest in genetics. The Bawas, along with Keese and Rita Tenhove, bred the two cats together to try and establish a hairless line of cats. The resulting litters contained some normal-coated kittens and some hairless ones. It was realized that the hairlessness was caused by a recessive gene, meaning it requires two copies of the gene for the trait to express itself. Therefore if each parent has only one copy of the hairless gene, the number of hairless kittens in a litter is about one in four. These first hairless kittens were originally termed Moonstone Cats or Canadian Hairless Cats. The Bawas and the Tenhoves bred their cats but because of the amount of inbreeding required, the development of the breed was hampered by health issues. The Cat Fanciers' Association (CFA) initially granted the young breed new breed and color status. David Mare, who sat on the CFA board, recounts that the breed was given its current name when one of the cats sat on the board

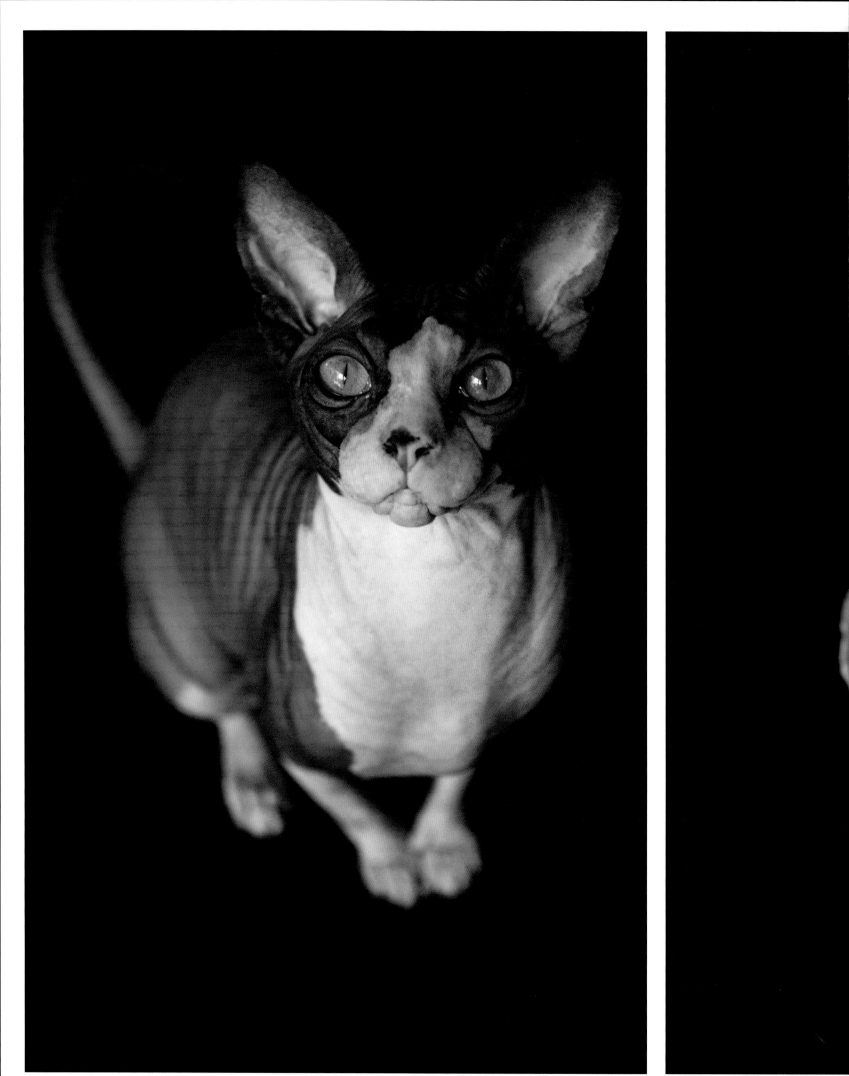

table during the discussions surrounding the breed, and looked exactly like a Sphynx. In 1971 the CFA withdrew their recognition of the breed due to health issues and infertility. The lines bred by the Bawas and the Tenhoves became obsolete during the 1980s.

In the late 1970s or early 1980s three hairless kittens were discovered by Shirley Smith abandoned in the streets of Toronto, Ontario. The two females, Punkie and Paloma, were sent to the cat breeder Dr. Hugo Hernandez in the Netherlands. Hernandez bred the kittens to a white Devon Rex called Curare van Jetrophin. Within roughly the same timeframe some hairless kittens were discovered on a farm in Minnesota owned by Milt and Ethelyn Pearson. Their domestic shorthair Jezabelle produced a hairless kitten they called Epidermis, followed by another the following year called Dermis. Both these hairless cats were acquired by the breeder Kim Mueske in Oregon, who used them to develop the breed. At the same time another breeder, Georgiana Gattenby from Minnesota, bred kittens related to the Pearson's line and crossed them to Cornish Rex to produce hairless kittens. These hairless cats from Minnesota, Oregon, and the Netherlands formed the basis for the breed as it is today. The International Cat Association (TICA) accepted the Sphynx for championship status in 1979, although the breed was not shown in the United States until the mid-1980s. In 1998 the breed was resubmitted to the CFA into the miscellaneous class. It was advanced to championship status in the CFA in 2002.

The first Sphynx in the United Kingdom arrived in 1988 from the Netherlands. This was a female called Hathor de Calecat, or Tulip for short. She had been bred by Hattie Nathon, who worked closely with Hugo Hernandez. Tulip, owned by Jan Plumb and Angela Rushbrook, was taken to three different Governing Council of the Cat Fancy (GCCF) shows to bring the breed to the awareness of the judges and the public. Although Tulip was much admired, the GCCF was reluctant to recognize the breed. Despite this, The Sphynx Cat Club was formed in 1991 and has grown steadily. The Sphynx Cat Association was formed in 2005. That same year the GCCF granted pre-affiliation to The Sphynx Cat Club, thus allowing the cats to be shown once again. The following year the GCCF granted the breed preliminary recognition. Breed numbers, although still modest, have grown steadily.

TONKINESE

MODERN – CANADA/UNITED STATES – UNCOMMON

APPEARANCE
Medium -sized, dense, and muscular with beautiful velvet coat. Surprisingly heavy when picked up, medium-length body, well-muscled. Legs in proportion to body and fairly slender, hind legs slightly longer than front legs. Paws more oval than round. Head is modified and slightly rounded wedge, a little longer than wide with a blunt muzzle. Ears tilt slightly forward, broad at base and oval at tip. Eyes are an open almond shape, aqua blue the preferred color. Tail proportionate to body and tapers to tip.

SIZE
Medium

COAT
Medium-short, soft, silky, and dense with a glossy sheen. Comes in a variety of colors, which may differ in different associations, and three patterns: solid, pointed, and "mink."

PERSONALITY
Gregarious, lively, extrovert, energetic, playful, very affectionate, humorous

ADMIRERS OF THE TONKINESE often describe this wonderful breed as combining the best parts of the Siamese and Burmese, the two breeds at its foundation. Certainly the Tonkinese makes a lively and captivating companion, full of energy and playfulness, and given to an occasional comic turn. The Tonk is very active and loves to climb, chase, fetch, jump, and explore, either in the confines of its house or the great outdoors. When playtime is over, however, the Tonk likes nothing better than to lavish its owner with affection and soak up as much love as possible in return. It is relatively vocal and likes to chat, sometimes at length, to whoever is around, but its voice is much softer than the Siamese and generally it is less demanding.

In terms of appearance, the Tonkinese is a moderate cat in all respects. Its body type is in proportion, with nothing being exaggerated. It comes in a range of magnificent colors, which can include lilac, fawn, chocolate, seal, blue, cream, red, and cinnamon, although accepted colors may vary between different associations. Its coat is in three patterns, which are basically varying degrees of intensity between the pointed Siamese and the solid Burmese. The pointed pattern is closest to the Siamese pattern and has the higher contrast in the coat; mink is the pattern most associated with the breed and a medium contrast; and solid is the lowest contrast pattern and closest to the sepia Burmese. All Tonkinese have beautiful, sparkling eyes. The most preferred—and those seen in the mink pattern—are a clear aqua, but Tonks' eyes can range in color from bright blue to violet in the pointed pattern and from green to gold in the solid patterns.

The Tonkinese is frequently described as an artificially created breed that was developed during the 1960s through crossbreeding Siamese and Burmese. However, these hybrid breedings have been randomly occurring for many centuries in Southeast Asia. Cats with Siamese and Burmese characteristics have existed in this area for a long time and it is only in the last century or so that they have been specifically bred. The earliest accounts of cats from Siam (now Thailand) arriving in the West in the 1800s names them as Siamese, but describes them as having coats of burnished chestnut with greeny-blue eyes. It is likely that these first cats were probably what would now be called Burmese, Havana Brown, and Tonkinese. The foundation cat for the Burmese breed, Wong Mau, who was brought into the United States in the 1930s was actually a Siamese and Burmese cross—that is, a Tonkinese!

In the 1950s in New York City the breeder Milan Greer began to cross Siamese and Burmese to produce Golden Siamese. He wanted to prove that this cross would breed true to type and produce cats with a rich, luscious coloring and a modified body type. His cats became very popular during the 1950s and 1960s, but he stopped breeding the hybrids once he felt he had proved he could.

The Tonkinese as it is now known was not specifically developed until the 1960s, and this occurred in Canada and the United States at around the same time. In Canada the breeder Margaret Conroy had a shy female Burmese cat called Khosoom from whom she wished to breed. Unable to find an appropriate local Burmese male and not wishing to ship her female, Margaret was at a loss for what to do. A cat judge suggested to her that she try breeding her female to a

local Siamese stud cat, which she did with great success. The kittens had pale tan or mink-colored coats with striking aqua-colored eyes; Margaret became interested in furthering this experiment. She called these cats Tonkinese and bred several generations true to the new type. In the United States a Siamese breeder from New Jersey named Jane Barletta decided to try and breed a moderate Siamese-type and set about breeding her Siamese to Burmese. Jane and Margaret began share their knowledge on the emerging breed and helped to establish what later became known as the Tonkinese. Jane was a driving force in the United States in getting the Tonk recognition. Breeders such as Mary Swanson on the west coast also began breeding Tonks and by the 1970s Tonk breeders on the west and east coasts were communicating to help advance the breed, leading to a very strong Tonk community.

The Canadian Cat Association was the first to accept the Tonkinese, and did so in 1971. That same year a group of breeders began showing the Tonkinese in the United States. The Tonkinese Breed Club began working on a breed standard and approached the Cat Fanciers' Association (CFA) with this in 1978. The next year the breed was accepted in the miscellaneous class. The CFA advanced the breed to provisional status in 1982, and the Tonkinese was finally awarded championship status in 1984. The acceptance of the breed took a long time because many in the cat fancy felt the breed represented a poor version of the Siamese; Tonk breeders asserted that the Tonkinese exhibits the best from the two different breeds and, more importantly, has its own unique identity.

One of the first Tonkinese to arrive in the United Kingdom was Chira Tan Tockseng, imported by a Burmese breeder, Mrs. Grove White, in 1958. Chira was a registered Burmese and Siamese cross. Mrs. Grove White wanted to use her as foundation stock for her Burmese breeding program. Tonkinese were initially known as chocolate Siamese in the United Kingdom as breeders strove to create a deliberate hybrid, mirroring efforts in Canada and the United States. The Cat Association of Britain recognized the Tonkinese in the mid-1980s and preliminary recognition was given by the Governing Council of the Cat Fancy (GCCF) in 1991. The Tonkinese Cat Club was formed in 1994 and in 1998 the breed was given full affiliation with the GCCF; it was advanced to championship status in 2001.

1960 TO 1969

AMERICAN WIREHAIR

MODERN — UNITED STATES — RARE

APPEARANCE
Muscular and solid with distinctive wire coat. Medium-sized and balanced cat with no exaggerated features. Back is level and shoulders and hips of equal length. Medium-length, muscled legs, rounded paws with heavy pads. Head is rounded with prominent cheekbones. Ears are set wide apart and slightly rounded at tip; eyes are large, round, and bright, color

dependent on coat color. Tail is medium length and tapers to tip.
SIZE
Medium
COAT
Unique wiry coat, dense, coarse, and ideally crimped over entire body. Whiskers are curly. Can be any color.
PERSONALITY
Active, attentive, affectionate, playful, easygoing, good with families, sense of humor

THE AMERICAN WIREHAIR is an all-American breed with a unique coat among cats. It makes a wonderful companion animal due to its superb temperament. The American Wirehair (AW) is a people-oriented cat—it loves attention without being demanding, and dotes on its human family. Given its easygoing nature, it adapts well to most situations and is good with children as well as being sensitive to its owner's moods; there is nothing like an AW to cheer one up when feeling sad!

The AW is essentially a version of the American Shorthair with an unusual coat, and is the result of a spontaneous mutation in the domestic cat population. The wirehair coat exhibits a range from being dense, short, and crimped all over the body—the ideal—to varying lengths of coat and sparseness. Sometimes the hair is spiky or curly with the individual hairs being crimped, hooked, or bent. Normally the coat is relatively soft to the touch, although the hairs spring back into place when displaced; occasionally the coat is very hard, leading to hair breakage. AWs can have sensitive skin, making them more prone to allergies; but this is not seen in every cat, and is remedied by keeping the coat clean. The wirehair gene is dominant, unlike the recessive gene that causes the coat of the Cornish and Devon Rex. Currently breed numbers are very low in the United States. They are not recognized in the United Kingdom, but are in Canada, Japan, France, and Germany.

The first wirehair kitten was discovered in 1966 in a litter of barn kittens in Verona, New York, on a farm owned by Nathan Mosher. Both parents were normal-coated domestic shorthairs, but the little male kitten, with his red and white coat, was distinctly different. His entire coat, including his whiskers, was of wiry curls. A local cat breeder named Joan O'Shea heard about the kitten and went to visit him—he had by now been given the rather grand name of Council Rock Farm Adam of Hi-Fi. O'Shea felt he might be a bit special, and in time he was bred back to his sister, who was straight coated. This mating resulted in two more wirehair kittens who were called Abby and Amy. Adam was bred to an unrelated straight-coated female, who again produced wirehair kittens, indicating that this particular coat gene was dominant. O'Shea sent hair samples from Adam to the British geneticist Roy Robinson, and Robinson deduced that the coat was unique and unrelated to the Cornish or Devon Rex. He also noted that the wirehair indicated the cat was closest to the American Shorthair than any other breed. The American Shorthair was then used to outcross to the wirehair cats to develop the American Wirehair.

O'Shea sold Amy to the noted Rex breeders Bill and Madeline Beck, who went on to work extensively with the AW. The Becks approached the Cat Fanciers' Association (CFA) in 1967 for recognition of the American Wirehair and this was granted the same year. The breed was awarded championship status in 1978. The standard for the breed was based on that for the American Shorthair, given that this breed had contributed so significantly to its development, and it still reflects this initial influence. The American Shorthair is also the only eligible outcross for the AW. While the use of outcrossing is vital in maintaining a healthy gene pool, it has led to some dilution in the wire coat. Also, litters do not always (or normally) contain all wire coats, but will include straight-coated kittens. Although these kittens are not viable for showing, they nevertheless make wonderful pets.

CHAUSIE

MODERN – UNITED STATES – RARE

APPEARANCE
Tall, lean, athletic, "wild" look. Long, rectangular-shaped body on long legs with medium boning. Chest is deep with flat sides, overall impression of a very athletic cat that resembles a wildcat. Tail is slightly short and medium width, tapering to end. Head is a modified wedge and slightly long with high, angular cheekbones. Ears are tall, erect, large, and sometimes tufted. Eyes are medium to slightly small, gold or yellow color preferred but hazel to light green allowed.

SIZE
Medium to large

COAT
Short to medium in length, dense with a resilient top coat and a soft undercoat. Colors are brown-ticked tabby, black, or black-grizzled-ticked tabby.

PERSONALITY
Very lively and energetic, highly intelligent, extrovert, very playful, devoted to owner, gregarious

THE CHAUSIE, PRONOUNCED "CHOW SEE," is not a breed for the fainthearted, but in the right home it is a delightful, highly entertaining, and rewarding companion. With an abundance of energy, this cat is not suited to a sedentary lifestyle. It not only wants to be at the center of the action, but will demand to be. Chausies are extremely playful and many will play with water. They are also very intelligent and are excellent at problem solving—this can be both good and bad for the unwitting owner! They tend to form strong bonds with a single member of the family, although will be affectionate to all. Chausies thrive on company and it is recommended that they be kept with other cats or in a home where the owner is present for most of the time. They also get along well with dogs and children.

Apart from its alluring temperament, the Chausie is most distinctive due to its appearance. It can be mistaken for a wildcat, and the breed is a hybrid of wildcat and domestic cat. It takes its name from the *Felis chaus*, also often called the Jungle Cat—although, confusingly, it does not come from the jungle. Chausies that are less than three generations removed from their Jungle Cat heritage may display some characteristics that reflect this wild heritage. They might, for example, be slightly more difficult to litter-box train and have a tendency to chew (and destroy) items, although this is not always the case. However, Chausies

that are three generations or more, which most are, are not really very different from other domestic cat breeds, apart from being more active than most. Some Chausies can show a higher than normal allergy to various cat foods as their digestive tract remains most suited to meat, although again this is not seen in every cat. This is easily remedied by feeding top-quality wet foods containing a high percentage of meat and avoiding excessive cereals.

The *Felis chaus* is found in parts of Central Asia, the Middle East, and in Africa along the Nile River Valley. It is currently on the Red List of Threatened Species by the IUCN (International Union for Conservation of Nature). This small, gregarious wildcat is thought to have lived on the periphery of human settlements for thousands of years and is far more tolerant of humans than other wildcat species. It will also breed with domestic cats and it is believed that this has occurred sporadically over time. The Jungle Cat, more accurately described as the Reed or Swamp Cat since this is the territory it naturally inhabits, was also occasionally domesticated and kept as a pet; archaeologists in Egypt have found mummified Jungle Cats alongside domestic ones. The easygoing nature of the Jungle Cat and its tendency to get along with domestic cats naturally led to it being a perfect candidate for using in the development of a hybrid breed.

Breeders began to experiment with producing a hybrid Jungle Cat and domestic cat in the United States in the 1960s, although it would take until the 1990s for the breed to be well established. These first breeding experiments were led by a growing fashion for exotic cats; breeders wanted to create a cat that looked wild but had a suitably domestic temperament. Offspring from the first cross of a Jungle Cat to a domestic invariably produces infertile male kittens, and reduced fertility in the females, so the progress was slow and difficult. Many different domestic cat breeds were used to crossbreed to the Jungle Cat in the initial development of the breed. A Chausie must have the look of

the wild Jungle Cat but be predominantly domestic in its heritage. Equally, to be a true Chausie, a cat must trace back to at least one Jungle Cat in its lineage. The trick with developing any hybrid breed is to fix the breed characteristics, so the kittens are born with largely uniform characteristics that identify them, while retaining the necessary elements from the original cross. Given the relative youth of this breed, there are still often kittens born that do not exactly reflect the look required by the breed standard. These make lovely companion cats, but will not be show ring material. This is particularly seen in the coloring of the breed. The Chausie has just three accepted colors, all of which reflect the Jungle Cat heritage. These are brown-ticked tabby, solid black, and black-grizzled-ticked tabby. This last coloring is completely unique to the Jungle Cat and therefore also to the domestic Chausie.

Early breeders to whom the Chausie owes its acceptance are Judy Bender and Sandra Cassalia of the Wildkatz Cattery, Florida. Judy was instrumental in bringing the Chausie to the attention of The International Cat Association (TICA). It was first registered in 1995 and was accepted to the evaluation class in 2000; in 2003 it was moved to the advanced new breed class and in 2013 it achieved championship status. Sandra and the Wildkatz Cattery have had a profound influence on the development of the breed and she is an authority on not only Chausies but also Jungle Cats.

A cat of influence in the breed's development was the male Tasurt Naabahi (Naabi). Naabi was the great-grandson of a Jungle Cat and therefore third generation. He was also the first male to be completely fertile and as such appears in a great many Chausie pedigrees. He fathered important early males all of good Chausie type and excellent fertility, including Willowind Dubai, Willowind MafiMushkla, Willowind Blackwater, and Tasurt Tashquin. Influential females in the breed development include Navajo Charisma, who produced numerous fertile males, including the first black-grizzled male, Tasurt Tehuti. Two other females, Wildkatz Cheetah of Willowind and Willowind Keetah, have contributed greatly to the breed development. To keep the gene pool of the breed healthy, careful outcrossing to Abyssinians and domestic shorthairs is still encouraged.

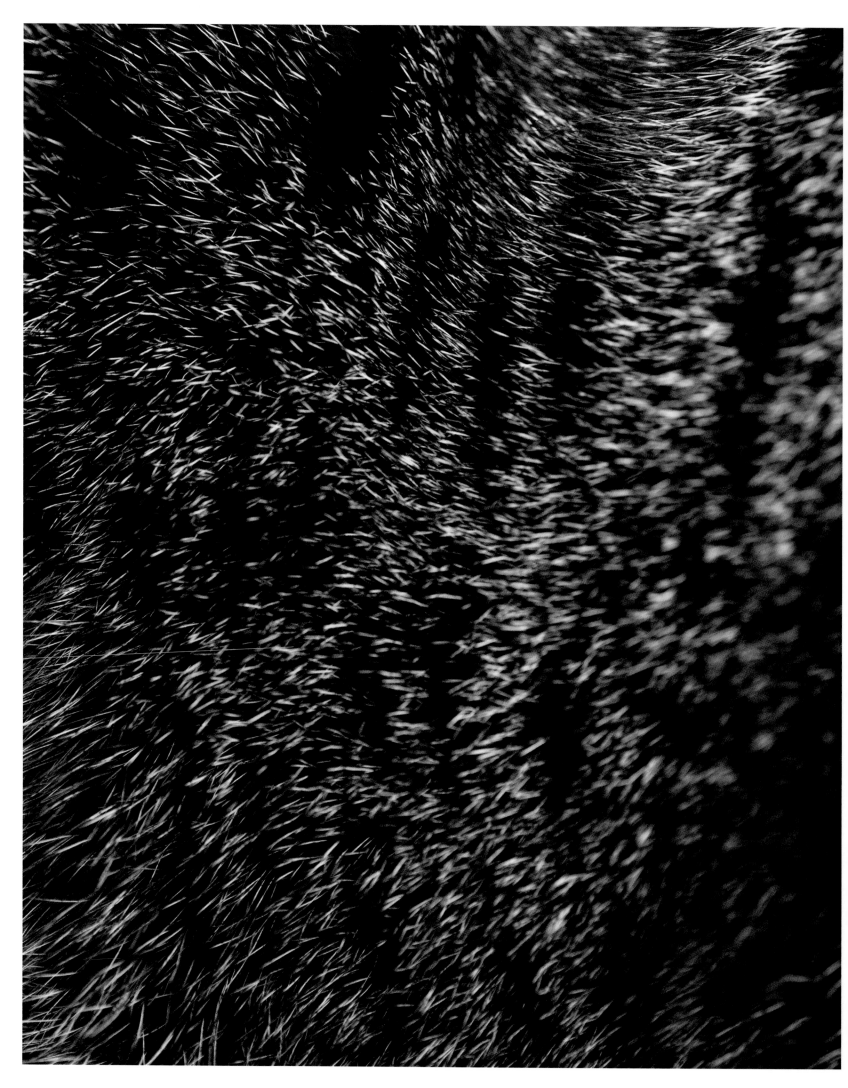

BENGAL

MODERN – UNITED STATES – UNCOMMON

APPEARANCE

Spotted or marbled coat and "wildcat" look. Athletic, solid, muscular build, long body, and medium-length legs; paws are large and round with prominent knuckles. Head is longer than it is wide and a broad modified wedge. Nose is wide and whisker pads prominent. Ears are medium to small and relatively short with rounded tops; eyes are large, almost round, and set wide apart. Tail is medium length, thick, and tapers to end.

SIZE

Medium to large

COAT

Short to medium-length coat, dense, luxurious, and very soft; hair can can be glittered, creating a sparkling effect. Brown tabby the most popular color, and pattern is either spotted (rosette two-toned spots) or marbled.

PERSONALITY

Lively, vivacious, active, highly personable, very affectionate, very playful, confident, interactive

THE BENGAL IS A UNIQUE MODERN CAT BREED, entirely created by humans through careful crossbreeding between the domestic cat and the wild Asian Leopard Cat (*Prionailurus bengalensis*). Bengals are breathtakingly beautiful cats that have the appearance of the wildcat with their extraordinary coats, but the temperament of the domestic cat. Most significantly, because of the wildcat heritage of the Bengal, enormous emphasis is placed on the temperament; unlike other cat breeds, the standard for the Bengal includes a description of the "ideal" temperament. Early breeding experiments resulted in some temperament problems—mostly shyness since the Leopard Cat is a small, shy, nocturnal creature—and there has been a concerted and successful attempt to address this. Consequently the Bengal is noted for its confident, playful, and interactive nature. Life with a Bengal is never dull; this is an energetic and intelligent cat with a huge personality, usually gregarious, curious, and devoted, and often fond of water—the Bengal may accompany its owner into the shower or even for a swim! The Bengal will insist on life lived to its own set of rules and is happiest when it is at the center of attention. The combination of superlative looks and affectionate nature has made the Bengal much sought after, and a dynamic addition to a home.

The concept of creating a hybrid cat breed between a wildcat and a domestic variety is not new. In 1889 the cat breed authority Harrison Weir described a Bengal that was housed at London Zoo in Regents Park, Britain, as "handsome but very wild." One of the first documented cases of crossbreeding between the Asian Leopard Cat and a domestic occurred in 1934, and was described in a Belgian scientific journal, though few details were given.

The Bengal's early history is one of several different strands that eventually came together many decades later. A driving force behind the breed was the American Jean Sugden Mill, who produced a paper as a student on the genetics of cat breeding a Persian and Siamese cross in 1946. Twenty years later Mill turned her attention to the Asian Leopard Cat, whose future was severely threatened. The striking beauty of these cats has, as for so many breeds, been their undoing, and they have been hunted almost to extinction by poachers after their pelts and to fuel the increasing exotic pet industry. Mill obtained a Leopard Cat from Southeast Asia in 1961 and, surprisingly, this queen bred to Mill's black shorthaired tom cat to produce a surviving kitten. Despite initial success, Mill's first project eventually failed, but would rekindle years later.

Another of the strands that led to the breed's development was pursued in the United States by Dr. Willard Centerwall, who was a noted human geneticist. It had been discovered that domestic cats carry the type C feline leukemia genome in the DNA molecule and pass this potentially lethal leukemia virus to their offspring. Very occasionally this virus is released into the system of the cat, which causes leukemia and death. However, the Asian Leopard Cat does not have this virus built into its system. Dr. Centerwall, in conjunction with Dr. Raoul Benveniste from the National Cancer Institute in Bethesda, Maryland, were investigating what happens to the leukemia genome in hybrids of the Asian Leopard Cat and domestic cat. Since feline leukemia acts in a similar way to

human leukemia, by understanding why Asian Leopard Cats were resistant to the disease, Dr. Centerwall hoped to be able to better understand the disease in humans. To this end, Dr. Centerwall established a number of Asian Leopard Cat and domestic cat hybrids.

A further key figure behind the Bengal's development, and the man responsible for naming the breed, was American William (Bill) Engler, who was a great advocate of exotic cats, including the ocelot. During the 1960s Bill imported and sold exotic cats, but found it increasingly difficult to source them. He decided the only way to preserve them in healthy numbers was to breed them domestically and to create hybrids. In 1970 Bill bred one of his Asian Leopard Cats, Shah, to two different domestic females, Cybele and Cyclemnestra. These two produced nine kittens, which Bill referred to as "Bengals." The following year he bred another two litters and had a further six kittens. Bill wanted to produce a cat with all the characteristics of the domestic, but with the appearance of the exotic cats that he was having problems locating for people. By 1975 Bill stated he had produced over sixty Bengal cats, and by the end of that year he said they had reached their third generation (F3). This was some achievement given that all first-generation crosses produce infertile males. Bill presented the Bengal breed to the American Cat Fanciers Association (ACFA) and they were accepted. Sadly Bill died in 1977 and his cats passed to some friends who cared for them.

During the 1970s a group of breeders concerned with exotics and hybrids founded the Walk on the Wild Side Cat Fanciers (WOW). These breeders included people developing the Bengal, Safari, and other hybrids of wild and feral cats with domestic cats. In 1979 WOW members presented the Cat Fanciers' Association (CFA) with a substantial document on hybrid breeds, including the Bengal and Safari, in an effort for these breeds to be better understood and accepted. Initially the Bengal was allowed to be registered as a domestic cat, but later the CFA banned them from registration, dealing a heavy blow to enthusiasts.

In 1980 Dr. Centerwall was introduced to Jean Sugden Mill and gave her several of his first generation (F1) hybrid kittens. Another enthusiast, Gordon Meredith, had also acquired some of Dr. Centerwall's hybrid cats, and when Meredith fell ill, these cats too made their way to Jean Mill.

She restarted her breeding experiments. In the first crossing of wild to domestic, the offspring (F1) were generally wild and shy in nature, with all of the males being infertile. To this day males are generally not fertile until they are at least four generations from the Asian Leopard Cat. However, with successive selective breedings (F2, F3, F4), the temperament began to align with the domestic cat. In 1982 Mill introduced a feral Indian street cat called Millwood Tory of Delhi to her breeding program (from which the glittery coat was introduced), and other outcrosses were also used to try and increase the size of the gene pool; Tory is often described as an Egyptian Mau. Through dedicated breeding, Mill produced the "ideal" Bengal, Millwood Penny Ante, a beautiful and very affectionate cat who Mill took to innumerable shows where she won the public's heart.

By now other breeders had become interested, including Greg and Elizabeth Kent, who developed their own lines using Asian Leopard Cats and Egyptian Mau. The public became hooked on the exotic-looking cats, and in 1986 The International Cat Association (TICA) accepted the Bengal as a new breed, awarding it championship status in 1991. In order to maintain and perpetuate the all-important character of the Bengal, TICA requires that show cats be bred Bengal to Bengal for at least four generations. Not every cat registry and association recognizes the Bengal, although several do in North America in addition to TICA.

Bengals were first introduced to Britain in the late 1980s. It has been more of a battle in the United Kingdom to gain breed recognition with the Governing Council of the Cat Fancy (GCCF), and it was not until April 2006 that brown-spotted Bengals were awarded championship status; the first to win this prestigious title was Grand Premier Admilsh Zabari—Ziggy to his friends. It would be another two years before the brown marbles and snow-spotted Bengals were awarded championship status. It was also in 2008 that the beautiful silver-spotted and silver-marbled Bengals were upgraded from "experimental" to "preliminary" status. Silver-colored Bengals have become increasing popular in the last few years and are now recognized by the international association, Fédération Internationale Féline (FIFe).

CHAPTER 5
1970 TO PRESENT

Perhaps surprisingly for owners of purebred cats, the majority of domestic cats are in fact of mixed breed or unknown origin. Internationally the figure is estimated to be as high as 96 to 98 percent mixed breed. Despite these figures, breeding purebred cats is on the increase, and through the twentieth century and into the twenty-first many new breeds have been established. These are generally artificially created as opposed to natural—they have come about through deliberate breeding programs initiated by breeders to achieve a certain result. These new breeds are achieved either through crossbreeding existing

breeds to strengthen some desirable characteristics (and eliminate others), or have been sparked through the sudden emergence of an unusual trait.

An example of careful crossbreeding is the Savannah, which was developed by crossing the wild African Serval with domestic breeds. When developing these hybrid breeds using wildcats, breeders face the additional challenges of fertility. Male offspring will generally be infertile until the fourth or fifth generation crosses, which makes the establishment of the breed both lengthy and difficult. In addition breeders have to overcome other

hurdles such as establishing the domestic cat temperament, and different gestation periods between the domestic breeds and the various wildcat breeds used. Not all new breeds with the wild look contain wild blood, however. The Toyger (developed since the 1980s) and the more recent Serengeti (1994) have the exquisite appearance of wildcats without using any wildcats in the breed development.

Other recent breeds to emerge from crossbreeding are the beautiful Nebelung, a longhaired Russian Blue, and the RagaMuffin, which was developed by crossing the Ragdoll cat with other breeds to increase the gene pool and introduce other characteristics.

An example of the sudden emergence of an unusual trait is the hairlessness (or greatly reduced coat) exhibited by the Don Sphynx and Peterbald breeds. Mutations affecting the coat are also seen in the wavy, curled, or kinked coats of the Rex breeds, such as the Selkirk Rex and LaPerm, developed since the 1970s and following on from the earlier Cornish Rex and Devon Rex breeds. The mutation that defines the American Curl is a folded ear, while the Munchkin has a reduced limb length. These traits and other similar ones were initially caused by spontaneous genetic mutations, the reason for which is unknown. In simple terms, when a genetic mutation occurs that produces a nonviable result, the kitten will die. However, if a mutation occurs that does not significantly reduce the kitten's chance of survival then the gene will become part of the gene pool and be reproduced. By careful selective breeding, breeders have been able to fix and perpetuate these certain characteristics and in so doing, have created the variety of new breeds that have appeared over the last decades. There are new breeds in constant development, some of which will inevitably fall by the wayside, while others will flourish. There is a fine line between producing viable, healthy cats and anomalies of nature, and it is one that breeders have a responsibility to adhere to; there are some genetic mutations that might produce a desired trait, but might also produce harmful traits such as bone disorders or other negative health implications.

The Pixiebob and the Singapura were both developed from naturally occuring groups of cats with distinctive traits, which breeders then went on to try to maintain. The Pixiebob is the only cat breed whose standard allows for polydactyl toes (up to seven per paw), and it recalls the American Bobcat in its appearance. The Singapura was developed as a breed from a strain of feral cats found in the streets of Singapore.

As new cat breeds emerged, cats also continued their rise in the world of animation and movies. The 1970s saw the appearance of one of the most recognizable cats in the world—Garfield. The lovable, overweight, lazy, lasagna-loving, ginger cat was created in 1978 by cartoonist Jim Davis and is still in circulation as a comic strip, appearing in over 2,500 newspapers and being read by over 2.5 million people daily. His insouciant attitude to life, love of food, enthusiasm for napping, and wholesomely unapologetic attitude appeal to a wide public, who perhaps secretly aspire to such behavior. He is surely the king of the antiheros and—pleasingly for all cat lovers—outsmarts dogs at every opportunity.

Cats have also appeared frequently and memorably in Hollywood movies. One of the most entertaining performances must be that of Mr. Bigglesworth, Dr. Evil's cat in the original *Austin Powers* film of 1997. Mr. Bigglesworth, a Sphynx, was played by a champion show cat named SGC Belfry Ted Nude-Gent, bred by Michelle Berge at the Belfry Cattery. Ted was actually something of a trailblazer in feline acting, being cast in a role that would normally have been given to a dog due to the degree of training required (lying still for long periods of time). A further three Sphynx kittens were also used in the second *Austin Powers* movie in 1979. Mel Gibskin, Paul Nudeman, and Skindiana Jones played Mini Mr. Bigglesworth, the tiny cat of Dr. Evil's diminutive clone Mini-Me.

The movie actress Whoopi Goldberg has long been a champion of cats and has often talked humorously about her cat Oliver Hoyt Goldberg. In 2009 Oliver "wrote" an open letter to newly elected President Barack Obama suggesting that instead of considering a dog for residence in the White House, he should opt for a cat. Although Oliver made a valiant case for feline residence, the President chose a Portuguese Water Dog. Prior to President Obama, cats have had a long tenure at the White House, perhaps none more famously than President Bill Clinton's cat Socks, who became a firm favorite with the public.

The former Australian Prime Minister Kevin Rudd had a black Oriental cat called Jasper, whose death in 2012 sparked a national wave of sympathy. Rudd had coauthored a children's book about the adventures of Jasper and his friend Abby, a golden retriever, and the cat's huge personality endeared him to the Australian public. Humphrey was a famous feline mouser of the British Prime Minster's residence, 10 Downing Street in London, where he lived from 1989 to 1997. Subsequent Downing Street cats have included Sybil and Larry.

The "Canadian Parliamentary Cats" were employed at Parliament Hill, Ottawa, home to Canada's parliamentary buildings until 1955, when poison began to be used to control rodents. Despite being laid off, a number of cats stayed on in the area as strays and eventually in the late 1970s Irène Desormeaux began to care for them. A series of volunteers took on the welfare of the cats and a small shelter was started with donated money. The cats were vaccinated, fed, and cared for as well as being spayed and neutered. The program of sterilization was so effective that by 2012 there were only four elderly residents left. They were adopted by the volunteers and the shelter closed in 2013.

The Hermitage Museum in St. Petersburg, Russia, is home to around sixty or seventy cats that patrol the storerooms, administration areas, and some public areas, keeping them free of rats. The tradition for cats at the Hermitage goes back to the eighteenth century but their welfare has only been addressed in the last couple of decades. Reputedly, during the Siege of Leningrad (1941–1944) nearly all the cats in the city died, including those at the Hermitage. The resulting rat infestation was profound. Cats were brought in from the countryside to combat the problem and gradually some strays made their way back to the Hermitage where they took up self-sufficient residence in the basement. Toward the end of the 1990s steps were made to improve their lives; the basement was converted into a small cat hospital and areas improved for the cats' living accommodation. Maria Haltunen, assistant to the museum director, led the way for the improvements and now the cats are cared for by three full-time volunteers and have a stipend of money to pay for their food. They have become firm favorites among the staff and visitors alike and can frequently be found catnapping in the museum offices and corridors.

In 1993, new life was breathed into a derelict archaeological site in Rome, Italy, through the efforts of former opera singer Silvia Viviani, who founded a cat sanctuary among the ruins in a cave-like space below ground level. This was in the Largo di Torre Argentina, a square in Rome containing the partial remains of four Roman temples and part of the Theatre of Pompey where Julius Caesar was stabbed to death in 44 B.C.E. The area had long been home to a horde of feral cats who took shelter in the subterranean area and had been fed by a succession of kindly people when Silvia and her partner Lia decided to help. Italy is home to a roughly estimated 7.5 million cats, of which a great many live in Rome. Cats are virtually an integral feature of the cityscape and trace their history here back to the time of the Etruscans; they have been designated part of Rome's bio-cultural heritage by the city council. Many of these cats are feral or neglected and their fate lies in the hands of inspired enthusiasts such as Silvia Viviani whose sanctuary has cared for around 200 of these felines at any one time, over the past two decades.

The latter decades of the twentieth century saw another extraordinary demonstration of the bond between people and cats in the form of the Dutch Cat Boat Foundation, a floating cat sanctuary found in the watery environs of Amsterdam and possibly the only one of its kind in the world. It began in the late 1960s when Henriette van Weelde found a stray cat with kittens hiding under a tree opposite her house. Henriette, who became known throughout the city as "the cat lady" took the cat into her home and cared for her. Suddenly another stray cat appeared, then another and another, and shortly Henriette's house was full to overflowing with rescued strays. It was then that she decided to move the cats onto an old Dutch sailing barge opposite her home. The barge was fitted out appropriately for feline occupants, and quickly filled up. Another barge was added and suddenly the Cat Boat became a popular destination for visitors keen to see the cats in their custom home and adopt them. In 1987 the city authorities agreed to register the Cat Boat as a charity and it became known as the Cat Boat Foundation.

The last few decades have also seen change and progress in (general) animal welfare laws across many countries in the world. Animals are becoming better protected, but at the same time there are increasing numbers of strays and feral cats. New Zealand, a country said to have one of the highest cat populations per capita with an estimated 48 percent of households owning a cat, has recently entered a cat controversy. Cats are being held accountable for the death of a large number of small animals and birds, and environmentalists are calling for a cull of strays, mandatory neutering and spaying, and keeping cats confined indoors. In addition, a recent research study in the United States has revealed an alarming increase in the deaths of birds and small mammals by cats in the last few years—of course some of those small mammals are the very same ones that cause destruction to food stores and homes, not to mention spread disease. Attacks on birds are a less appealing side to cat behavior, but there are some measures that can be taken to reduce fatalities, such as bells on collars or confining cats at certain times when fledglings are learning to fly.

As the twenty-first century progresses it is hoped that intelligent, responsible pet ownership and consideration for welfare will continue to advance and improve the inherent problem of an increasing feral population as well as attacks on wildlife. Cats, it would seem, are still dividing opinions and inspiring the highest emotions at each end of the scale, just as they have done throughout their history.

The many new breeds that have been recognized and the many others that are presented to the different cat organizations annually are making for interesting times in the world of cat fancy, marking the continual development of the domestic cat. Many breeds, both new and old, are rare and in need of preservation, however. With dedication, these can all live on, alongside the equally captivating and beautiful non-pedigreed cats.

SINGAPURA

MODERN — SINGAPORE/UNITED STATES — RARE

APPEARANCE
Small, dainty, beautiful, with warm sepia-colored coat. Small, moderately stocky body, legs well muscled at the body, tapering to small, oval paws. Head is rounded with medium-short, broad muzzle and blunt nose. Large ears with a deep cup, slightly pointed. Large almond-shaped eyes, brilliant green, copper, yellow, or hazel.

Slender tail, not whippy, ending in a blunt tip.
SIZE
Small
COAT
Very short and fine, close to body. Sepia-ticked tabby is rich sable ticking on a ground of old ivory.
PERSONALITY
Lively, curious, playful, intelligent, affectionate, loyal, mischievous

THE SINGAPURA IS THE SMALLEST BREED of domestic cat, and has an exquisite, even angelic, appearance. It also has enormous character and is extremely intelligent, with endless humor, playfulness, and affection. With its heavenly looks and winning temperament, it tends to get its own way. It adores its family and insists on being in the limelight at all times. Equally it displays an inherent affinity with emotions and moods and is as sensitive to the sadness of its owner as their joy.

The story of the Singapura's origins is an interesting one, and not without a little drama. The breed is a naturally occurring one that can be traced back to the feral cats of Singapore in the 1970s and before. Here large numbers of cats in many shapes and sizes lived an unglamorous life among the drains and sewers, and were often referred to as drain cats by the island's inhabitants. Because of their large numbers, they were unpopular among the residents. Although there was great variety among the cats, there are accounts of distinctive small, brown cats with ticked coats that resembled what we now know as the Singapura. The breed began its journey toward recognition with an American couple, Hal and Tommy Meadow. Tommy had bred cats, including Burmese, over the years and was interested in genetics; she had undertaken a number of genetic studies on rats. Hal worked in Southeast Asia as a geophysicist. In the early 1970s they moved to Singapore for Hal's job, and lived there for several years before returning to the United States in 1975. They took their cats back with them—a neutered, sable-colored Burmese and five others. These others were the male Ticle, females Tess and Pusse, and two kittens, George and Gladys, by Ticle and Pusse. These five cats shared very similar characteristics, including their distinctive brown-ticked coloring, and they became the first Singapuras.

Back in the United States the Meadows began to breed their cats to produce kittens of fixed characteristics, thus starting to develop a new breed. They worked extremely hard at promoting their beautiful cats, exhibiting them at shows to garner awareness for the fledgling breed both from the judges and the public. In 1978 the breeder Barbara Gilbertson acquired a pair and she was followed by several other breeders including Helen Cherry, Catherine MacQuarrie, Gerry Mayes, Jo Cobery, and Tord Svenson. The following year The International Cat Association (TICA) accepted the Singapura for championship status. At this time the gene pool for the breed was still extremely small; a major step was made in 1980 when Chiko, a female Singapura residing at the Society for Prevention of Cruelty to Animals (SPCA) in Singapore was located by Sheila Bowers. Bowers sent the cat back to the United States, complete with all the correct documentation, to Barbara Gilbertson. In 1982 the Cat Fanciers' Association (CFA) accepted the Singapura for registration and in 1988 the breed was awarded championship status.

By this time the little Singapura had created quite a stir and had attracted a core group of dedicated enthusiasts. They established the breed club, The Singapura Fanciers' Society. In 1987 breeder Gerry Mayes went to Singapore for an extended trip and, through the help of the Singapore Cat Club, located a number of Singapuras and arranged their export back to the United States. In the 1980s there was a difference of opinion among breeders, which led to the formation of a second breed club, the International Singapura Alliance. Both breed clubs were affiliated with the CFA. In 1990, a reporter interviewed Tommy Meadow for *The Straits Times,* and Meadow admitted that Tess, Ticle, and Pusse had all been born in the United States, and not in Singapore as everyone had supposed. She explained that her husband, Hal, had sent her some brown-ticked cats from Singapore in the early 1970s on a cargo ship with no import papers attached to them. These cats had given rise to Tess, Ticle, and Pusse; the Meadows had then taken them over to Singapore with them, and returned with them. This caused considerable controversy, and the Meadows were asked before the CFA board in 1991 to offer a full explanation. Despite the confusion, the fact remained that the cats were ultimately from Singapore, plus the breed as a whole had been greatly influenced in the intervening years through the import of documented cats from Singapore. There is, in addition, no denying the work that the Meadows put into establishing the breed.

The Singapura first arrived in the United Kingdom in 1988 when Carole Thompson from Gloucestershire imported a pregnant female, Imagos Faye Raye of Usaf from the United States. Faye produced her kittens Muffy, Mimi, and Kuan while in quarantine. Kuan was later sold back to the United States and became a four-times grand champion with the American Cat Fanciers Association (ACFA). Thompson also imported a male, Sricoberys Indah, who was bred to Faye, Muffy, and Mimi. Pat and Eddie Bell from Northumberland purchased cats from Carole, and later Debbie Van Den Berg and her partner Mal Burns bought two females, Tolgoblin Sweet Saffron and Tolgoblin Esmirelda Ofmine, from the Bells. Van Den Berg and Burns went on to import an American male. Debbie and Mal exhibited their cats at many shows with the Governing Council of the Cat Fancy (GCCF). In 1993 a breed club was established and by 1997 the GCCF granted the breed preliminary status. This was promoted to provisional status in 2002, and full championship status in 2004. In 2007 two Singapuras earned the U.K. Imperial Grand Champion title.

Rather ironically given that Singapore had previously held a dim view on its feral cats, the Singapura was adopted by the Singapore Tourist Board as a key part of their advertising campaign and has now been designated a national mascot. The breed has a strong international following and is found in continental Europe, Australia, Canada, Russia, Japan, South America, and South Africa.

AMERICAN CURL
MODERN — UNITED STATES — RARE

APPEARANCE

Distinctive through their curled ears and sweet expression. Moderate, well proportioned and well balanced. Body is rectangular and longer than height at shoulders. Well muscled and athletic rather than cobby. Head is a modified wedge without flat planes; straight nose with gentle curve from bridge of nose to forehead, moderate in length. Eyes are moderately large, clear, and walnut shaped, color no relation to coat except in Colorpoint class. Ears distinguish the breed; they are moderately large, set equally to the side and top of head and curl back at the tip between 90 and 180 degrees. Ear tips are flexible and rounded and furnishings preferable. Legs in proportion to body, paws rounded, and tail wide at base, flexible, and tapering to end.

SIZE

Medium

COAT

Longhaired has silky coat that lies flat with little undercoat, tail is full and plumed. Shorthaired has a shorter silky coat that lies flat with little undercoat. All colors and patterns allowed.

PERSONALITY

Very affectionate, people oriented, intelligent, very playful, curious, easygoing

THE AMERICAN CURL IS A TRULY DELIGHTFUL BREED that is particularly people oriented without being overdemanding. This cat likes nothing better than to be in the company of its owner at all times, taking an active and not always very helpful role in events. It tends not to voice its requests loudly but instead gently uses its paws to pat one for attention, or vocalizes softly. The American Curl (AC) is also noted for its extremely gentle, kind nature, a disposition that is easily read on its face. Given this, it is generally excellent with children, and tends to get along with other cats and with dogs. ACs are smart cats and love to play—they will learn fetch quickly and will often retain their playful kittenlike behavior throughout their lives.

The excellent temperament characteristics of the AC are seen throughout the breed, although in physical appearance it can vary a fair amount. American Curl kittens are born with straight ears; they start to curl back when the kitten is between one and seven days old, and can continue to change in degree of curl up to about four and a half months. After this age the angle of the ear should not change and should be within a range of 90 to 180 degrees. These lovely cats can be long- or shorthaired and any color or pattern.

The origins of the breed are well documented, but are not without a little mystery, too. They trace back to 1981 to Lakewood, California, when two skinny kittens aged about six months appeared on the doorstep of Joe and Grace Ruga; the Rugas later established the Curlniques Cattery. Both kittens were female; one was black with longhair and the other black and white with semi-longhair, and both had unusual ears that curled back. The Rugas named the black cat Shulamith and the other kitten Panda. After two weeks or so Panda suddenly and sadly disappeared.

Shulamith settled into life with the Rugas and some months later produced a litter of kittens, which contained two with the same distinctive curled ears. The Rugas realized that there was something special about these cats and began to undertake some experimental breeding with Shulamith. The two kittens went to Grace Ruga's sister, Esther Brimlow, where they were seen by a dog breeder named Nancy Kiester. Kiester was entranced by the lovely kittens with their unusual ears and acquired them. Kiester had seen an article about the Scottish Fold cat and wondered if her kittens might represent a new breed. Kiester and the Rugas made contact, and within the same time period Cat Fanciers' Association (CFA) judge Jean Grimm, who also bred Scottish Folds, began to help establish the American Curl as a recognized breed.

In 1983 the Rugas and Kiester exhibited Shulamith and some of her progeny at a CFA show in Palm Springs, California, bringing these new cats into the public realm and to the awareness of the judges. Shulamith, the original American Curl, was used as the ideal on which to base the breed standard and was recognized as the foundation cat of the breed. However, in order to keep the tiny gene pool of the AC healthy, it was necessary to outcross to other cats, and it was dictated that these should only be nonpedigree domestics. This was to prevent distinguishing characteristics from pedigree breeds appearing or diluting the features of the American Curl. Early breeders enlisted

the help of two geneticists, Solveig Pflueger and Roy Robinson, to better understand the science behind the genetics of the breed. Subsequently it was revealed that the curled ear was caused by an autosomal dominant gene, which means that a cat need only have one copy of the gene to exhibit the curled ear. It was also discovered that this dominant gene carried no adverse health problems or deformities and had occurred as a spontaneous mutation.

In 1984 the first AC to AC breeding took place, which resulted in Playit By Ear, the first homozygous AC—because he had two copies of the same gene, he would pass the ear-curling trait on to all of his offspring whether he was bred to an AC or a domestic. Since then AC to AC breeding has taken place frequently with no genetic abnormalities reported. In fact, ACs are known for their robust health, which is in great part due to the large nonpedigree domestic input to the breed at its foundation. Unusually for a new breed, the American Curl was accepted very quickly by all the cat associations, and in 1986, just five years after Shulamith and Panda had been discovered, the breed was recognized by The International Cat Association (TICA) and the CFA. In December 1989 the geneticist Roy Robinson published a piece in the *Journal of Heredity* based on his analysis of data from 383 AC kittens. It was a significant moment for breeders because he reported that there were no defects in any of the kittens he had studied, and this underlined how healthy the American Curl is.

The CFA advanced the American Curl to championship status in 1993 and, interestingly, the breed became the first admitted into the CFA championship class as one breed with two coat lengths. The two coats lengths traced back to Shulamith, who produced shorthaired curled-ear kittens in her third litter. She went on to produce more shorthaired AC kittens over the years and now shorthaired varieties are not infrequent.

The American Curl has now become popular across the United States and in Japan as well as the United Kingdom. In England the breed was established by Claire Winman of the Overear Cattery, Lincolnshire, in 2007. Claire acquired her first two AC cats in 2007 from the noted Procurl Harem Cattery in New York, owned by Caroline Scott and Michael Tucker. At the moment there are still very few American Curls in England, but given this breed's tremendous qualities, this seems sure to change in the near future.

LAPERM

MODERN — UNITED STATES — RARE

APPEARANCE

Striking curly coat with soft ringlets; large, expressive eyes. Medium to long body, athletic, muscular, and with medium boning. Medium to long legs, front legs slightly shorter than hind, and rounded paws. Head is a modified wedge with slightly rounded contours. Slightly broad muzzle and straight nose. Eyes are medium large, almond shaped, very expressive; eye color has no relation to coat color. Ears are medium to large with tufts and earmuffs. Tail in proportion to body.

SIZE

Medium

COAT

Medium longhaired has light curls and ringlets, longer on ruff and neck, kinked eyebrows, and curled whiskers; coat is light and airy, hair textured like mohair and stands away from body; tail has a full plume. Shorthaired also exhibits waves and curls, though of shorter length and with no ruff; tail is like a bottlebrush.

PERSONALITY

Intelligent, very curious, determined, problem solving, very affectionate, loyal, clownish

WITH ITS COMPELLING LOOKS and bewitching personality, the LaPerm is a wonderful cat that will take over one's life and home with characteristic good humor, affection, and charm. It is an active cat and loves to engage in a riotous play session, tear up a tree, fly off ledges, and generally be acrobatic; when the fun is done it likes nothing better than to curl up on one's lap. It possesses great intelligence and has a particularly high problem-solving ability. It is also determined, in the nicest possible way—if it wants something it will generally either access it after careful thought and planning, or persuade its owner to do so. Easygoing by nature, it gets along with all the family.

As with many of the modern cat breeds, it is possible to trace the roots of the LaPerm breed directly back to its origins and to a single cat called Curly. The breed came into being in March 1982 in a barn in a cherry orchard belonging to Linda Koehl near to The Dalles in Oregon. Linda watched one of her barn cats, a tabby called Speedy, give birth to a litter of kittens, which included one ugly female kitten who was entirely bald. The little female had a classic tabby pattern on her skin, but no hair. Given that Linda had a number of barn cats on her farm that were there to keep the rodents at bay, she gave little thought to

the odd-looking kitten. Within around eight weeks, though, the kitten began to grow a soft, downy, and curly coat, and by the time she was four months old she was covered in a full coat of curls, earning her the name Curly.

One day Curly had an accident that called for a trip to the veterinarian. Back at home, Linda moved Curly into her house to recuperate and realized that not only did she have the most beautiful, soft coat, but she also had a very sweet temperament. Curly took herself back outside to the other barn cats and sometime later produced a litter of five bald, male kittens. All five grew their curly coats as Curly herself had, and were left unneutered to go about their lives on the farm. Curly herself had just this one litter before she sadly disappeared, but her five boys bred with the other domestic farm cats unchecked for ten years, by which time Linda had quite a number of these unusual curly-coated cats.

Linda referred to her cats as LaPerm and finally, at the urging of friends, decided that she had something special going on at her farm. She set about trying to organize the breeding of her cats, and to earn them official breed recognition. She took several of her curly-coated cats to a Cat Fanciers' Association (CFA) cat show to exhibit them; they caused something of a sensation, leaving Linda in little doubt that she had to pursue her new breed.

During the ten years of unsupervised breeding on her farm the cats had developed long and short coats and were appearing in all sorts of colors and patterns due to the influence of non-pedigree domestic barn cats. This wide gene pool also initially contributed toward the LaPerm's robust health. Early in the breed's development about 90 percent of the kittens were born bald and then developed their curly coat by around four months of age. Now very few LaPerm kittens are born bald (BB), instead they are born with a curly coat (BC). Some are born with a straight coat (BS), but will pass on the curly-coated gene. The coat of the LaPerm can also change during the seasons, becoming sparser in hot weather and denser when it cools down.

The breed is referred to as one of the Rex breeds, along with the Selkirk Rex, Cornish Rex, and Devon Rex; all are notable for their wavy or curly coats. The LaPerm derives its coat from a natural mutation, leading to a dominant gene that causes the coat to be curly. Dr. Solveig Pflueger, a noted geneticist, has determined that the LaPerm gene is unique in being completely dominant and therefore differs from the other Rex breeds. The LaPerm also differs in that its whiskers are long and flexible, often with a wave in them; the other Rex breeds generally have short, brittle whiskers.

Some LaPerms, known as heterozygous, can carry the gene for straight hair, and occasionally straight-haired kittens are born. Although not eligible for showing, they are useful for breeding programs. Outcrosses are used when breeding in order to maintain a healthy gene pool, but the type of outcrossing allowed varies between associations on an international basis. In the CFA, for example, outcrossing to domestics is allowed until 2015. In the United Kingdom, unregistered domestics and their registered progeny are allowed in the pedigrees of LaPerms registered prior to June 2004; outcrosses to some pedigreed breeds such as the Somali are also permitted. However, most breeders now concentrate on breeding LaPerms with each other because the genetic diversity has been established.

The LaPerm was given new breed status by The International Cat Association (TICA) in 1995; this was progressed to championship status by 2002. The first TICA champion was Ch Dennigan's French Maid of Shoalwater. The LaPerm Society of America was established in 1997 and in 2000 the CFA allowed the breed entry to the miscellaneous class. This was advanced to provisional in 2005 and championship status in 2008, with the first CFA grand champion being Pacific Gem BC Saguaro of Bosque. Although the breed is still rare, it has spread across much of the world with LaPerms now in Japan, Russia, Australia, New Zealand, South Africa, Canada, continental Europe, and the United Kingdom. The first to arrive in the United Kingdom was Uluru BC Omaste Po of Quincunx, a lilac tortie and white female imported in 2002. Shortly after her arrival she had a litter of five kittens that are recognized as the foundation stock for the breed in England. Further LaPerms have since been imported and a careful breeding program has been developed using some outcrosses. The LaPerm Cat Club was founded in 2004.

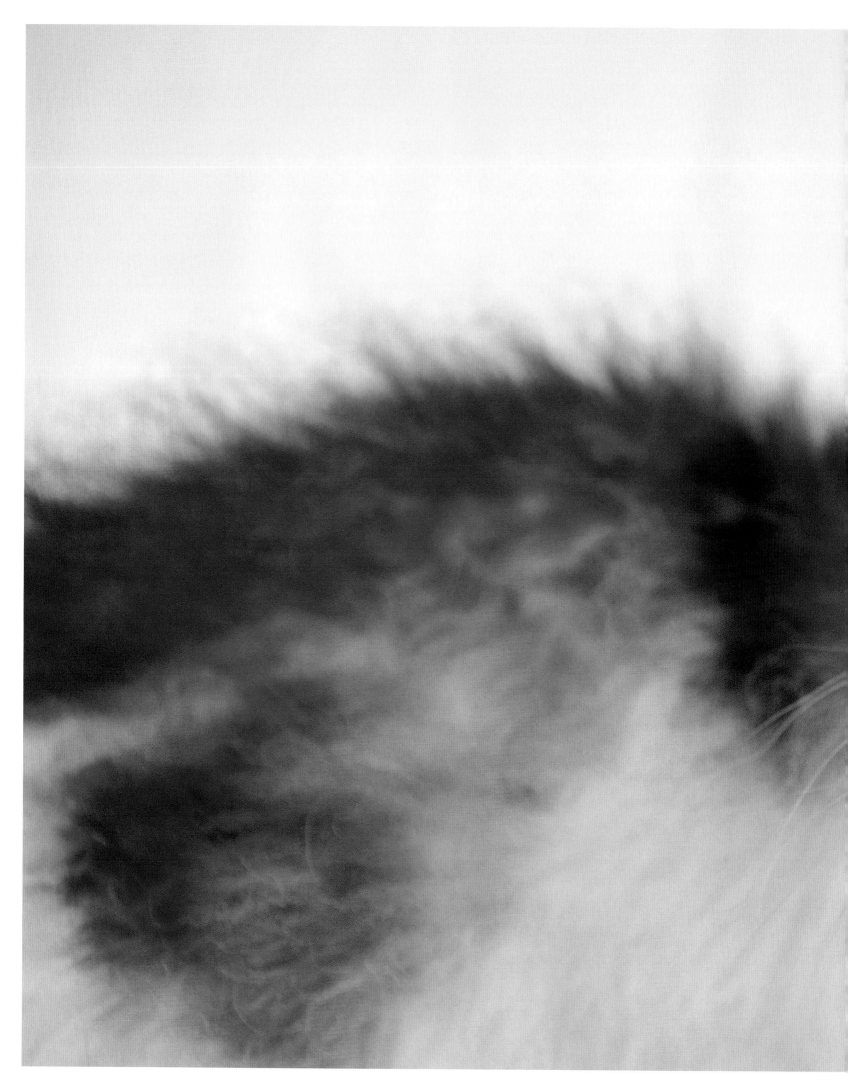

MUNCHKIN
MODERN – UNITED STATES – MODERATE

APPEARANCE

Short-legged, either shorthaired or semi-longhaired. Thick, semiforeign body, back slopes upwards from shoulders to tail. Legs are short, paws round and compact. Head is a modified wedge with high cheekbones, eyes are walnut shaped and rather wide apart; color has no relation to coat color. Ears are in proportion to head with slightly rounded tips. Tail is equal in length to the body, tapers to a rounded end, and is carried erect when in motion.

SIZE

Small

COAT

Shorthaired is semi-plush and resilient, semi-longhaired is silky with moderate ruff. Can be any color or pattern.

PERSONALITY

Very active, playful, sociable, outgoing, loving

THE MUNCHKIN HOUSES A LARGE PERSONALITY in a relatively small body. It is a naturally occurring dwarf cat, meaning that it has short legs but in all other respects is the same as an ordinary cat. What this cat may lack in height, however, it more than makes up for in character and energy. In fact, the Munchkin is an extremely active breed and exhibits astonishing athleticism and determination. It is an affectionate and fun-loving cat that makes a very rewarding pet and is overwhelmingly cheerful in nature.

The breed is still fairly controversial and not accepted by all the major associations, although this is likely to change over time. Dr. Solveig Pflueger, chairperson of The International Cat Association (TICA) genetics committee in the United States, determined through studies in the 1990s that the short legs are the result of a dominant genetic mutation that affects only the long bones of the front and rear legs. This mutation is thought to have occurred spontaneously, though it is not known why. A cat that has this gene (the Munchkin gene) from one parent will produce roughly 50 percent Munchkin kittens and 50 percent normal kittens.

Given that this is a naturally occurring mutation, it is likely that there have been short-legged cats for some time. Certainly documented occurrences date back to 1944 to an entry in the English Veterinary Record by Dr. H. E. Williams-Jones. In this he describes four generations of short-legged cats, all in apparently good health and including an eight-year-old black female. This line of cats is believed to have died out during the years of World War II. Another account is found in Germany and dates to 1956 when Max Von Egon Thiel of Hamburg described a short-legged kitten he had seen in Stalingrad three years earlier. He wrote about the kitten sitting on its haunches with its front legs in the air, a position that the modern Munchkin will often adopt. More of the same type of cats were seen in the United States in New England in 1970.

It is to 1983 that the breed traces its systematic development, and to Rayville, Louisiana. Here Sandra Hochendel, a music teacher, discovered two short-legged cats hiding underneath her pickup truck. Hochendel took the cats in, later realizing they were both pregnant. She named them Munchkins after the little characters in *The Wizard of Oz*. Hochendel kept the black female, who was called Blackberry, and gave away the gray female, who was called Blueberry. After Blackberry had her kittens, Hochendel gave one of the short-legged ones, named Toulouse, to her friend Kay LaFrance in Monroe, Louisiana. Toulouse went on to breed freely with a number of neighborhood and feral cats, and subsequently a feral population of Munchkins developed in the Monroe area.

TICA controversially accepted Munchkins into its new breed development program in 1994, and in 2003 the Munchkin was afforded championship status. Munchkins can be outcrossed with any domestic cat that is not a member of a recognized breed. As a result, they can be short- or longhaired, and come in many colors and patterns. Some felt that Munchkins would be prone to back, hip, and leg problems because of their short legs, but breeders report no signs of this in older cats. Although these cats are still not universally accepted, they have found their way into the hearts of a dedicated following, and have become increasingly popular as pets and show animals.

NEBELUNG

MODERN – UNITED STATES/RUSSIA – RARE

APPEARANCE
Longhaired blue cat with green or yellow-green eyes. Long, semiforeign body type with medium boning and graceful, athletic appearance. Long legs with medium boning, medium-sized paws with tufting between toes. Appears to stand and walk on balls of feet. Head is a modified wedge, more pointed than rounded. Ears are large and pointed and eyes almost almond shaped and green or yellow-green

mixture in color. Tail is equal to body length with hair longer than that on body.

SIZE
Medium

COAT
Long, double-coated, and very soft with outer coat being fine and silky. Blue in color with lustrous silver tipping.

PERSONALITY
Devoted to owner, can be shy with strangers, playful, highly intelligent, active, and patient

NEBELUNGS ARE BEAUTIFUL AND ENIGMATIC CATS that make exceptional companions because they are so affectionate to their owners. They are known for their intelligence and perhaps as a result of this are often wary of strangers. They can be shy and will invariably disappear to a safe vantage point when someone new arrives, but once they have decided that no danger is present, they become very interactive and personable. They are of course also particularly attractive with their lustrous, long, blue coats and intense eyes.

The breed takes its name from the German word *nebel*, meaning "mist" or "fog," and the epic German poem *Nibelungenlied* (translated as *The Song of the Nibelungs*), which relates the story of a dragon-slayer hero called Siegfried. The German origins of the breed's name are slightly unusual because the breed itself has greater ties with Russia, but the name was chosen by Cora Cobb, who developed the breed in the United States. Some of the foundation cats of the breed also take their name from the same epic poem. The male, Siegfried, was born in 1984; his mother was a black shorthaired domestic called Elsa, who belonged to Cora's son, and his father was a longhaired cat that resembled a black Angora. This pairing produced two shorthaired black females and Siegfried, who had the appearance of a longhaired Russian Blue. Siegfried had a

special quality about him from the very beginning. He was extremely handsome and well built with great charisma. Some months later Elsa bred back to Siegfried's father, producing seven kittens, of which two were longhaired females, one black and one blue. The blue kitten was special, like Siegfried, and closely resembled him in coat and build; Cora called her Brunhilde after the Icelandic queen in the *Nibelungenlied*.

Cora took her two cats with her when she moved from Denver, Colorado, to El Paso, Texas, and in 1986 they produced their first litter of three kittens that were all blue longhaired and with the Russian Blue build. At this point Cora realized that she may be witnessing the emergence of a new breed and she approached The International Cat Association (TICA) for advice on how best to proceed and how to apply for new breed status. This status was granted in 1987. Cora was encouraged and advised by Dr. Solveig Pflueger, who was TICA's genetics specialist, and who suggested that she describe her new breed as a longhaired Russian Blue, and write a breed standard based on that of the Russian Blue.

In her quest for recognition for the breed, Cora also encouraged other breeders to work with the Nebelung to try and expand the gene pool and keep it healthy. In addition she needed to get the public interested in these gorgeous new cats. Cora did this by taking one of her cats, Schatzi, to a cat show where she was able to exhibit her in the new breed category. At the show she made contact with a Russian Blue breeder who allowed her to breed Schatzi to one of her champion Russian Blues. The resulting kittens were all blue and shorthaired, although they in turn produced blue longhaired progeny.

Next Cora acquired a male Russian Blue cat who had unusually long hair, although he was not classed as longhaired. His name was Universal Concord and he was of tremendous influence in the fledgling breed. By this time other breeders were involved, including Karena

Carlso (CK Cattery) and John Hruza, as well as Kim di Nubilo, whose breeding stock of Nebelungs later tragically died during an epidemic of feline infectious peritonitis. A further tragedy was the death of both Cora's original cats, Siegfried in a road traffic accident and Brunhilde through unknown causes. Undeterred, Cora continued to travel widely and even internationally, exhibiting her cats in new breed classes, determined to bring them greater coverage and inspire the public and judges alike.

Cora returned to Denver in 1992 and she continued to breed and exhibit her cats in new breed classes, with her cats and their progeny winning many times. By this time the breed was also becoming recognized in Europe and Cora was contacted by a Dutch breeder, Letty van den Brock, who had a male Nebelung called Timofeus who had been bred in Russia. This was one of the first clues that the breed had probably originated in Russia as a natural mutation within the Russian Blue. The Nebelung is considered by some to be a longhaired Russian Blue, and in some countries is defined as such—this led to initial skepticism from some Russian Blue breeders who were not willing to accept a longhaired variety.

Cora applied to TICA for championship status in 1995, but was turned down. The same year Cora was contacted by her old friend Sue Bower, who had founded the El Paso Compadres Cat Club and who had seen a Nebelung being exhibited in Moscow. The following year Cora took one of her cats, Silver Streak, to the cat show in St. Petersburg where he won the best of the best new breeds and was awarded Best in Show. In 1997 she again approached TICA, taking Sigrdrifa, a five-month-old female, with her and the board voted unanimously to advance the breed to championship status. Shortly afterwards she was able to acquire a male Nebelung, George, from Russian breeder Natasha Stolyarova. The Russian Blue has continued to be an important outcross in the establishment of the Nebelung and the continuance of a healthy gene pool.

The Nebelung is supported by a group of dedicated breeders worldwide but still exists in relatively small numbers. In the United Kingdom the Nebelung was recognized by the Governing Council of the Cat Fancy (GCCF) in 2011 and granted preliminary recognition in 2012. Breeders in the United Kingdom and continental Europe are working hard to promote this delightful breed.

PIXIEBOB

MODERN — UNITED STATES — UNCOMMON

APPEARANCE

Wild bobcat look, short tail, can have polydactyl toes. Long, muscular, and rangy bodies with long, heavily boned legs; front legs slightly shorter than hind. Large, round paws with fleshy toes; can have up to seven toes. Tail is minimum of two inches (5 cm) and can reach the hock, can be kinked or knotted. Medium to large head shaped like an inverted pear with a heavy brow and fleshy chin. Ears are wide and deep at base, lynx furnishings preferred.

Eyes are heavily hooded and a soft triangular shape; color can be golden brown or gooseberry green.

SIZE

Medium to large

COAT

Can be long- or shorthaired. Thick, double coat that stands away from body. Longhaired are slightly silkier to touch. Brown-spotted tabby is the ideal color, any shade of brown allowed.

PERSONALITY

Gregarious, lively, intelligent, loyal, affectionate, interactive

THE PIXIEBOB IS A STRIKING CAT in every way. Its appearance reflects the wild American Bobcat, but it has a delightful and entertaining temperament and is devoted to its family. It is sometimes described as being "doglike," and this is true in many ways; it can even be trained to walk on a leash. Pixiebobs love to accompany their owners wherever they go. They have a laid-back temperament and an ability to take most things in their stride, and usually with apparent good humor.

There is an air of mystery surrounding the Pixiebob's origins. It is described as a naturally occurring cat and was developed as a breed by Carol Ann Brewer of Washington State. In 1985, a couple living in the foothills of Mount Baker in the northern Cascade Mountains of Washington State heard a terrible noise outside their barn. On investigation they saw what appeared to be a bobcat wrestling with their domestic barn cat, who was a short-tailed female with polydactyl (more than the usual number of) toes. Sometime later this female cat produced kittens and it is widely assumed that this was the result of the bobcat breeding the barn cat. Carol Ann Brewer acquired one of the kittens, a spotted male, again with polydactyl toes and a short tail. A few months later Carol Ann acquired another bobtailed cat, this one being distinguished by its

large size; she named it Keba. Given the similarities in these cats with their short tails, wild appearance, polydactyl toes, and lovely temperament, Carol Ann felt that she had stumbled upon a "breed" of cat and, after further research, discovered other people across the Pacific Northwest of the United States who had seen cats of similar wild appearance. Due to the lack of evidence, however, Carol Ann initially called these cats Legend Cats, since their history appeared to be based on legend rather than fact.

Keba bred her neighbor's cat and Carol Ann chose a kitten from the ensuing litter, a beautiful female called Pixie, who went on to be the foundation cat for the Pixiebob breed. Carol Ann set about a breeding program to recreate as closely as possible the appearance of her beloved Pixie through breeding to cats of similar appearance and character. Because of the wide genetic base in its development, the Pixiebob can be short- or longhaired and is also known for its robust health. In 1989 Carol Ann wrote a breed standard and named the breed the Pixiebob, and in 1993 she approached The International Cat Association (TICA) to start the process for breed recognition. The following year TICA accepted them for exhibition status, and in 1996 they were advanced to new breed color status. This was upgraded to championship status in 1998.

Pixiebob breeders have worked long and hard to gain acceptance for their breed, but it is still not recognized by some of the major associations. This has not however diminished the enthusiasm of breeders for these cats, and is certainly not a reflection on their admirable qualities. Although they are still relatively low in numbers they are found internationally, including in the United Kingdom. Here, the first Pixiebobs arrived in 2004 at the foundation cattery Alsoomse Pixiebob on the edge of Exmoor in southwest England. The bloodlines of these cats traced back to Pixie herself, and the cattery has since bred over seven champions and exported Pixiebobs to a number of European countries.

SAVANNAH

MODERN – UNITED STATES – RARE

APPEARANCE
Tall, lean, spotted, wildcat look. Slender and graceful, athletic with long, muscular body and longer than average, elegant legs; paws are medium sized and oval. Head is small in proportion to body and face has triangular form with wide nose and low-set nostrils. Ears are very large, set on top of head, wide and deep at base, very upright, and can have ear furnishings. Eyes are small to medium sized and set under a slightly hooded brow, tearstain marks present; eyes can be any color. Tail is medium length and medium to thick in width; tapers slightly to a blunt end.

SIZE
Medium to large

COAT
Short to medium in length, loose and nonresilient with a softer undercoat. Black brown-spotted tabby, black silver-spotted tabby, black smoke. Spotted pattern only, spots should be bold, dark brown to black, and round, oval, or elongated.

PERSONALITY
Extrovert, very active, playful, very curious, very adventurous, loyal to family

THE SAVANNAH CAT brings a little piece of the wild into the home. Quite apart from its svelte, striking looks, which recall the wild African Serval, the Savannah is an energetic cat that is extremely interactive. It will use any available items as its own personal gym and will impress with its athletic maneuvers, jumping to a much greater height than an ordinary domestic cat. The Savannah has many doglike traits and can be trained to walk on a leash quite happily. It will also invariably greet one at the door like a dog and is often chosen by former dog-owning homes. It is not a lap cat, although it is very affectionate. Much time and consideration has gone into breeding the Savannah for its temperament as well as its stunning looks, and consequently it is easygoing and will get along well with other cats, dogs, and children.

Breeders have developed the Savannah by crossing the wild African Serval with the domestic cat. It was intended specifically to imitate a wildcat in appearance, but with the superb temperament of the domestic cat. Several other cats have been bred for the same purpose, including the Toyger, which was also initiated during the 1980s, and the Bengal, Chausie, and Ocicat, which were developed some years earlier. The first Savannah was born in 1986. A domestic

cat belonging to the Bengal breeder Judy Frank was bred by an African Serval. Judy's domestic was a seal point Siamese, and the kitten exhibited a grayish-brown background color (from the mother) with dark spots (from the father). The kitten was acquired by another breeder, Suzi Wood, who called her Savannah, which later gave rise to the breed name.

Breeders of hybrids face a number of problems. In the wild an African Serval would not naturally breed to a domestic cat, so any hybrid breeding program would need to use Servals that have been raised or lived among domestics for some time. Another problem facing potential breeders of this hybrid was the difference in size between the domestic cat and the much larger Serval; additionally Servals can have a slightly longer gestation period (up to ten days longer) than domestics. One of the biggest hurdles, however, is fertility in the males. The offspring from the first cross (domestic to Serval) are referred to as F1. Not all F1 kittens will survive and those that do on the male side will be infertile. F1 females are fertile and when they are bred back to domestics they will produce F2 kittens. When F2 kittens are bred back to domestics they produce F3 kittens, and so on. Male F3 kittens will also be infertile, but the likelihood of male fertility increases with each generation, and F4 male kittens may be fertile. This gives some indication as to how extremely difficult it is to establish a breed such as the Savannah, and just how much hard work has gone into it. An SBT (Stud Book Traditional) Savannah is one that has been bred Savannah to Savannah for at least three generations, with no outcross to domestic. The earlier generation Savannah cats (F1, F2) may be larger in size than the SBT Savannah and exhibit more traits in common with the Serval than the SBT. These are still lovely cats, but should be homed with experienced individuals.

Suzi Wood's original female Savannah proved fertile and produced a number of F2 kittens, which indicated to Suzi that it might be possible to create a new breed. Suzi published a couple of articles on the Savannah and these came to the attention of Patrick Kelley, who wanted to develop a new domestic breed with the spotted appearance of a wildcat. He purchased one of Savannah's female kittens from Suzi and bred her back to a domestic to produce F3 kittens. At the same time he approached a number of Serval breeders to see if he could encourage them to come on board with his project to develop a new breed. By this time Suzi had withdrawn from the process.

Breeder Joyce Sroufe took up the gauntlet and she is considered one of the main driving forces behind the establishment of the Savannah breed; her cattery was called A1 Savannahs, and when she retired from breeding she sold this prefix. The A1 Savannah cattery remains active, but is not now associated with Joyce Sroufe. Joyce was one of the first Savannah breeders to breed down through the generations and produce fertile males, and in 1996 she and Patrick Kelley wrote the first breed standard and presented it to The International Cat Association (TICA) board. The following year Joyce showcased the new breed at the Westchester Cat Show in New York, bringing it to the public and cat fancy's attention. Kelley meanwhile wrote a number of articles about the Savannah for cat fancy magazines and began to promote the breed on the internet. He too is recognized as instrumental in popularizing the new breed.

Breeder Lorre Smith was the first person to write a book about the breed. Lorre became the first TICA Savannah breed working group chairperson and was instrumental in obtaining recognition for the breed and unusually rapid advancement through TICA. Lorre also worked along with other Savannah breeders to update and refine the breed standard. The Savannah was granted championship status in 2012, much to the delight of breeders and owners alike. Lorre Smith is still very much involved with the breed. Breeder Brigitte Cowell of Kirembo Savannahs became the first TICA Savannah breed chair after the breed received championship status.

Savannahs can be found internationally as well as in the United States. They are popular in Canada, Japan, continental Europe, and the United Kingdom, although their numbers are still relatively low in Europe. In the United States in 2011 they were the fourth most-registered breed in TICA.

DON SPHYNX

MODERN — RUSSIA — RARE

APPEARANCE

Hairless with pronounced wrinkles. Solid, robust, and muscular through frame. Body is medium long with sturdy bone structure, broad chest and croup, and visibly rounded abdomen. Front legs shorter than hind, paws are oval with very long, slim toes; thumbs bend inward not downward on front paws and webs separate the toes. Head is medium sized and a modified wedge with flat forehead and finely outlined cheekbones; medium-length muzzle, nose has Roman curve in profile. Large, wide ears tilt forward slightly. Medium to large, almond-shaped eyes, color no relation to coat. Tail is medium long and tapers to a rounded tip.

SIZE

Medium

COAT

Four types: born bald; flocked, has appearance of hairlessness and feels like chamois; velour, born with bald spot on top of head, body has wavy coat that gradually disappears; brush, bristly, soft, wiry, or wavy coat on most of body, not eligible for show classes.

PERSONALITY

Gregarious, very affectionate, very playful, energetic, charismatic, devoted, loyal, easygoing, very intelligent, curious

THERE IS SIMPLY NO MISTAKING THIS BREED, with its striking combination of hairlessness and wrinkles. This is a cat with enormous personality, full of charisma and charm, which will win one's heart in an instant. The Don Sphynx loves to play and will entertain itself with endless games if no one is around to join in. It is just as happy to curl up on one's lap though, and it feels warm and soft to the touch. Generally Don Sphynx are extremely outgoing and friendly cats that will get on with other animals and visitors alike.

The defining physical feature of the Don Sphynx is its coat, or lack thereof, and this is caused by a dominant hairless gene. It should be noted that the Sphynx and the Don Sphynx are completely unrelated; the Sphynx's hairlessness is caused by a recessive gene. The Don Sphynx can have one of four coat varieties: born bald; flocked, with the appearance of hairlessness and the feel of chamois; velour, meaning that it is born with a bald spot on top of its head, while the body has wavy coat that gradually disappears; and brush, with a bristly, soft, wiry, or wavy coat on most of its body. Its skin is particularly distinctive, being extremely elastic and having pronounced wrinkles

on the cheeks, jowls, and under its chin. Vertical wrinkles run down its forehead between its ears and spread into thick horizontal lines above the eyebrows. The base of the neck also has deep wrinkles, as does the chest area, around the base of the tail, the underbelly, and the front and undersides of the legs. Like humans, the Don Sphynx can be prone to sunburn.

The Don Sphynx breed came into being by accident, and owes its origins to the compassion of Elena Kovaleva, a professor at the State Pedagogical Institute in Rostov-on-Don in the Southern Federal District of Russia. One day in 1986 Elena was returning home when she encountered a group of young boys playing soccer with a sack in a local playground. Elena heard a terrible mewling and realized that they had a kitten in the bag. She retrieved the bag from the boys and took the kitten home with her, naming her Varvara. The little tortoiseshell kitten was thought to be about three to four months old when Elena rescued her and appeared to be in perfect health other than her scare. However, not long after her rescue, she began to lose her hair and Elena embarked on a series of visits to the veterinarian to try to determine why. After many tests and expensive courses of treatment, and with Varvara still appearing to be fine in herself, the veterinarian suggested they leave her alone to see what happened.

Over the next couple of years Varvara continued to lose her hair, but remained in all other respects in perfect health. Elena was by now very attached to and proud of her little cat and when in 1989 a cat show was held in her home town, she persuaded her friend Irina Nemykina and her daughter Inna to take Varvara along. The charming little cat was poorly received, much to Elena and Irina's chagrin, so the next time a cat show was held Elena decided to enter Varvara herself. By this time she had lost nearly all of her coat and had only a little fur on her tail, legs, and behind her ears. Elena had heard about hairless cats called Sphynx that had been developed in Canada relatively recently, and

when she got to the cat show she described her cat as a "sphynx." No one there had heard about these cats and she was not believed.

In 1990 Varvara was bred to a neighbor's cat, a European domestic shorthair, and produced a litter of kittens. Elena gave one of the kittens, a female with a brushy coat to Irina Nemykina, who called her Chita. Chita began to lose her hair, as did her litter-mate Patchy. Elena and Irina took Chita, Patchy, and Varvara to the next cat show, where it was realized that these were not sick, but exhibiting a new trait; they were awarded a prize at the show. This inspired Irina Nemykina to start breeding Chita to try to develop this new hairless cat. Chita initially bred with a stray tomcat. The resulting four male kittens all had her original brushy coat, but after two months began to lose their hair. Next Irina bred Chita to a smoky blue tabby called Dima, with whom she produced three litters. All the kittens exhibited the same coat and hair loss with one exception—a female kitten in the third litter was born completely bald.

This little bald female went to live with Irina Katzer in St. Petersburg, who also owned one of her brothers from a previous litter, Anton Mif. Brother and sister were bred together and the resulting litter again had a single hairless kitten, a male called Viscount Mif. Other breeders became interested and the unusual hairless cats started to develop as a breed. Irina Nemykina named the new breed Don after the river Don, near where Varvara had been rescued, and Sphynx after the hairless cats of Canada and America. Given the genetic difference between the Sphynx and the Don Sphynx, some breeders began to call them either Donskoys, Don Hairless, or Russian Hairless. However the majority of breeders favor the name Don Sphynx. These cats are recognized by The International Cat Association (TICA) as a preliminary new breed (called Donskoy); all other registries recognize them as Don Sphynx.

Don Sphynx kittens are very delicate. They are born with their eyes open and need to be weighed daily and sometimes bottle-fed to maintain their weight. These are very family-oriented cats. The father will comfort the mother before she goes into labor and will be very loving and nurturing with the kittens once they are born. Kittens are nursed and nurtured within their family group until they are around three months old, and even older unrelated Dons, both male and female, will help to nurture the kittens.

SELKIRK REX

MODERN — UNITED STATES — UNCOMMON

APPEARANCE
Fairly substantial and of semi-cobby type with good musculature and relatively heavy boning. Rectangular in shape with medium-length legs; front legs slightly shorter than hind. Paws large and round. Head is broad and rounded with short, squarish muzzle and full cheeks. Medium-sized ears set well apart; eyes are large and round with color no relation to coat color.

Tail is medium length and tapers to a rounded tip.

SIZE
Medium

COAT
Longhaired has thick, soft, and plush coat with loose individual curls. Shorthaired has medium-length coat also thick, soft, and plush with curls present.

PERSONALITY
Patient, affectionate, people oriented, tolerant, easygoing

THE SELKIRK REX is often referred to as the "cat in sheep's clothing," and it is easy to see why. It has a wonderful soft, curly coat, either long- or shorthaired. This is combined with a patient and loving nature, derived from the British and American Shorthair in the breed's early foundations, along with Persians and Exotics. Selkirks are very sociable cats and thrive on feline or human company, though they do not do well on their own for long periods of time.

The Selkirk Rex owes its existence to Jeri Newman, a Persian breeder of Livingston, Montana, in the United States. Jeri received a phone call in 1987 from a shelter about an unusual, curly-coated kitten looking for a home. Jeri collected the kitten, which she called Miss DePesto (Pest). It occurred to Jeri that Miss DePesto may have represented a new spontaneous genetic mutation, perhaps different from the Cornish and Devon Rex. This was later confirmed by geneticist Roy Robinson, who reported on the differences between the breeds to the Cat Fanciers' Association (CFA).

Jeri set about a breeding program to see if she could recreate Pest's coat and personality, but add substance and frame. She bred Pest to her Persian male, Ch Photofinish of Deekay, and the resulting litter of kittens contained three curly coated and three straight coated. This percentage indicated that the curly coat was caused by a dominant gene—unlike the Devon and Cornish Rex coat, which is caused by a recessive gene. One of the kittens, NoFace

Oscar Kowalski, represented the type that Jeri wanted to produce; he was heavier in frame than his mother and was black and white with white, curly whiskers and eyebrows. Jeri bred Oscar to Persians, British Shorthairs, and Exotics, and back to his mother Pest. This latter breeding produced four kittens, three curly coated and one straight coated. NoFace Gracie Slick, one of the curly-coated kittens, went to Mary Harrington in Switzerland and was featured in an article in the French cat magazine *Atout Chat*. This created a stir in the French cat fancy world and Gracie was bought by Regine Lohre (Cattery du Clos des Anges) where she became the foundation for the breed in France. Through her progeny the breed was established in Germany.

Pest, the founder of the breed in the United States, was only bred five times (one being an accident), and of her progeny just fifteen went on to be registered with the CFA, making the original gene pool small. Jeri and a small group of breeders worked hard to produce a consistent type—one that most closely resembled the British Shorthair in the body. Jeri chose Selkirk as the name of the breed in honor of her stepfather whose family name was Selkirk. Rex was added to describe the curly coat. The fledgling breed was presented to The International Cat Association (TICA) in 1990 and was accepted into the new breed and color class; it was advanced to championship status in 1994. The CFA accepted the breed into their miscellaneous class in 1992 and awarded championship status in 2000.

The breed first arrived in England in 2002, with three kittens being imported from the Austrian breeders Christiana and Karl Aichner. One female went to breeder Lisa Peterson (Trueblu Cattery), who was a driving force in getting the breed established in the United Kingdom and provided many other British breeders with foundation stock. Lisa later moved to Australia and is a noted breeder of the Selkirk Rex there under the Islarey prefix. The breed was recognized by the General Council of the Cat Fancy (GCCF) in 2003, and gained championship status in 2009.

TOYGER

MODERN — UNITED STATES — RARE

APPEARANCE

Like a small toy tiger with beautiful, glistening, glittered coat. Long and muscular body, deep chest, strongly built without being cobby. Long, muscular neck, medium length legs of equal height in front and hind; paws appear large with long toes. Rolling gait. Tail is very long with blunt tip, set and carried low. Longer face with an inverted heart-shaped muzzle, puffy whisker pads. Small ears with rounded tip and thick fur covering. Eyes are small to medium, hooding to eyelids and rounded with rich deep color.

SIZE

Medium

COAT

Short, thick, luxurious, and soft coat with some "glittering." Brown mackerel tabby in color with dark markings on brilliant orange background or silver with light basecoat with black markings. Unique coat pattern of broken or branched vertical stripes in random pattern. Facial markings should have circular pattern to cheeks and chevron markings on forehead.

PERSONALITY

Easygoing, affectionate, playful, intelligent, sociable, very trainable

THE TOYGER IS A DESIGNER CAT, very specifically created through extremely considered breeding. This lovely cat has the appearance of a tiny tiger in its distinctive coat markings, which are unique to the breed. Also reminiscent of the tiger is the glittering sheen of its coat, and its slightly rolling gait, with the tail carried low. The Toyger, however, has a charming temperament and is a wonderful addition to any cat-loving home. It is easygoing and gregarious, accepting other cats and dogs in the household and enjoying a riotous game. Lively and playful, the Toyger is also relatively easy to train (for a cat) and can be coaxed into walking on a leash or engaging in games of fetch.

The breed owes its development to Judy Sugden (EEYAA Cattery), the daughter of noted U.S. cat breeder Jean Sugden Mill, who was the driving force behind establishing the Bengal cat. During the 1980s when the Bengal breeding program was in full swing, Judy was also actively trying to improve the clarity of mackerel markings in the domestic tabby. At this time there was a great interest in purchasing exotic (basically wild) cats for the domestic environment, driven primarily by their beautiful coats and markings. While some people provided proper care and housing for these cats, many were not able to cope with their needs and temperament. In addition there was an alarming decrease in some populations of exotics in the wild, through illegal hunting for pelts and partly due to the pet trade. Breeders like Judy Sugden and her mother were attempting to create a totally domestic cat with the appearance of an exotic cat, to fill a market need and protect wild populations.

Two cats of great significance early in the Toyger development were a striped domestic shorthair called Scrapmetal, who had uniform tabby stripes and dorsal stripe, and a large Bengal called Millwood Rumpled Spotskin. Judy, supported by other breeders such as Anthony Hutcherson of JungleTrax Cattery and Alice McKee of Windridge Cattery, spent years trying to establish the correct body type and unique markings now seen in the Toyger. In 1993 Judy imported Jammu Blu, a street cat from Kashmir, in the north of the Indian subcontinent, who had beautiful (and unusual) spots between his ears. She used him in her breeding program. Even now there is very careful ongoing breeding to fix the tiger characteristics in this domestic breed, which contains no wild blood at all. In 1993 The International Cat Association (TICA) accepted the breed, then known as the Californian Toyger. It was not until 2007 that TICA awarded them championship status.

Toygers first arrived in the United Kingdom in 2004 when British breeder Gaynor Jean-Louis of Queenanne Cats imported a male and female directly from Judy Sugden. Gaynor was the first person outside the United States to breed Toygers. Her two imported cats were a male, Eeyaa Thunder and female, Eeyaa Aglow. Aglow was already pregnant when she was shipped to Gaynor, and shortly after her arrival produced four stunning kittens. One of the males from this litter, Queenanne Tobias, was shipped to Dee Zimmer in Australia; Dee became the first breeder of Toygers in Australia under the name Xquizit Toygers. There are now several breeders worldwide, although breed numbers of these amazing cats are still relatively low.

PETERBALD

MODERN – RUSSIA – RARE

APPEARANCE
Long, slender, and generally appears hairless. Graceful, lean body with long, medium- to fine-boned legs; hind legs slightly longer than front. Medium-sized, oval paws with long, prominent toes. Tail is long, very slender, and whippy. Head is long, inverted triangle with flat forehead and high cheekbones. Ears are very large, pointed at tip, and broad at base; eyes are medium sized and almost almond shaped, color has no relation to coat color.

SIZE
Medium

COAT
Bald, which ranges from ultra-bald to flock to velour. Can also have a brush coat, which is dense and wiry of irregular texture.

PERSONALITY
Vivacious, highly affectionate, very intelligent, playful, active, prone to comic behavior, extremely sociable

THE DISTINGUISHING FEATURE OF THE PETERBALD is of course its coat, or lack of it, but this is also a captivating cat that exudes personality. It is very interactive and loves nothing better than a long game with its owner followed by a sleep on its owner's lap or shoulders. It seems to possess a sense of humor, engaging in comic turns, flying leaps, and balletic behavior. It thrives in company and is not happy on its own for long periods; it will firmly became a key member of a family and delight in as much attention as possible. That said, it is not demanding in an obsessive manner, but will most often get what it wants in the end!

The Peterbald coat is caused by a hair-losing gene rather than a hairless gene. The Peterbald can be either bald or have a brush coat. It is the bald variety for which the breed is best known, ranging from ultra-bald to flocked and velour. Ultra-bald Peterbalds are born without any coat, eyebrows, or whiskers and never grow any. They are warm and soft to the touch with the skin having a slightly sticky feel, like chamois. Flocked Peterbalds are about 90 percent hairless, although they may have a light down on their extremities. Their eyebrows and whiskers are curled, kinked, or broken. Their skin has a silky-smooth feel. The velour Peterbald is about 70 percent hairless. Its coat has a suede-like feel; from a distance it appears hairless, but if the coat is dense the cat has a very sleek and shiny look. As

these cats age they may lose their coat. The second type of Peterbald is the brush coated. Brush-coated Peterbalds are covered in wiry hair to less than one-quarter of an inch (5 mm) long, varying from wavy to curly. The coat should be dense and irregular in texture ranging from coarse to smooth; this is a unique coat not seen in any other breed and should not feel like a normal cat coat. Occasionally Peterbalds will exhibit a combination of coat types, having a brush coat on their extremities and a flocked coat on their body, for example. Very occasionally, straight-coated Peterbalds are found that do not have the hair-loss gene.

The Peterbald was developed in St. Petersburg in the 1990s through crossing another Russian breed, the Donskoy, with an Oriental Shorthair. The foundation cats are a male brown mackerel tabby Donskoy and a female tortie Oriental, both bred by the Russian breeder Olga S. Mironova. These cats produced four kittens. One, a male called Nocturne, was widely bred to pedigreed Oriental and Siamese females, producing quality offspring. The new cats were a great success in St. Petersburg, where they quickly earned the name Peterbald. In 1996 they were accepted into the Russian Selectional Feline Federation; in 1997 they were accepted by The International Cat Association (TICA) into new breed status, and upgraded to championship status in 2005. The Peterbald brush coat division was accepted into TICA for championship status in May 2008.

To keep the gene pool healthy on this young breed, Peterbalds are still crossbred to Donskoy as well as Orientals and Siamese, and so a wide range of colors is found. An outcross that is not allowed is to the Sphynx. Although the Sphynx and the Peterbald appear to have hairlessness as a similarity, they are not at all alike in body shape or, most significantly, on a genetic level. The Sphynx's hairlessness is caused by a recessive gene, while the hairlessness of the Peterbald is caused by an essentially dominant gene. Crossing the two results in full-coated kittens and offers no benefit to either breed.

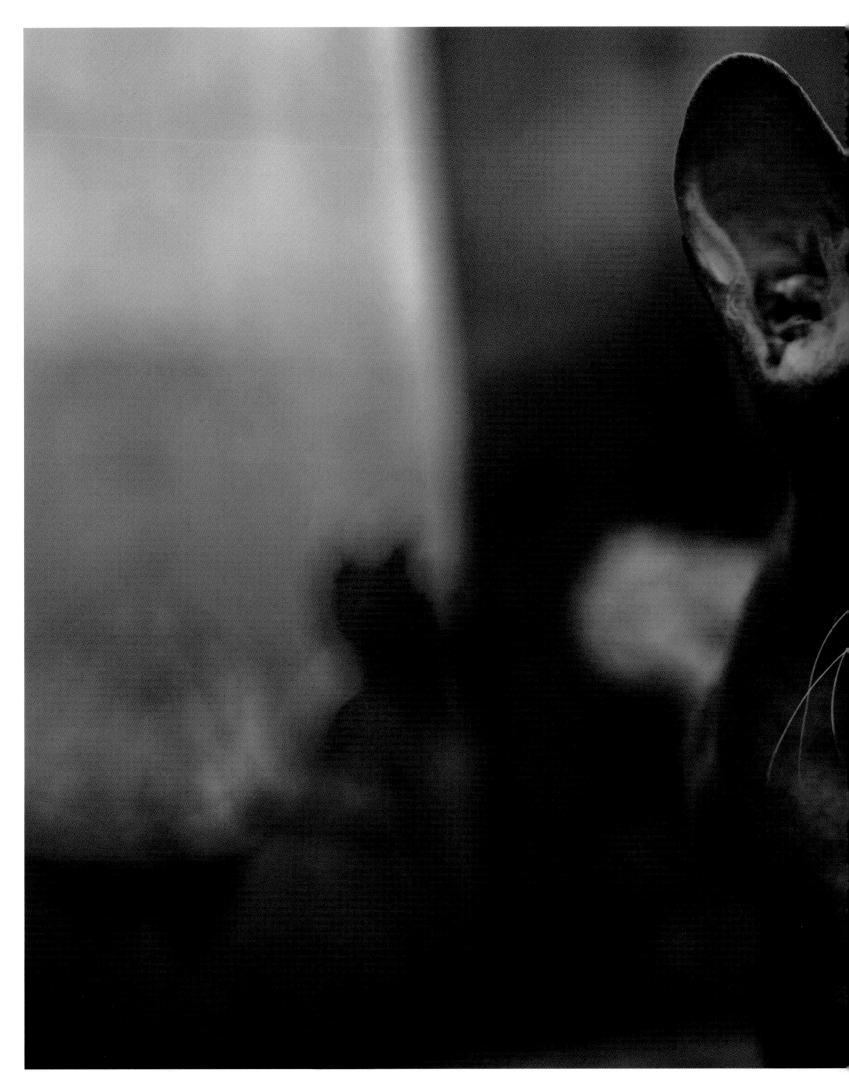

RAGAMUFFIN

MODERN – UNITED STATES – MODERATE

APPEARANCE

Substantial cat with luxurious, thick fur, and sweet expression. Rectangular body, broad chest and shoulders, solid boning, and moderately heavy musculature. Fatty pad to lower abdomen, ribs and spine well covered with flesh. Legs are medium to medium long and heavily boned; back legs slightly longer than front. Paws are large and round with tufts of hair between toes. Long tail is fully furred and plumelike. Head is a broad, modified wedge with rounded appearance. Broad, slightly short muzzle, full cheeks, and puffy whisker pads. In profile

nose has obvious dip. Medium-sized ears tilt forward slightly with furnishings. Eyes are large, walnut shaped, and moderately wide set. Intense color preferred.

SIZE

Large

COAT

Medium to medium long, soft, thick, and silky to touch. Longer hair forms ruff round neck, hair on front legs shorter than hind. Any color or pattern accepted (varies in different associations).

PERSONALITY

Sweet, kind, gentle, very affectionate, playful, easygoing, gregarious

THERE IS SOMETHING INSTANTLY CAPTIVATING about the RagaMuffin, which is a bundle of purring fur. A large cat, the RagaMuffin does not fully mature until it is about four years old, and the male will normally be considerably larger than the female. This cat possesses a particularly equable temperament and is extremely affectionate, very loyal, and easygoing, making it an ideal family pet. Although quiet, it is far from lazy and loves a serious play session, as long as it is followed by a dedicated nap. The RagaMuffin is very striking in appearance with its beautiful, soft coat and plumed tail. Its coat does not require extensive grooming.

The RagaMuffin shares a common origin with the Ragdoll breed that was developed during the 1960s by Ann Baker of Riverside, California. In an unusual step, Baker decided to take control of the Ragdoll breed; she established her own registry, the International Ragdoll Cat Association (IRCA), and developed strict rules for anyone wishing to breed Ragdolls. These control measures were bitterly opposed by a number of breeders, who split from Baker and began to make their own breeding choices; they further developed the Ragdoll and eventually gained mainstream recognition for the breed.

In 1994 another group of Ragdoll breeders, led by Janet Klarmann, Curt Gehm, and Kim Clark, attempted to persuade Ann Baker to retire so they could take control of the IRCA and steer the breed back in a more healthy direction. Sadly Baker was unable to relinquish control and so the group left the registry; they were required to find a new name for their cats, which now included all colors and patterns. The name RagaMuffin was initially put forward rather jokily by Curt Gehm, but the name stuck (with the M capitalized), and seemed to aptly describe these lovely cats. To increase the rather diminished gene pool, breeders sensibly outcrossed to Persians, Himalayans, and domestic longhairs, which has resulted in physical differences between the Ragdoll and the RagaMuffin, and a more robust cat. The RagaMuffin Associated Group (RAG), the parent club for the new breed, was established in 1997; Janet Klarmann was a driving force and the first president of the club, serving from 1997 to 2008.

The United Feline Organization (UFO) was the first association to recognize the RagaMuffin; it is also recognized by the American Cat Fanciers Association (ACFA). Laura Gregory (Ragtime Cats) was a leading force in gaining recognition with the Cat Fanciers' Association (CFA). The CFA accepted the breed into the miscellaneous class in 2003; in 2009 it was advanced to provisional, and in 2011 it achieved championship status. The CFA does not accept pointed colors to emphasize the difference from the Ragdoll. Some major organizations do not recognize the RagaMuffin due to its similarity to the Ragdoll.

The breed is well supported in the United Kingdom and is promoted by the U.K. RagaMuffin Cat Society. The RagaMuffin was recognized by the Governing Council of the Cat Fancy (GCCF) in 2010, when it was granted preliminary recognition. Breeders are now working toward having this status advanced; they do not allow any crossbreeding between RagaMuffins and Ragdolls to maintain the separateness of each breed.

SERENGETI

MODERN – UNITED STATES – RARE

APPEARANCE
Statuesque with upright posture and large, round-tipped ears. Solidly built and of semi-foreign type, athletic through frame, muscular, and long legged with medium boning; paws are medium sized and oval. Tail is medium short, thick, and tapers slightly to the end. Head set on a long, thick neck. Head is longer than it is wide and a modified wedge shape with a moderately wide nose. Eyes are large and round, gold or yellow preferred, hazel to light green allowed. Ears are large and equal in height to the length of face; broad at base and round tipped, set to the top of head, and upright.

SIZE
Medium

COAT
Short and even with silky texture. Must be spotted tabby with any shade of brown and high contrast between ground color and spots, can be glittering; solid black, ghost spots may be visible; silver smoke with black spots on silvery body.

PERSONALITY
Very active and curious, highly affectionate, loyal, playful, can be shy with strangers

BEAUTY, ELEGANCE, AND BOTTOMLESS AFFECTION are all rolled into one amazing package with the Serengeti, which must certainly be one of the more striking cat breeds. These gorgeous cats are highly distinctive and unusual in their appearance, particularly in their very upright posture, which recalls ancient statuary, as do their very large, upright, and alert ears. This, combined with their silky coats and stunning pattern, lends the Serengeti the appearance of a wildcat that has simply strolled into the home. In fact, and unlike the Savannah, no wildcats were used directly in breeding the Serengeti; it is a breed that has been entirely "man-made" using domestic crosses.

Serengetis make a delightful addition to any home, and while they might initially be shy with strangers—not always a bad thing—they are extremely affectionate with their loved ones, and very reliant on their human family for both companionship and love. They are also relatively vocal cats and love a good discussion with anyone who is willing to listen—and perhaps even with those who are not. Given their athletic appearance, it is unsurprising that these cats are also extremely agile and active, prone to vigorous play sessions and even a little showing off!

The breed owes its development to one woman in the first instance, Karen Sausman of Kingsmark Cattery, California, who began her breeding program in 1994. Karen, who is also a conservation biologist, wanted to create an entirely domestic breed of cat that conjured up such wildcats as the African Serval in appearance, without using wildcat blood in the process. As it turned out, although she had plans in place to begin this breeding program, her very first "Serengeti" was the product of an accident; one of her male Oriental kittens called Shetani managed to successfully breed a female Bengal when he was only five months old, and without Karen's knowledge! Shetani later became important in the breed foundation.

Karen based her program primarily on crossing Bengals with Oriental Shorthairs, although she also used other cats when they exhibited the traits she was wishing to reproduce and fix in the emerging Serengeti breed. Some of the foundation cats of the breed were the Bengals, Leopardlane Zulieka, Kingsmark Emir, and Joykatz Black Jag, and the Orientals, Andiescats Shetani, Andiescats Magpie, Andiescats Dobro Man, and Pizzaz Sweet Mister. The "wild" element of the breed's appearance is mostly derived from the use of Bengal cats in its foundation; the Bengal has the wild Asian Leopard Cat crossed with a variety of domestic breeds at its foundation. In particular Karen chose for her breeding Bengals that exhibited a longer leg in proportion to their body, large, round eyes, and random clear spotting in their coats. She chose Orientals with a spotted pattern, ebony silver, or solid ebony and with ears set higher on their heads than Oriental breeders would want.

The development of a new breed takes time and enormous care and dedication, and it is still an ongoing process. It took several litters before the features emerged that Karen wished to "fix" for the breed; these were the longer leg length and the higher ear set. Taking these features and making them more extreme, however, takes many generations. The hardest element has been fixing high-contrast spotting due to the ticking present in the Oriental side of the family. Once Karen had begun the process it was necessary to try and involve other breeders in the project to widen the gene pool and help further the breed's development. Another early breeder who joined with Karen is Lynn Palmer (now Bundy) of the Mystic Hills Bengal Cattery in Bozeman, Montana, and her help as a major breeder for The International Cat Association (TICA) was invaluable in establishing the breed. Other significant breeders in the United States who have been or remain involved with the Serengeti are Susan Karakash, Michelle Bryant, Dr. Susan Sehn, Rise Mikolowski, Pat Killmaier, and Anthony Hutcherson.

Several breeders had begun to work with the Serengeti in the United Kingdom by the early 2000s, including Paul Starling Ozalet. Breeders have begun their own lines using British Bengal and Oriental Shorthair, as well as some early lines including Siamese in their background; TICA initially allowed this as an acceptable outcross, though this is no longer the case. When Paul passed away unexpectedly in 2004, his breeding stock passed to Lesley and Emily Dart (Neverneverland Cattery and Littlefancy Cattery). Lesley had first come across the breed in 2003 and had been instantly captivated. In 2007 she was one of the first to import Serengeti from the United States, and acquired the female Kingsmark Shakeria Stardust direct from Karen Sausman; Stardust quickly went on to have a litter of kittens. Karen exported several of her young adult Serengetis to the United Kingdom in 2007, 2008, and 2010, including Kingsmark Baraka and Spotsonthelake Cougar of Kingsmark. Other British breeders who have contributed to establishing the breed are Sue Threapleton and Janice Boden.

Karen Sausman also sent some of her Kingsmark Serengetis as foundation stock to breeders in Germany, Austria, Russia, and Canada from 2006 onward. Serengetis are now registered with TICA in their preliminary new breed category and can be shown in these classes, which is also bringing them greater exposure to the public and other judges. Breeders are now working towards the Serengeti being advanced to championship status.

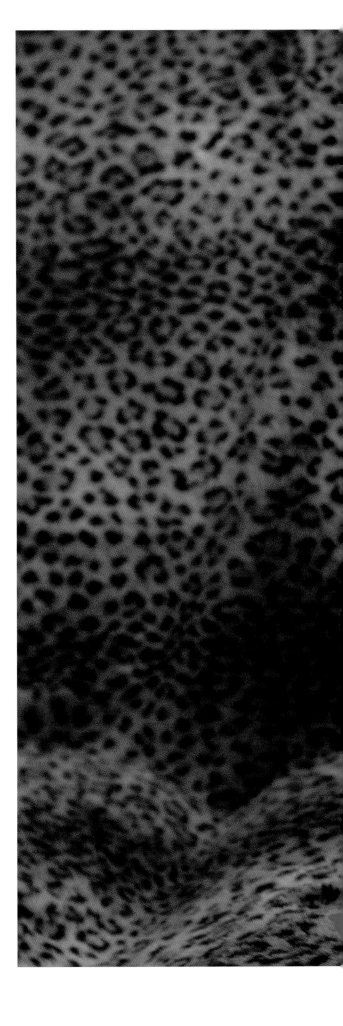

INDEX

Abandonment of Animals
    Act 1960 162
Abyssinian 21, 51, 85, 91,
    114–17, 136, 148, 161, 187,
    188, 209
allergies 154, 162, 194
American Bobtail 161, 192–3
American Cat Association
    (ACA)
    Snowshoe 183
American Cat Fanciers'
    Association (ACFA)
    Bengal 215
    Cornish Rex 167
    RagaMuffin 275
    Singapura 226
American Curl 221, 228–31
American Shorthair 46, 84,
    96–9, 154, 156, 161, 167,
    170, 179, 183, 188, 205, 259
American Wirehair 161,
    204–5
Amsterdam 222–3
Animal Boarding
    Establishments Act 1963
    162
Animal Welfare Act (US)
    1966 162
Antarctic bases 120
archaeology 20, 22, 29
artistic representations 20,
    21, 22, 23, 51, 83
Atout Chat 259
Australian National Cats
    (ANCATS)
    Snowshoe 184

Baker, Ann 174, 275
Balinese 60, 121, 124–7, 136
Barrymore, John 120
Bastet 21–2, 25
Battersea Dogs and Cats
    Home, London 120

Baudelaire, Charles 85
Bengal 161, 212–19, 249, 275
bird populations 223
Birman 23, 72–5
Black Death 82
Bobcat (Lynx rufus) 104,
    193, 221, 245
bobtail cats
    American Bobtail 192–3
    Japanese Bobtail 23, 50–3,
        193
    Kurillian Bobtail 112–13
    Pixiebob 221, 244–7
Bombay 121, 156–9, 167
Book of Rites 23
Brewer, Carol Ann 245
British Havana 142, 147
British Longhair 46
British Museum, London 119
British Shorthair 22, 34,
    44–9, 91, 100, 118, 156,
    167, 169, 170, 259
Buffon, Comte de Histoire
    Naturelle 100
burials 20, 22, 82
Burmese 46, 60, 121,
    128–33, 154, 156, 161, 167,
    179, 198
Byron, Lord George 85

Canadian Cat Association
    201
Canadian Hairless Cat see
    Sphynx
Carroll, Lewis Alice's
    Adventures in Wonderland
    45
Carter, Jimmy 60
cartoon cats 163, 221
Cat Aficionado Association
    56
Cat Book Poems (Tamra
    Maew) 23, 59, 67, 122, 129

Cat Fanciers' Association
    (CFA) 51, 119
    American Curl 228, 231
    American Shorthair 96
    American Wirehair 205
    Balinese 125
    Bengal 215
    Birman 75
    Bombay 156
    Burmese 129, 130
    Chinese Li Hua 54, 56
    Colorpoint Shorthair 136
    Cornish Rex 154
    Devon Rex 167
    Egyptian Mau 26
    Exotic Shorthair 179
    Havana Brown 147
    Himalayan 135
    Javanese 127, 136
    LaPerm 232, 235
    Maine Coon 107
    Manx 34
    Ocicat 188
    Oriental 142
    RagaMuffin 275
    Ragdoll 177
    Russian Blue 92
    Scottish Fold 170
    Selkirk Rex 259
    Siamese 59, 122
    Singapura 225, 226
    Snowshoe 183, 184
    Somali 148
    Sphynx 194–7
    Tonkinese 201
    Turkish Angora 89
Cat Fanciers' Federation 125,
    183
cat food 163
cat litter 162
cat sanctuaries 222–3
Cat, African (Felis sylvestris
    lybica) 20, 25, 77, 115

Caffre 115
Chinese Mountain (Felis
    sylvestris bieti) 54
Egyptian Spotted Fishing
    187
Jungle (Felis chaus) 161,
    206–9
Leopard (Prionailurus
    bengalensis) 161, 212–15,
    216, 279
Pallas's (Octolobus manul)
    77
cats 18–19
    1960 to 1969 160–3
    1970 to present 220–3
    ancient history 20–3
    crossbreeding 220–1
    late nineteenth century to
        1959 118–21
    Middle Ages to nineteenth
        century 82–5
Cats Protection 162
Centerwall, Dr Willard
    212–15
Champion, D. B. Everybody's
    Cat Book 81
Chartreux 46, 82, 100–3
Chausie 161, 206–11, 249
Chestnut Foreign Shorthair
    141, 147
China 82–3
Chinese Li Hua 23, 54–7
Churchill, Sir Winston 120,
    162–3
Clinton, Bill 222
Cobb, Cora 241–2
Colorpoint Persian 135
Colorpoint Shorthair 60,
    121, 127, 136–9, 141
Conroy, Margaret 198–201
Cornish Rex 121, 152–5,
    164, 197, 205, 221, 235, 259
Cox, Beryl 164

Crusades 22, 29, 82, 100
Crystal Palace Cat Show
  1871 40, 45, 59, 81, 91, 115,
  118
curly-haired cats
  American Wirehair 161,
    204–5
  Cornish Rex 121, 152–5,
    164, 197, 205, 221, 235,
    259
  Devon Rex 161, 164–7, 205,
    221, 235, 259
  LaPerm 221, 232–7
  Selkirk Rex 221, 258–61,
    235
Cymric 23, 32–5

Daly, Virginia 187–8
Dante Alighieri 82
Darwin, Charles 77
della Valle, Pietro 78, 86
Devon Rex 161, 164–7, 205,
  221, 235, 259
Dickens, Charles 85
DNA 23
Domestic Shorthair 96
domestication 20–1
Don Sphynx 221, 254–7
Donskoy 268
double-coated cats
  Manx 23, 32–5, 51, 91, 118,
    170, 193
  Nebelung 221, 240–3
  Norwegian Forest Cat 23,
    36–9, 86, 104
  Russian Blue 46, 85, 90–5,
    100, 118, 141, 147, 179,
    221, 241
Downing Street, London
  222
Dumas, Alexander 85
dwarf cats
  Munchkin 221, 238–9

Egypt, ancient 20–2, 115,
  206
Egyptian Mau 21, 22, 24–7,
  216
Exotic Shorthair 178–81,
  259

Fédération Internationale
  Féline (FIFe) 119
  Bengal 216
  Norwegian Forest Cat 38
  Snowshoe 184
  Sokoke 30
Feline Defense League 85
feline infectious peritonitis
  242
feline leukemia 212–15
feral cats 222–3
films 163, 221
Ford, Gerald 60
Foreign White 141
Freret, Elizabeth 51
fur 82, 91, 100

Gainsborough, Thomas 107,
  264
genetic drift 22
genetic mutations 160–1
genetic studies 20, 21, 23,
  212
  American Curl 228–31
  American Wirehair 205
  Burmese 129
  Cornish Rex 152
  Munchkin 239
  Ocicat 187
  Persian 81
  Ragdoll 177
  Scottish Fold 161, 169,
    170
  Sokoke 30
Gethers, Peter The Cat Who
  Went to Paris 170

Governing Council of the
  Cat Fancy (GCCF) 60, 118
  Balinese 127
  Bengal 216
  Birman 75
  British Shorthair 46
  Burmese 130
  Cornish Rex 154
  Devon Rex 167
  Havana Brown 147
  Himalayan 135
  Japanese Bobtail 51
  Maine Coon 107
  Nebelung 242
  Ocicat 188
  Oriental 141–2
  Persian 77
  RagaMuffin 275
  Ragdoll 177
  Russian Blue 91
  Scottish Fold 170
  Selkirk Rex 259
  Siamese 59
  Singapura 226
  Snowshoe 184
  Sphynx 197
  Tonkinese 201
  Turkish Van 29
Gray, Thomas On a
  Favourite Cat 85
Greece, ancient 22, 25

hairless cats 221
  Don Sphynx 221, 254–7
  Peterbald 221, 268–73
  Sphynx 161, 167, 194–7,
    221, 268
Halliday, Sonia 29
Harper's Weekly 115
Havana Brown 121, 141, 142,
  146–7, 154, 198
Hayes, Rutherford B. 60
Henry VIII 84

Hermitage Museum, St
  Petersburg 222
Herodotus 21
Himalayan 43, 60, 77, 121,
  134–5, 179, 275
Hindley, Greta 122
Hochendel, Sandra 239
Holland, Sylvia 125
Horner, Nikki 156
hotel cats 120

International Cat
  Association, The see TICA
IUCN (International Union
  for Conservation of
  Nature) 206

James VI and I 84
Japanese Bobtail 23, 50–3,
  193
Javanese 60, 121, 127, 136
Jennings, John Domestic and
  Fancy Cats 40
Johnson, Samuel 85
Journal of Heredity 129, 231

Karelian Bobtail 112
Keats, John 85
Kelley, Patrick 250
Kennedy, John F. 162
Koehl, Linda 232
Korat 23, 66–71, 129
Kotofei Cat Club 43
Kovaleva, Elena 254–6
Kurilian Bobtail 112–13

LaPerm 221, 232–7
Lear, Edward 85
Leonardo da Vinci 84
Lewis Hind, C. Turner's
  Golden Visions 34
Life 152
Lilac Havana 141, 147

long-haired cats 22–3, 120–1
American Curl 221,
228–31
Birman 23, 72–5
British Longhair 46
China 78
Cymric 34
Himalayan 43, 60, 77, 121,
134–5, 179, 275
Kurilian Bobtail 112–13
Maine Coon 104–11
Munchkin 221, 238–9
Nebelung 221, 240–3
Norwegian Forest Cat 23,
36–9, 86, 104
Persian 22–3, 46, 76–81,
86–9, 100, 104, 118, 121,
135, 174, 179, 259, 275
Pixiebob 221, 244–7
Siberian 23, 40–3, 86
Turkish Angora 77, 78, 81,
84, 86–9, 104–7, 174
Turkish Van 22, 28–9
Longhair 60, 77
Longhaired Colorpoint 135,
193
Loxton, Howard *Guide to the
Cats of the World* 169
Lushington, Laura 29

Mague, Evelyn 148
Maine Coon 84, 85, 104–11
mammal populations 223
Maneki-Neko 23, 51
Manx 23, 32–5, 51, 91, 118,
170, 193
Mayflower 84, 96
Meadow, Hal and Tommy
225, 226
medium-haired cats
American Bobtail 161,
192–3
Balinese 60, 121, 124–7,
136

Chartreux 46, 82, 100–3
Egyptian Mau 21, 22, 24–7,
216
Exotic Shorthair 178–81,
259
Havana Brown 121, 141,
142, 146–7, 154, 198
Japanese Bobtail 23, 50–3,
193
RagaMuffin 221, 274–7
Ragdoll 161, 174–7, 275
Scottish Fold 161, 168–73,
228
Somali 121, 148–51, 235
Tonkinese 60, 129, 161,
198–203
military uses 119–20
Mill, Jean Sugden 212,
215–16, 263
Moeldrup, Gloria 30
Moncrif, François Augustin
de Paradis de *Histoire des
Chats* 85
Moonstone Cat *see* Sphynx
mouse, house (*Mus
musculus*) 20, 119
Muhammad 86
Munchkin 221, 238–9

National Cat Fanciers'
Association (NCFA) 174
Nebelung 221, 240–3
neutering 162
New Zealand 223
Newman, Jeri 259
Nibelungenlied 241
Nightingale, Florence 85
Nordane, Carl Frederik 38
Norwegian Forest Cat 23,
36–9, 86, 104

Obama, Barack 221–2
Ocelot 161, 187, 215
Ocicat 60, 161, 186–91, 249

Ocicat Classic 188
Oriental 60, 121, 140–5, 268,
275, 280
Oriental Longhair 142

Pallas, Peter Simon 77
Parliament Hill, Ottawa 222
Pasteur, Louis 85
pedigrees 118
Peiresc, Nicolas Claude
Fabri de 86
persecution 82, 83–4
Persian 22–3, 46, 76–81,
86–9, 100, 104, 118, 121,
135, 174, 179, 259, 275
Peterbald 221, 268–73
Petrarch 82
Pflueger, Dr Solveig 177, 231,
235, 239, 241
Phoenicians 22, 23, 33
Pierce, F. R. 107
Pixiebob 221, 244–7
Post Office cats 119

RagaMuffin 221, 274–7
Ragdoll 161, 174–7, 275
Rama V of Siam 67
rats 82, 84, 119
Brown Rat 85
Red List 206
retrieving cats 25, 33
Richelieu, Armand Jean Du
Plessis, Cardinal de 84, 86
Robinson, Roy 231, 259
rodent control 20, 22, 23, 82,
84, 119, 120, 222
American Shorthair 96
Birman 75
British Shorthair 45
Chartreux 100
Chinese Li Hua 54
Japanese Bobtail 51
Maine Coon 104
Norwegian Forest Cat 37

Russian Blue 91
Siberian 40
Roman Empire 22, 25, 45
Rome, modern 222
Rudd, Kevin 222
Runas, Edel 38
Russian Blue 46, 85, 90–5,
100, 118, 141, 147, 179, 221,
241, 242
Russian Longhair 89
Russian Selectional Feline
Federation 268

Safari 215
Sausman, Karen 279–80
Savannah 248–53
Scott, Sir Walter 85
Scottish Fold 161, 168–73,
228
Selkirk Rex 221, 258–61,
235
Serengeti 221, 278–81
Serval 220, 249, 279
Shackleton, Ernest 120
Shelley, Percy Bysshe 85
short-haired cats
Abyssinian 21, 51, 85, 91,
114–17, 136, 148, 161, 187,
188, 209
American Curl 221,
228–31
American Shorthair 46, 84,
96–9, 154, 156, 161, 167,
170, 179, 183, 188, 205,
259
Bengal 161, 212–19, 249,
275
Bombay 121, 156–9, 167
British Shorthair 22, 34,
44–9, 91, 100, 118, 156,
167, 169, 170, 259
Burmese 46, 60, 121,
128–33, 154, 156, 161,
167, 179, 198

Chausie 161, 206–11, 249

Chinese Li Hua 23, 54–7

Colorpoint Shorthair 60, 121, 127, 136–9, 141

Korat 23, 66–71, 129

Kurilian Bobtail 112–13

Munchkin 221, 238–9

Ocicat 60, 161, 186–91, 249

Oriental 60, 121, 140–5, 268, 275, 280

Pixiebob 221, 244–7

Russian Blue 46, 85, 90–5, 100, 118, 141, 147, 179, 221, 241

Savannah 248–53

Serengeti 221, 278–81

Siamese 23, 58–65, 118, 121, 129, 135, 136, 141, 147, 154, 161, 167, 183, 187, 188, 198, 268

Singapura 221, 224–7

Snowshoe 60, 161, 182–5

Sokoke 20, 30–1

Thai 60, 121, 122–3

Toyger 221, 249, 262–7

shows 118–19

Siamese 23, 58–65, 118, 121, 129, 135, 136, 141, 147, 154, 161, 167, 183, 187, 188, 198, 268

Siberian 23, 40–3, 86

silkworms 23

Simpson, Frances *The Book of the Cat* 81, 91, 194

Singapura 221, 224–7

Skogkatt *see* Norwegian Forest Cat

Slater, Jeni 30

Snowshoe 60, 161, 182–5

Sokoke 20, 30–1

Somali 121, 148–51, 235

Southampton, Earl of 84–5

Soviet Felinology Federation 43

space exploration 160

spaying 162

Sphynx 161, 167, 194–7, 221, 268

spotted cats

Bengal 161, 212–19, 249, 275

Egyptian Mau 21, 22, 24–7, 216

Ocicat 60, 161, 186–91, 249

Pixiebob 221, 244–7

Savannah 248–53

Serengeti 221, 278–81

Sroufe, Joyce 250

Stirling-Webb, Brian 135, 141, 152–4, 164

striped cats

Toyger 221, 249, 262–7

Sugden, Judy 263

Surlusson, Snorri *Prose Edda* 37

swimming cats 29, 112

tailless cats 33–4

Manx 23, 32–5, 51, 91, 118, 170, 193

Thackeray, William Makepeace 85

Thai 60, 121, 122–3

theater cats 119

Theft Act 1968 162

Thompson, Dr Joseph 129

TICA

American Bobtail 193

American Curl 231

Bengal 216

Bombay 156

Chausie 209

Cornish Rex 154

Devon Rex 167

Don Sphynx 256

Exotic Shorthair 179

Havana Brown 147

Himalayan 135

LaPerm 235

Munchkin 239

Nebelung 241, 242

Oriental Longhair 142

Peterbald 268

Pixiebob 245

Ragdoll 177

Savannah 250

Scottish Fold 170

Selkirk Rex 259

Serengeti 280

Singapura 225

Snowshoe 184

Sokoke 30

Sphynx 197

Thai 122

Toyger 263

Tonkinese 60, 129, 161, 198–203

Topsell, Edward *The History of Four-footed Beasts* 84

Toyger 221, 249, 262–7

triple-coated cats

Siberian 23, 40–3, 86

Troubetskoy, Nathalie 25–6

Turkish Angora 77, 78, 81, 84, 86–9, 104–7, 174

Turkish Van 22, 28–9

Turner, J. M. W. 34

Twain, Mark 85

United Feline Organization (UFO) 275

Van Vechten, Carl *The Tiger in the House* 119

Victoria 81

Vikings 23, 33, 37, 104

Wain, Louis 69, 118

Wales 82

Walpole, Horace 85

water-loving cats 212

Chausie 161, 206–11, 249

Kurilian Bobtail 112–13

Maine Coon 84, 85, 104–11

Manx 23, 32–5, 51, 91, 118, 170, 193

Siberian 23, 40–3, 86

Turkish Van 22, 28–9

Weir, Harrison 45, 91, 212

Our Cats and All About Them 40, 81, 115, 118

wild cats

African Cat (*Felis sylvestris lybica*) 20, 25, 77, 115

Bobcat (*Lynx rufus*) 104, 193, 221, 245

Egyptian Spotted Fishing Cat 187

Chinese Mountain Cat (*Felis sylvestris bieti*) 54

Jungle Cat (*Felis chaus*) 161, 206–9

Leopard Cat (*Prionailurus bengalensis*) 161, 212–15, 216, 279

Ocelot 161, 187, 215

Pallas's Cat (*Octolobus manul*) 77

Serval 220, 249, 279

Winslow, Helen 81

Concerning Cats 40–3

witch hunting 83–4

Wolsey, Thomas, Cardinal 84

World Cat Federation (WCF)

Kurilian Bobtail 112

Thai 122

Wyatt, Sir Henry 84

CREDITS

Endpapers
Coco (British Domestic)
Owners: Mr. & Mrs. D. Brewerton

2 *Honey & Ariel* (Ocicat)
JumpnSpots Honey Nugget &
JumpnSpots Ariel
Cattery: JumpnSpots Ocicats
Owner: Mrs. S. Klusman
jumpnspots@verizon.net
www.JumpnSpotsOcicats.com

5 (Siamese)
Cattery: Mapu Siamese
Owner: Mrs. G. Baughan
www.mapusiamese.co.uk

6 *Bart* (Kurilian Bobtail)
Ainu Bartholomew
Cattery: Ainu Cattery
Owner: T. Gurevich
tgurevich@gmail.com
www.ainucattery.com

7 *Coco* (British Domestic)
Owners: Mr. & Mrs. D. Brewerton

8–9 *Gherkin* (Pixie Bob)
CH Special Agent Grand Canyon
Cattery: Special Agent Pixie Bobs
Owners: J. & P. Deacon
wind@agentcats.com
www.agentcats.com

10 *Oshie* (Nebelung)
DGCA Brumeux Oscian
Cattery: Brumeux Nebelungs &
TrueVine Cattery
Owner: K. Stewart
kristi@truevinecattery.com
www.facebook.com/NebelungCats

11 *Kennedy* (Oriental)
SGC Purrsia Jackie Oh Kennedy
Cattery: Purrsia Cattery
Breeders/owners: Mr. & Mrs. S. Shon
purrsiaoriental@yahoo.com
www.purrsiaoriental.com

12 *Coley* (Bengal)

13 *Bali* (Ocicat)
JumpnSpots Bali Hai
Cattery: JumpnSpots Ocicats
Owner: Mrs. S. Klusman
jumpnspots@verizon.net
www.JumpnSpotsOcicats.com

14 *Dewey Miller* (Siberian)
Cattery: Usta Siberians Cattery
Owners: Mr. & Mrs. Miller
jhirsch27@gmail.com

16 *Zen* (Chausie)
Sarsenstone Psusennes
Cattery: Sarsenstone Cattery
Owner: Dr. C. Bird
sarsenstone@pacific.net
www.chausie-kittens.com

19 *Sunshine* (American Shorthair)
Char's Rae of Sunshine
Owner: C. Swanson
summertymeblues@charter.net
www.catterycorner.com/char/char.html

20–21 *Rikki Tikki Tavi* (Korat)
Cattery: Ithacats
Owner: Mrs. J. Wiegand
jmwiegand@verizon.net

22–23 *Khyssa* (Egyptian Mau)
Maunarch Khyssa ní Erin
Cattery: Maunarch Cattery
Owner: Mr. C. Caines
cc@christophercainesdance.org
www.christophercainesdance.org

24, 26, & 27 *Khyssa* (Egyptian Mau)
Maunarch Khyssa ní Erin
Cattery: Maunarch Cattery
Owner: Mr. C. Caines
cc@christophercainesdance.org
www.christophercainesdance.org

28 *Mika* (Turkish Van)

31 *Kianu* (Sokoke)
Sunbright Kianu
Cattery: Sokoke Cats
Owner: L. Schafer Russell
sokokecats@yahoo.com
www.sokokecats.org

32, 34, & 35 *Murray* (Manx)
Danzante White Fire
Owner: Mrs. M. Della
marilyn.della@btinternet.com

36, 38, & 39 *Osi, Lago, & Hugo*
(Norwegian Forest Cat)
GB* Jotunkatts Osiana Rose, GB*
Adkelekatts Lago, & GB* Adkelekatts
Hugo
Cattery: Adkelekatts
Owner: Mrs. C. Harrison
adkelekatts@hotmail.co.uk
www.adkelekatts.co.uk

41–43 *Denny Miller* (Siberian)
Cattery: Usta Siberians Cattery
Owners: Mr. & Mrs. Miller
jhirsch27@gmail.com

44 & 46–49 *Izzie* (British Shorthair)
Isabelle
Breeder: G. Denny
Owners: Mr. & Mrs. James

50, 52, & 53 *Tabitha & Juliet** (Japanese
Bobtail)
GC GP Ginchika Juliet Burke*
Owner: J. Reding
jennifer@janipurr.com
www.janipurr.com

55–57 *China* (Chinese Li Hua)
Lihua China Zhong Guo of C2C
Breeder: Li Yu Zhang

Owner: Z. Liyu & J. & E. White
ranchapurr@yahoo.com

58 & 60–65 *Maiko, Pippa, Lady, & Rosie*
(Siamese)
CH Mafdet Maiko, Mapu Pippa, Mapu
Lady Arwin, & CH Mapu Rosie
Cattery: Mapu Siamese
Owner: Mrs. G. Baughan
www.mapusiamese.co.uk

66 & 68–71 *Rikki Tikki Tavi* (Korat)
Cattery: Ithacats
Owner: Mrs. J. Wiegand
jmwiegand@verizon.net

73 & 74 (Birman)
Cattery: Birman Cat La Pommeraye
Owner: Mr. L. Triqueneaux
omertri@aol.com
www.birmanlapommeraye.com

76 & 80 *Ruby* (Persian)
Owner: Mrs. J. Rilon

79 *Tigger* (Persian)
Cattery: Kismet Kittens
Owners: Mr. & Mrs. Myers
persiankittyinfo@aol.com
www.kismetkittens.org

82–83 *Copper* (Chartreux)
RW GP Charleval's Copper of House of
Blues—Charleval
Owners: D. Giannoni & M. Yaneza
dgiannoni@yahoo.com
www.houseofbluescattery.com

84–85 *Billy* (Maine Coon)
Owners: P., G., & P. Reidy

87 & 88 *Pascha & Thunder* (Turkish
Angora)
Stenbury Pascha & Stenbury
Thunderball
Cattery: Stenbury Cats
Owner: Mrs. T. Barker
stenbury@yahoo.co.uk
www.stenburycats.co.uk

90 & 92–95 *Angel & Enchantress*
(Russian Blue)
GCH Valnika's Angeloina of Cynful
CH Cynful's Enchantress
Cattery: Cynful Cats Russian Blues
Owner: Mrs. C. Wagner
cynfulcats@aol.com

97–99 *Sunshine* (American Shorthair)
Char's Rae of Sunshine
Owner: C. Swanson
summertymeblues@charter.net
www.catterycorner.com/char/char.html

101–103 *Copper & Gerber* (Chartreux)
RW GP Charleval's Copper of House of
Blues—Charleval & RW GP House of
Blues Gerber—House of Blues (CFA)
Owners: D. Giannoni & M. Yaneza

dgiannoni@yahoo.com
www.houseofbluescattery.com

105, 106 & 110–111* *Rita & kittens**
(Maine Coon)
CH Whatatrill Lovely Rita of CaliCats
Cattery: CaliCats Maine Coons
Owner: M. Thorsness
mthorsness@aol.com
www.CaliCats.net

108 & 109 *Chelsea* (Maine Coon)
Chelsea of Malibu

113 *Morgan & Bart* (Kurilian Bobtail)
Ainu Morgan & Ainu Bart
Cattery: Ainu Cattery
Owner: T. Gurevich
tgurevich@gmail.com
www.ainucattery.com

114, 116, & 117 *Pharlap* & Sea Biscuit*
(Abyssinian)
*Breeder: Amberize Abyssinians
Owner: J. Moran
amberizecats@msn.com
www.amberizeabyssinians.com

118–119 *Gemmie* (Thai)
RW SGC Pangaea Argemone of
Sarsenstone
Cattery: Sarsenstone Cattery
Owner: Dr. C. Bird
sarsenstone@pacific.net
www.siamesekittens.info

120–121 *Willow* (Oriental)
Willow Waltz D'Arnaid of Topeng
Cattery: Topeng Cattery
Owner: M. Siconolfi
topengcattery@gmail.com
www.topengcattery.com

123 *Gemmie* (Thai)
RW SGC Pangaea Argemone of
Sarsenstone
Cattery: Sarsenstone Cattery
Owner: Dr. C. Bird
sarsenstone@pacific.net
www.siamesekittens.info

124 & 126–127 *Cookie* (Balinese)
Bali Dancer Captain Hook
of Topeng
Cattery: Topeng Cattery
Owner: M. Siconolfi
topengcattery@gmail.com
www.topengcattery.com

128 & 130–133 *Coffee* (Burmese)
Coffee Cream
Owners: Mr. & Mrs. R. Garran

134 *Darci* (Himalayan)
Prancenpaws Darci
Cattery: Prancenpaws Himalayan
Owners: R. Avery & V. King
rhondajavery@yahoo.com
www.himalayans.org

137, 138, & 139 *Be* (Colorpoint Shorthair)
Penelane Be
Cattery: Penelane
Owner: M. Lukic
mpkl@aol.com
www.penelane.com

140, 144, & 145 *Kennedy* (Oriental)
SGC Purrsia Jackie Oh Kennedy
Cattery: Purrsia Cattery
Breeders/owners: Mr. & Mrs. S. Shon
purrsiaoriental@yahoo.com
www.purrsiaoriental.com

142–143 *Willow* (Oriental)
Willow Waltz D'Arnaid of Topeng
Cattery: Topeng Cattery
Owner: M. Siconolfi
www.topengcattery.com

146 *Gatsby* (Havana Brown)
Ch St Evroult Gatsby
Cattery: Eastpoint Havanas
Owner: Mrs. L. Spendlove
lindaspendlove1@aol.com
www.eastpointsiamese.co.uk

149, 150, & 151 *George* (Somali)
Owner: Mrs. E. Minden
johnminden@dancer.com

153 & 154–155 *Far Out* (Cornish Rex)
RW GC Ranchapurr Far Out of Roseric
Owners: C. Page & J. & E. White
ranchapurr@yahoo.com

157 & 158–159 *Loony* (Bombay)
GCH Typha Huntersmoon
Cattery: Typha Typhast
Owners: Mr. & Mrs. Alger-Street
barrieandrosie@typha-typhast.co.uk
www.typha-typhast.co.uk

160–161 *Nibbler* (Ocicat)
JumpnSpots Zodiak
Cattery: JumpnSpots Ocicats
Owner: Mrs. S. Klusman
jumpnspots@verizon.net
www.JumpnSpotsOcicats.com

162–163 *Sarsenstone Tarn* (Chausie)
Cattery: Sarsenstone Cattery
Owner: Dr. C. Bird
sarsenstone@pacific.net
www.chausie-kittens.com

165 & 166–167 *Macey & Carmella*
(Devon Rex)
RW QGC LuvbySu Macey Grey of Nada
& DGC Nada Carmella Apples
Breeders: S. Henley & C. Kerr
Owner: C. Kerr
nadasphynx@gmail.com
www.sphynx.us.com

168 & 170–173 *Poppy & Humphrey*
(Scottish Fold)
Sheephouse Poppy & Mister Humphrey
of Sheephouse

Cattery: Sunrise Folds
Owner: Mrs. J. Bradley
jandybull@btinternet.com
www.sheephouse.co.uk

175 & 176–177 *Matilda* (Ragdoll)
The Algonquin Hotel, Times Square, NYC
matildaalgonquincat@algonquinhotel.com

178 & 180–181 *Kirsti & Katya* (Exotic
Shorthair)
Zendique Kersti (SH) & Zendique Katya
(LH)
Breeder: Ms. J. Allen
Owner: Miss. S. Balston
balston09@btinternet.com
www.zendique.com

182 & 184–185 *Flash* (Snowshoe)
Glittakitz Flash
Breeder: Mrs. T. Rhodes
Owner: Mrs. V. Jobbins
jobbinsford@yahoo.co.uk
www.snowdustsnowshoes.co.uk

186 & 188–191 *Sebastian, Honey, &*
Shakira (Ocicat)
JumpnSpots Merlin Black Magic,
JumpnSpots Honey Nugget, &
Jumpnspots Shakira
Cattery: JumpnSpots Ocicats
Owner: Mrs. S. Klusman
jumpnspots@verizon.net
www.JumpnSpotsOcicats.com

192 *Chase* (American Bobtail)
Magicbobs Chasing My Blues Away
Owner: G. Hayes
gwynethayes@hotmail.com

195, 196, & 197 *Jack & kitten* (Sphynx)
GC RW PinUpCats Pirate Flag
Cattery: PinUpCats Sphynx Cattery
Owner: C. Gause
gauseabode@charter.net
www.pinupcats.com

199 & 200–203 *Lucy, Jules, Barbie, &*
Midge (Tonkinese)
RW SGC Elvessa's Lucy Ricardo, RW
SGCA Channelaire Julie Newmar of
Elvessa, Elvessa's Barbara Roberts, &
Elvessa's Midge Hadley
Cattery: Elvessa
Owner: L. Schiff & M. Yates
elvessa@fatpet.com
www.fatpet.com/elvessa

204 *Pia* (American Wirehair)
Owner: C. Swanson
summertymeblues@charter.net
www.catterycorner.com/char/char.html

207–211 *Zen* (Chausie)
Sarsenstone Psusennes
Cattery: Sarsenstone Cattery
Owner: Dr. C. Bird
sarsenstone@pacific.net
www.chausie-kittens.com

213 & 214 *Khan* (Bengal)
Cattery: Giradelle Bengals
Owner: Mr. & Mrs. M. Cauvain
www.giradellecats.com

216 & 217 *Leo* (Bengal)
Leonidas
Breeder/Cattery: B. Boizard-Neil/
Bambino Bengals
Owner: O. Garran & T. Boon
olieygarran@gmail.com

218–219 *Pollock* (Bengal)

220–221 *Ruby* (Singapura)
RubyRose of Tamangambira
Cattery: Tamangambira
Owner: M. Thomas
www.singapuracats.org

222–223 *Oshie* (Nebelung)
Brumeux Oscian
Cattery: Brumeux Nebelungs &
TrueVine Cattery
Owner: K. Stewart
kristi@truevinecattery.com
www.facebook.com/NebelungCats

224 *Snowy* (Singapura)
SnowWhite of Singville
Cattery: Singville Cattery
Owner: M. Bolonkowska
mbolonkowska@aol.com
www.singapuracats.org

226–227 *Ruby* (Singapura)
RubyRose of Tamangambira
Cattery: Tamangambira
Owner: M. Thomas
www.singapuracats.org

229 & 230–231 *Ektorp* & Sundae*
(American Curl)
Procurl Harem Ernest Curlingway* &
America Runs on Duncurl
Cattery: Procurl Harlem
Owners: A .Delphine*, C. Scott, & M.
Tucker
caroline9@earthlink.net
www.procurlharem.com

233, 234–235, & 236–237 *Mouse &*
Beau* (La Perm)
Quincunx Fliberrstygibbet &
Quincunx Beau*
Cattery: Quincunx Cats
Owner: Mr. A. Nichols & M. Weston*
anthony@quincunxcats.co.uk
www.quincunxcats.co.uk

238 *Max* (Munchkin)
Creators Lilboy To The Max
Breeder: M. Gardiner
Owner: S. Rivero
sueb68@aol.com

240 & 242–243 *Oshie & Brindie*
(Nebelung)
Brumeux Oscian & Brumeux Brindie

Breeder Cattery: Brumeux Nebelungs
Owner: K. Stewart
kristi@truevinecattery.com
www.facebook.com/NebelungCats

244 & 246–247 *Seal, Mystery, & Sniper*
(Pixiebobs)
Special Agent Seal Six
Special Agent Canyon Sniper (fondly
known as "The Diva")
RW SGC Special Agent Sniper (Sniper)
Cattery: Special Agent Pixie Bobs
Owners: J. & P. Deacon
wind@agentcats.com
www.agentcats.com

248 & 250–253 *Jassy & Lightning*
(Savannah)
Jas Queen (F1) & SGC A1 Savannahs
Lightning (F5 SBT)
Owner: J. Spain
alistsavannahs@yahoo.com

255 & 256–257 *Smeagol* (Don Sphynx)
Anatollja Rijhik
Breeder: G. Khudyakova
Owner: K. Demeanour
kat@sphynxcatassociation.co.uk
www.sphynxcatassociation.co.uk

258 *Iffy* (Selkirk Rex)
Kicsi-Macska Iffy of Elegance
Owner: S. Rauch

260–261 *Whisty* (Selkirk Rex)
Gr Ch Sheephouse Whisteria
Cattery: Sunrise Folds
Owner: Mrs. J. Bradley
jandybull@btinternet.com
www.sheephouse.co.uk

262 & 264–267 *Taitan & Hercules*
(Toyger)
Eeyaa Taitan & Eeyaa Hercules
Breeder/owner: J. Sugden
eeyaa@uia.net
www.toygers.com

269–273 *Nikolas* (Peterbald)
SGC Purrsia au Contraire
Cattery: Purrsia Cattery
Breeders/owners: Mr. & Mrs.
S. Shon
purrsiaoriental@yahoo.com
www.purrsiaoriental.com

274, 276, & 277 *Flower* (Ragamuffin)
Finesthour My Boy Flower
Cattery: Finest Hour Cats
Owner: Mrs. T. Chennell
tam@ralph768.orangehome.co.uk
www.finesthourcats.webs.com

278 & 280–281 *Emmi* (Serengeti)
Kingsmark Silver Emiri
Cattery: Kingsmark Serengeti Cats
Owner: K. Sausman
kserengeti@aol.com
www.kingsmarkfarms.com

ACKNOWLEDGMENTS

This book would not have been possible without the very great help and advice from a number of individual breed experts, breeders, clubs, and organizations in both the UK and the US. Although our book is not affiliated with any one organization we would like to acknowledge the amazing work that these organizations do, and in particular TICA, CFA, GCCF, and FIFE. The breed descriptions in this book are general descriptions and do not specifically reflect any one organization or their standards.

We would like to extend our very great thanks to Mark Fletcher, Jane Laing, Dean Martin, Elspeth Beidas, and the rest of the team at Quarto for their patience, support, and expertise. Particular thanks also go to Bobbi Tullo for her sage advice and help, to Innis and John MacEachin for their wonderful support, Stephen Rew for his everlasting support and patience, and to the following individuals (with sincere apologies if anyone has been accidentally left out):

Alexis Mitchell
Andrea and David Brewerton
Annabel Cailles
Anne McCulloch
Annette Wilson
Brigitte Cowell
Carl and Marion Ainscoe
Caroline Scott
Carolyn and Douglas Menzel
Cheryl Hague
Clare Willoughby
Colleen and Andrew Brown
Cora Cobb
Cristy Bird
Cynthia Tunello
Dennis and Judy Ganoe
Dennis Gannoe
Diane Castor
Donna Madison
Donna Verba
Elaine Gleason
Ellen V Crockett
Erica Tadajewski
Esther and Joann White
Evelyn Jacobs
Gaynor Jean-Louis
Harold Bourgeois
Hellen Pounds
Iris Zinck
Judith Mackey
Judy Harper
Judy Sugden
Julie Keyer
Kara Fox

Karen Bishop
Karen Sausman
Katherine Bock
Kathrine Marshall Ruttan
Kathryn Sylvia
Kathy Black
Laura Gregory
Lynn Miller
Marcia Owen
Marilyn Della
Marion Yates
Martina Gates
Mary Desmond
Michele Punzel
Nicki Esdorn
Norma and Ron Thayer
Norma Placchi
Norman and Martha Auspitz
Robin Higgins
Sally Patch
Sandra Bell
Sharon Ann Paradis
Sherri Mcconnell
Susanna Tally
Virginia Wheeldon